In Devil's Den
Journals of a Park Interpreter
Wallace F. Keck

In Devil's Den Journals of a Park Interpreter

Wallace Keck

Published by Wallace Keck, 2024.

IN DEVIL'S DEN JOURNALS OF A PARK INTERPRETER

First edition. July 3, 2024.

Copyright © 2024 Wallace Keck.

ISBN: 979-8227261427

Written by Wallace Keck.

Table of Contents

Note to the Reader

The following is a true story of the life and experiences of a park interpreter (naturalist, ranger) in Devil's Den State Park, living in a log cabin in the Ozark Mountains of Arkansas during the years 1988-1994). One employee continues to work at the park, but the rest have moved on to other positions or retirement. Some have passed away. The day quickly approaches when few or none will remember the stories, the experiences, or histories of life in the Upper Lee Creek Valley unless perchance someone writes them down. The historic record of the park is lost more quickly than it is made.

The audience for this book is first and foremost the park visitor who surveys the awe-inspiring landscape and ponders, "What's the story here?" How did this come to be? Other audiences include local historians, naturalists, and college students preparing to enter the profession. A larger readership might include the men and women who protect the nation's treasured places. May they be encouraged regardless of where they serve, that theirs is a noble calling.

About the Author

Wallace Keck was born in St. Joseph, Missouri, in the last year of the baby boom and coincidentally, the first year of the Wilderness Act. At age seven, the family of six picked up and moved to the resort/retirement community of Bella Vista, Arkansas. In 1972, the journey from Bella Vista to the nearest town (Bentonville) was still a wild one. The school bus routes were chert-covered hill-climbs and low-water crossings that consumed two to three hours each day. Weekends offered free time and woodland places to explore. Every bluff overhang was a potential cave, and every stream promised a secret waterfall. The wilderness began where the lawnmowing ceased. Such was the environment that fostered the boy in the woods to be a ranger and park manager of Idaho's wilder landscapes.

Keck earned a BS in Fisheries and Wildlife Management from Arkansas Tech University. His 43-year career spanned employment in five public land management agencies in three states, and at eight state and federal parks. <u>In Devil's Den: Journals of a Park Interpreter</u> encompasses approximately five and a half years of his career working for Arkansas State Parks.

A Word About the Journals

Every year for as long as I can remember, World Book Encyclopedia automatically sent my mother a planner entitled <u>Today 1981</u>, (<u>Today 1982</u>, etc.). Whether she offered it to me, or I asked for it, I cannot now recall, but without fail, I received an orange-colored journal in the mail (and still do!). It comes in October to overlap the current year with the one that approaches. The planner serves well as a journal, and from day one (more than 15,700 entries ago), every day has some note or entry. Daily, I record my deeds *ad nauseam*.

Why is this background important? What is written here is based on the journals, and the journals are true from my perspective and experience. The facts were often written within hours of their occurrence. The stories, events, and characters are verifiable. No attempt has been made to disguise a person's name or identity, for we were all public officials.

Finally, it should be noted that while the events of the book are written in chronological order, not every event is included. At times, I have skipped as much as a week or more. For one reason, there would be a considerable and excessive amount of material to cover, and secondly, much of it would begin to feel redundant, tedious, and ordinary. I have cherry-picked the most interesting and relevant content to illustrate the life of a park interpreter assigned to and living in Devil's Den State Park. The chronology remains true to demonstrate that a ranger's life is quite frenetic and uncontrolled from day to day, and sometimes by the hour. No two days were ever the same.

Table of Contents

Chapter One: Closure

Poking through the saturated darkness, I can just make out the distant flicker of cottages scattered along the ridges. Winter rain conspires with fog to swallow the faint yellowish headlights of my Isuzu Trooper. On the road, I am alone – somewhere west of Winslow (the one in Arkansas). Making use of the silence, I encourage my thoughts to wander with the weavings of state highway 74. Subtly, I plot my escape from yet another government job to a new way-of-life where work and adventure are inseparable, where the park is my home.

The most euphoric moment in the life of a traveler is the departure upon *the road less traveled*, along the nearly imperceptible path. Hours earlier, I concluded my employment at DeGray Lake Resort State Park as the self-titled pathfinder, naturalist, historian, and storyteller. I learned to embrace the pockets of wildness there – the undeveloped shoreline and secret coves. But that place could never offer the life I dreamed of for me. I had no real ties, no binding kinship. That way was already worn and well-trodden.

"*Better is the end of a thing than its beginning.*"

(Ecclesiastes 7:8)

As soon as a position opened, I requested a transfer from the foothills of the Ouachita Mountains to the dissected plateaus of the Ozarks. It felt good to reach the end. But DeGray had been my park; its wildness my responsibility and stewardship. At age 24, I never expected to be so conflicted. *Parting is such sweet sorrow.* Yes Juliet, I get that now. Who will remember to check in on the nesting Red-shouldered Hawk near the fairway? Who will recount the *Legend of the Cove of No Return* aboard the full moon cruise? Will anyone know where the Saginaw Railroad goes after the trail signs fade?

The Lee Creek Valley entraps the inattentive driver from the first hairpin curve. There is no turning back for the next several miles, and the time for checking brakes has passed. A gray fox appears from the shadowy woods to observe my descent. He gives no opinion, no warning of things to come. Devil's Den State Park sits at the bottom of the Boston Mountain Plateau and the nineth pigtail of Arkansas Highway 74. A quick steering to the left and I am down the driveway and at the doorstep of cabin four.

Susan arrived earlier in the daylight with all the furniture we own, which is little more than what occupied our dorm rooms four years ago at Arkansas Tech University. The cabin is small but as cozy as a married naturalist could hope. The front door opens into the living room. Large windows frame Lee Creek further below. A native sandstone fireplace with oak mantle, dominates a corner of the room. The living room transitions into the dining room and kitchen. Bed and bath complete the floor plan. The walls are knotty pine, and oak beams support the rafters. The cabin is old, built by the Civilian Conservation Corps (CCC) in 1936, but recently renovated by skilled craftsmen and is rent-free. It is the most romantic place we have called home.

Saturday, December 17, 1988, 10 p.m. I scribble a few lines in the journal. The next chapter – a very new chapter in my life is about to begin. I can barely comprehend it. All I know for sure is that I am meant to be here at this place and for this time.

Chapter 2: New Beginnings

December 18, 1988

Susan and I intentionally oversleep. I have the day to settle in. Other residents of the valley (now population 11) have long since risen. Employees that live on the plateau have also arrived and gather at the park office to converse about the weather over a steamy pot of coffee. Phyllis Ulm calls from the office to confirm our connection to the phone system and to welcome us to the park family. Phyllis is the receptionist who lives on a farm 10 miles down the worst road in the area, which is to say a great deal as all roads in and out of Devil's Den are the worst if such a ranking were possible to give.

Harry Harnish calls to invite us for a walk. Harry, my cohort, is also a park interpreter. He lives in cabin ten, directly downhill from us. His wife, Pat, immaculately cleans the 13 rental cabins that are scattered about. I finish unpacking and walk down to the visitor center to investigate my assigned office. Tim Scott is there, and we become better acquainted. He is thirty-something, single, and the assistant superintendent who lives in the modern residence adjacent to the visitor center. His recent promotion from park interpreter has created the vacancy I now fill.

December 19, 1988

Work begins and ends this day, straining over maps and brochures. Devil's Den State Park is 2,000 acres situated in upper Lee Creek Valley of the Boston Mountain Plateau, the highest of three plateaus (including Springfield and Salem) collectively called the Ozark Mountains or Ozarks for short.

The park (named after its longest cave) exhibits the largest sandstone crevice area in the United States. Parks worth working at and living in must have a nationally significant and superlative feature. Additionally, the park and surrounding Ozark National Forest are filled with history, legend, and biodiversity. It will be my job to coax and tease these stories out of the landscape and share them with the unsuspecting visitor.

There is much to learn about the park's unparalleled resources, but more pressing skills need honing, like running the cash register and phone system, as well as the daily routine of recording the weather, feeding the birds, restocking the firewood bin, and raising the flag.

After work, Susan and I drive to town for supplies. "Town," referred to by park residents, is Fayetteville some 25 miles north. Winslow is closer (13 miles east), but has only a small grocery, gas station, post office, and school (home of the Winslow Squirrels). The town was named in 1882 in honor of the Frisco Railroad president, Edward J. Winslow. It is the highest incorporated town in Arkansas and a geographical divide of the Boston Mountain Plateau.

West Fork is eighteen miles north of Devil's Den and downstream of Winslow. It is passed on the way to "town." Larger than Winslow and more community-active, West Fork was established in 1848 on the west fork of the White River. This is the same White River that makes its way inevitably to the Mississippi River, but not before spending considerable time in Missouri.

Fayetteville is a world away. To get there, we drive north around the headwaters of Lee Creek along a ridge that separates this drainage from the watershed of the Illinois River – one of four such rivers in the US so named. At the divide, the road descends the plateau into the wide valley of West Fork.

Fayetteville is home to the University of Arkansas and the famed Razorbacks, the closest Wal-Mart, and other cultural icons. Established in 1828 as Washington Courthouse, the town's name was later changed to Fayetteville, honoring a similar town in Tennessee. Today, it is the heart and soul of Northwest Arkansas.

Resupplied and cargo stowed, we commence the 45-minute drive home. Trips to town will be infrequent and reserved for dire need or special occasions.

December 20, 1988

Up at 6:30 a.m. and down to work early. There is just so much to learn and so many exciting projects await. Fortunately, my transfer occurs during the off-season, allowing plenty of time for orientation. There are very few park visitors and virtually no interpretive programs to conduct.

I meet with Wally Scherrey, park superintendent, and listen to his orientation spiel. We walk to the cave and crevice area to discuss ideas, projects, and interpretive philosophies. He cares deeply for the park, its frequent visitors, and rich natural and cultural history; however, it is apparent change comes reluctantly. He asks what I think should be done to improve the badly eroded Devil's Den Trail. "Pave it!", I say—half kidding, half serious. He is not impressed.

After work, the Harnishes invite Susan and me over for hamburgers. Harry is the quintessential griller. We play Trivial Pursuit, relax around the fire, and get properly acquainted.

December 21, 1988

Orientation continues. Yellow Rock is a prominent crag and popular overlook, upstream and north of most park facilities. It consists of a thick layer of Atoka sandstone as well as additional sedimentary beds of limestone, siltstone, and shale. "Yellow" Rock gets its name from the iron oxides present in the sandstone prior to exposure to water and air. The crag stands 300 feet above Lee Creek. Harry and I walk the three-mile trail, discussing geology of this and other complicated sites.

Most visitors (and frankly most employees) are content to accept the simple explanation of how geologically, this place came to be. A lesser guide and storyteller might lose their audience after using words like Paleozoic, sedimentary, or Atoka; but a professional interpreter would research a word like "Atoka" and ask, what is the story here?

First, I help the visitor understand that the Ozark Mountains once consisted of nothing more than layer upon layer of sediment deposited at a delta, shallow beach, or ocean. Sediments varied in size from silt to sand and also included the crushed bodies of calcareous creatures like seashells and corals. About 542 million years ago, these deposited sediments hardened into rock due to heat and pressure from the weight of sediments on top. Then, sedimentary rock began to uplift and bend like a dome. Once exposed above the ocean, erosional forces took over. Rivers formed on the surface and cut into the dome, exposing the layers of sedimentary rock created long before. For 200 million years, rivers created by exposure and erosion were being uplifted just as canyons and valleys were being incised and entrenched (cut and kept).

Of course, the good interpreter is prepared for two rebuttals: (1) the argument to which many subscribe – the earth is just not that old, - but the process may be verifiable, and (2) what caused the dome or sedimentary rock to suddenly uplift? Plate tectonics. The collision of crustal plates, including the crumbled portion of the tectonic plate associated with the formation of the Ouachita Mountains to the south? The point is not to have all the answers, but to plant an interest in the visitor to learn more, buy a book, find a new hobby, attend a class on the subject and support efforts to protect sites where the stories are best told and understood.

Imagine a clubhouse sandwich. From the top looking down, all we see is the toasted bread, but if we slice it in half we can see a layer of bread, pickles, lettuce, turkey, cheese, and tomato. The bread (aka) Atoka Sandstone is the thickest layer of the sedimentary rock (sandwich). There's no meatball (aka) igneous rock in this geologic formation! Geologist study and map formations – how thick they are, how far they go, in what other club sandwiches do they occur, and where are they similar?

Formations are typically named after a present-day natural feature in the geographic area where they were first studied and described. In this case – Atoka, Oklahoma. The story only goes deeper when we learn that Atoka the town and Atoka County are located on a centuries old Choctaw village located on the same site as present-day Atoka. The village honors one of its more famous chieftains named Atoka. The word itself means "ball grounds." The word might relate to a place where the Choctaw tribesmen would gather to conduct and play sports. All very interesting, but so far I have only a pocket full of facts. I will continue to research until a connection can be made between the visitor and the superlative. Until the question of "So what?" is answered, there is no point in going down the endless roads of information.

After lunch, winter projects begin. The first task is to repair the footbridge at Twin Falls. Boards are loose, some are missing, and the department is ripe for a lawsuit. The great fear of park administrators and agency solicitors is a tort claim, and many have succumbed to the practice of fencing overlooks and posting "keep out" signs to alleviate the problem. The problem doesn't go away, but at least with a sign, it is easier to assess blame for injury or death of a visitor. Too often these signs are nothing more than knee-jerk attempts to save the public from themselves. After being fully informed of hidden dangers, let the public draw their own lines of safety and choose the degree of risk. It is not madness, but wildness. How else can we perpetuate the American spirit? I fix the bridge because it needs fixing.

I now understand one of the reasons why my cabin is provided rent free. Tonight, I have phone duty. After eight hours of work, I return home to find the phone ringing incessantly. I answer with my rote script. *I'm sorry, we have no cabins available for Christmas weekend. I'm sorry, the office is closed; please call back tomorrow after 8 a.m."* Of course, the only thing I am sorry about is phone duty.

Between calls, Susan and I tour the county road southwest of the park. We are on an expedition to acquire a wild Christmas tree. Cutting a tree in the park would be the pinnacle of hypocrisy, culminating – I would imagine – in my swift termination; so, we drive just beyond the boundary to an abandoned parcel of private property. The overgrown field contains a dozen Eastern Red Cedars (*Juniperus virginiana*) of perfect size and shape. Ten quick strokes of the bowsaw and we lash and load the sacrificial tree. The pleasing fragrance of cedar permeates the Isuzu Trooper.

December 22, 1988

Orientation and research are combined today as Harry and I prepare to survey the cave. After decades of state park status and public access, conflicting estimates remain as to the cave's length and depth.

One enters Devil's Den through a small hole on a steep hill, a quarter mile from the visitor center. The passage is a fracture ranging from one to fifteen feet wide. Smooth sandstone walls rise to thirty feet and are damp to the touch. Pipistrelle bats (*Pipistrellus pipistrellus)* hibernate here but are frequently roused by spelunkers. We see a few bats as we stretch the tape measure. Cave salamanders and camel crickets are often found near the entrance as well. On this visit, I observe neither.

The cave was formed over seventy-five thousand years ago when a massive landslide occurred. During the uplift of the Boston Mountain Plateau, a syncline formed. Thick layers of Atoka Sandstone rest on thin beds of shale. Over time, Lee Creek cut deep into the axis of the syncline, leaving huge layers of rock stranded on the hillside and leaning downward. Meanwhile, surface water percolated through the porous sandstone, reaching the shale layer. Unable to permeate the shale, water flowed between it and the sandstone creating a slippery contact. Eventually thick sandstone layers, unable to fight the laws of gravity, slid. The result is a jumbled mass of gigantic sandstone blocks and crevices.

I stand inside, trying to imagine the sliding, grunting, and ferocious roar of a billion tons of rock hell-bent for the valley, but these are appropriate thoughts for outside the cave. I am inside the beast, the esophagus. Rocks hang precariously above my head like rotten teeth. I am told the cave's structure has not changed in the history of the park, and there is little fear it will in the next one hundred years.

The cave is five-hundred and fifty feet! Harry and I depart satisfied that we are the first to confirm it. We proceed to the upper crevice area, a sacred place now closed to visitors. In the 1930s the CCC built an elaborate trail system amongst the crevices, crags, and caves. Equestrians used these trails as recent as the 1960's, giving name to the largest and deepest crevice called "Dead Horse." Harry says it is our job to avoid renaming the fifty-five-foot chasm, "Dead Tourist"; although, the latter is a constant possibility. Several years ago, administrators decided the crevice area could be ruined by litterbugs, potheads, and rappelers. Some still believe the only solution is to keep the area closed.

We wander through like priests, pondering the rationale and reason. Harry and I agree that the crevice area should be protected and cherished but subscribe to the doctrine: *We preserve what we appreciate.* To educate we must at least be allowed to lead interpretive hikes into the area for which the park is most famous. Down Imp's Leap Ravine we scramble, discussing and agreeing perfectly.

Susan and I attend the employee Christmas party this evening – the social event of our little valley. Finally, I meet the rest of the staff who work here but live in Winslow, Strickler, Brentwood, and West Fork.

December 27, 1988

Brent Daugherity and I are assigned the task of removing the Christmas decorations. Brent is the park ranger – the one who carries the gun. In the public's eye, anyone who wears the uniform and Smokey Bear hat is a ranger. "Rangering" is the profession of law enforcement. Interpretation is the profession of education, research, and inspiration. Confusion results because rangers frequently perform interpretation, and interpreters frequently enforce regulations and respond to emergencies. We haul the Christmas tree from the visitor center to the eight-acre lake to create additional fish habitat.

Later, Brent introduces me to Holt Road, which serves as the park's eastern boundary. The road follows a ridge dividing Blackburn Creek and Lee. It is not a road by modern standards, merely a long stretch of parallel ruts interrupted by frequent mud holes. The road is a four-wheeler's playground and virtual Venus flytrap for lesser autos. Holt Road, Holt Ridge, and Holt Vista are all named for Benjamin Holt who settled land at its southern end during the early 1900's. One story tells how Ben, tired of single life, advertised for a wife in a New York City newspaper. Facts are sketchy, but I am told he found one. She bore him a child, but she died during labor, which was somewhat common in those days.

I learn quite a bit more about the park and Brent after spending the day with him. Like Wally, Brent came to Devil's Den straight from college to be the park interpreter or "naturalist" as they were called back then. One summer he fell in love with a local girl who was working as a lifeguard. They married, settled on land near the original CCC camp, and started a family.

As we leave Holt Road it begins to sleet. By the time we reach the visitor center, it turns to snow and covers the grass.

December 31, 1988

Alone, I drive the so-called fire road (probably a CCC designation) north of camp area "A". According to a General Land

Office map, this road existed in 1837. The road is gated at the campground and again at the north boundary, one mile beyond.

Chapter 3: Getting Down to Business

January 4, 1989

Rural phone and postal routes can be confusing. Winslow is the closest town, but the park's address is West Fork. Despite these two locations, our telephone company is in Prairie Grove; however, our exchange is listed as Strickler. Winslow is a long-distance call, but a call to Lincoln (three times farther) is considered local. These realizations occur today when the phone bill arrives. Wally, Tim, Harry, and I share one phone line. We circulate the bill, initial our long-distance calls, and write a personal check to Prairie Grove Telephone Company. My first bill is fourteen dollars and fifty cents.

Alone again, I hike the Lee Creek Trail to the walk-in campground. Immediately at the trailhead, the hiker is required to wade the creek. At this location in 1941 through the spring of 1942, the CCC was busy constructing a second, larger lake in the valley. Evidence of an earthen dam, concrete spillway, and native stone tower are within sight. World War II and the CCC's declining popularity led to disbandment despite projects in progress such as this one. The project was to include construction of additional cabins and campgrounds.

January 5, 1989

I ride with Harry three miles to get our mail. It used to be delivered to the visitor center, but in March 1987 a section of Arkansas Highway 170 collapsed and later became impassable. The occurrence was like the creation of the crevice area. Reconstruction continues but will take several months. The landslide is bypassed by taking the old dirt highway built by the CCC in 1933-34. After the mail run, Harry drives the county roads pointing out Brent's place on the way to Phyllis'. We stop for a minute to visit Phyllis and her husband, Clyde.

January 7, 1989

While I am registering cabin guests, a young woman reports hitting a deer last night. I am not surprised. They are everywhere. I have already seen a herd of 20, and recently counted 29 while driving the length of the park. Today, I have been given the assignment of feeding the snakes we keep on display. Caging wildlife at visitor centers is controversial. Some naturalists theorize that a snake safely displayed before a juvenile urbanite will suddenly stir within them a sense of awe and wonder. Instead, they tap incessantly on the cage, terrorize the reptile and brag of killing one bigger. I do not believe the visitor's need to see a snake is greater than the snake's need to be wild. The best service a park can offer is to guide visitors to see wildlife in their natural element. I often think of freeing the snake, but another would only be forced to take its place.

January 10, 1989

Susan and I have planned a rendezvous on the quarter-mile Woody Plant Trail for a walk. The creek is impressive here as it cuts through Pitkin Limestone and Fayetteville Shale, the oldest exposed rocks in the park. For a winter day, the valley seems full of color. The sky is a dreamer's blue; the leaves milk chocolate, while oaks and hickories stand naked and gray. Mosses paint the limestone bluffs and Christmas Ferns bask in winter sunlight. Even more captivating is the color of Lee Creek. It is often described as green, but its hue is not so bold. Indeed, there is the mixture of blue and yellow, but only enough of these to suggest a green. Scientifically, the appearance is due to the refraction of light when striking suspended sediment. Its color is a pleasing contrast with the white, foaming rapids.

January 15, 1989

The morning is cold, but perfect for a long hike. I set out to cover 11 of the 13-mile Butterfield Hiking Trail. It is named in honor of the Butterfield Overland Express which carried mail from Tipton, Missouri to San Francisco, California in 1858-1860, and the same which passed through adjacent Fall Creek Valley. After a shuttle to the wood-carved entrance sign on Arkansas Highway 74, I begin the hike at mile marker two. I am the park's self-appointed geographic explorer, prepared to document the region with notes and photographs. The adventure is not solely for orientation but to be the subject of an audio/visual production to be shown in the upcoming season. I leave sight of the road at 9 a.m. Patches of snow lie beside the trail, and ice-laden branches bow to my passing. Around mile three, silence breaks with the witch-like call of a Pileated Woodpecker, and of icicles dripping on leaves, yielding to the day's warmth.

Quaill Valley (spelled today with only one "l" in Quail) is by far the best attraction. The valley is named for Jack Quaill, a retired Tourism Department Assistant Director. He enjoyed hiking in this region and admired its seventy-foot bluffs, waterfalls, caves, and crevices. On his recommendation, Butterfield Hiking Trail was rerouted through here. I take several photographs to capture the essence of this relatively undiscovered area. I meet two hikers at Rock Hole campsite and trade the usual greetings. Relaxing on the bank of Blackburn Creek, we make small talk over cheese and crackers.

At Junction Camp, I soak my feet in the rapids along a gravel shoal below a large Sweet Gum. (Note: This tree has the most fascinating seeds, leaf-shape and scientific name or binomial, to wit (*Liquidambar styraciflua*). This is the halfway point for most hikers, and by far the most popular of the three designated camping areas. Junction Camp, named for the confluence of Blackburn and Lee Creek, is the site of an old community called Anna. On April 29, 1893, a flood scoured the valley killing six of its residents. Five bodies were never found. One woman was discovered tangled by the hair several feet up a tree. A cemetery on the west side of the confluence contains a dozen graves of this forgotten community.

Around mile nine, walking becomes dreamlike. The rhythmic sound of footsteps upon wet leaves numbs the sense of hearing. The sense of smell, however, is acute and the aroma, pleasing. Around mile 10, an armadillo spooks me, as I am sure I have spooked him. Wildlife sightings are strangely few. I cue the hand-held radio from Holt Ridge Vista to determine if the visitor center is within range. Harry answers and warns of an approaching storm. From the vista I see what only he could know by listening to the National Weather Service. I have yet two miles to cover, and both storm and darkness are looming. Descending the ridge is treacherous. Much of Butterfield Trail was built in the 1960's with a bulldozer. My theory is that the operator reached this point around quitting time (or perhaps he caught wind of an approaching storm). Instead of constructing switchbacks, he plowed straight down, four-hundred-fifty feet of elevation. I name this section "Hell's Half Mile." At 4:50 p.m., I complete the trail on the verge of darkness. According to my notes, it has taken an average of thirty-nine minutes per mile including breaks.

January 19, 1989

Debbie Wells, the park bookkeeper, shuttles me to the Old Road Horse Trail on her way to get the mail. I hike to Yellow Rock, then south through cedar glades. Practically ignored by hikers, this horse trail is in many ways more interesting than the adjacent Yellow Rock Trail. "Old Road" pertains to the old CCC highway. Along the way I find an explosives bunker used during road construction.

January 20, 1989

Orientation to the park's forty miles of trails is nearly complete. I walk Vista Point Horse Trail with Harry as he points out two graves. Unmarked sandstone slabs serve as headstones. Called "Civil War graves" by the locals, they are more likely to be that of homesteaders than soldiers since the Bridges family settled here about the same time. In either case, I find these graves to be infinitely more fascinating than the pretentious monuments found in larger cemeteries. Persons passing this way cannot help but wonder who they were and what kind of life they lived on this high plateau. The trail continues through the lower quarry used by the CCC. Flagstones placed around the community building (store and cafe) came from here. Another, much larger quarry is off trail and several hundred yards uphill.

Brent stops by the cabin this evening to tell of a plane crash a few miles south in the Ozark National Forest. Volunteers are on the scene putting out the fire. Minutes later, the local news reports the evacuation of Devil's Den. This is news to us.

January 21, 1989

Around the coffee pot this morning we learn that the plane crash story was in error. Apparently, a piece of a Russian satellite fell and started a fire. The falling debris was observed by many including my older brother in Jane, Missouri, 65 miles to the north.

One of the more enjoyable duties of an interpreter is inventorying the park's natural and cultural resources. Armed with this knowledge, the interpreter can inform and enlighten visitors thoroughly and professionally. A park's natural resource inventory provides a baseline of knowledge allowing naturalists to monitor and document change in the environment. To study the more interesting plant communities, I establish three plots: Yellow Rock Glade, Imp's Leap Ravine, and an unnamed seep downhill from Devil's Ice Box.

A young couple in the cabin next door is requesting my assistance in starting a fire. The fireplaces were remodeled in the mid-1970's to prevent further deterioration; however, the new brickwork constricts the flue. The slightest draft from an open window or door draws smoke away from the flue. Over my shoulder they watch as I demonstrate proper fire building with the last match in the book. I begin with small sticks and newspaper placed in the very back. After igniting the paper, the flame is encouraged by blowing directly at the base. Like spoon-feeding a baby, I add more fuel, slowly. It is critical to maintain patience here. A good fire cannot be rushed in the early stages. Gradually the logs are offered, and the fire perpetuates itself. The process is an art, perfected when denied the use of a second match. Technique number 2: in your camp kit, carry a small plastic 35mm film canister containing dryer lint, lightly dipped in lighter fluid. This application will help the process along (especially for building outside campfires) by skipping the paper and going straight for the twigs.

January 22, 1989

Today's geographic exploration is charted to the Benjamin Holt homesite, and once again the Isuzu is tested. Accompanying me are two backpackers who request a shuttle to the top. The park offers free shuttling for backpackers and mountain bikers. Many prefer to shortcut the first two, mostly uphill miles of the Butterfield Trail. We part ways at the junction, and I continue south down Holt Road, shifting into four-wheel drive.

With only a pen, notebook, and odometer as cartographic tools, I map the prominent features and side trails encountered. Several threatening mud holes that may prove to be bottomless pits are navigated with the greatest of apprehension. The road is well-traveled in winter by hunters, turning ruts into canals. At mile one, I walk to an overlook and find camp area "E", 450 feet below. To the west I see the drainage of Ellis Creek and Arkansas Highway 170 climbing Hurricane Ridge. The ridge, named in 1912, was shaved by a tornado spawned from a gulf coast hurricane. It skipped over the valley but destroyed houses in the Blackburn community.

Continuing back on the road, I reach a point that requires serious soul searching. A steep hill choked with boulders appears to be the crux of the journey. The road forks midway. Left is the older route containing embedded boulders and ledges. The road slants, channeling the wheels into an Everest-size crevasse. The right fork avoids it but is better suited for descending vehicles. I breathe deeply, tighten the seat belt, and throw caution to the wind. Shifting into low-four, I race the engine and relieve the clutch. Bucking and whining, the Isuzu crests the hill triumphantly.

The road continues south, crossing into Crawford County. A stone wall on the right outlines a forgotten farm. Emerging from the woods I reach an abandoned and overgrown field. Downhill on the left, there is a spring-fed pond. Rocks around the spring are reinforced with cement containing the inscription June 30, 1954. I walk to the shore and find it completely frozen. There is an eerie silence here. Except for crows "cawing" in the distance, no other sound is heard. I attempt to remedy the situation by skipping pebbles across the ice, but the reverberations only add to the weirdness.

Up the road, stands a two-room house. Inside is an old stove crammed with sticks and acorns. An Eastern Woodrat or some other rodent has laid claim. This was Benjamin Holt's home. I continue, first taking the left fork which ends abruptly in a field. Backtracking, I take the right fork heading steeply uphill. This, too, terminates in a field, but one far more interesting. Winged Sumac (*Rhus copallinum*), Persimmon (*Diospyros virginiana*) and Coralberry (*Symphoricarpos orbiculatus*) have each colonized a portion. Broom Sedge (*Andropogon virginicus*) covers open ground. I am at the high, southern end of Holt Ridge. Scanning the edges of the field, I locate a 55-gallon drum stuck 30 feet up in an oak. On close examination, I find nails strategically positioned for climbing. Ah! It's a makeshift deer stand, and I cannot resist the temptation to climb. The view is spectacular. I imagine what it was like for Ben. He had to be inspired. Back in the Trooper, I return the way I came, more confident of surviving the mud pits and rocky ledges. I return to my cabin to refuel the body and plan the next map.

After lunch, the adventure continues now with greater confidence in my off-road driving skills and the Trooper's capabilities. I am determined to drive all the way up Lee Creek Valley. North of the park boundary sits a cabin on a shale bluff above the creek. I holler to the cabin, and a bearded gentleman appears on the deck. "Do you mind if I come up", I say, not wanting to barge in upon his private property. "Come on up", he says.

He introduces himself as Jim Boyd, then leads me to a chair beside the fire. He is holding Peterson's Field Guide to the Birds; a journal lies close by. I quickly introduce myself and explain my trespass. Once rapport is established, he confides in me the secrets of the upper valley. Jim is very protective of the area, and I understand why. He has a name for every prominent feature and seems to know the land intimately. I suspect neither Wild Turkey nor White-tailed Deer cross his land without him knowing. An hour later, I depart so as not to intrude any longer in his solitude.

Across the creek, I visit a place Jim calls the "Bubble Hole." A portion of Lee Creek flows underground and reemerges like an artesian well. Upstream, I consult a 1908 map which shows a church near the confluence of Lee Creek and Rich Hollow. After scouting the hollow, I proceed up to the first bench and discover the stone foundation of Old Bethlehem Church. On the west side there is a dilapidated iron gate and fence. A half dozen headstones and several unmarked graves hide amidst the undergrowth. How eerie it is to be alone, deep in this valley, and so close to death. I meditate upon the words of Psalm 23:4. A Pileated Woodpecker laughs in the distance, reaching my ears just before it fades. I am in the valley of the shadow.

The road continues across Rich Hollow then northeast out of Lee Creek Valley. Near the top I come to a house. A man standing on the porch gives me an unwelcome expression. Signs reading "NO TRESPASSING" are everywhere, but what am I to do? Either I continue, or retreat and retrace six miles of creek crossings, ruts, and mud holes. I wave apologetically as I pass the house. In the rear-view mirror I see several other signs hanging from the gate for the benefit of interlopers like me.

January 24, 1989

Shocked into silence, I watch a Cooper's Hawk attack a White-throated Sparrow just 20 feet away. The seeds that I disperse outside the visitor center attract sparrows, goldfinches, and juncos. These birds in turn attract Cooper's and Sharp-shinned Hawks. This hawk is hunting from a tall cedar near the building. I cannot help but feel complicit in this sparrow's demise.

February 3, 1989

The thermometer reads 15 degrees with a windchill of -20 degrees.

February 5,1989

Extremely cold this morning. Birds are crowding the feeders. Ice has formed huge columns over bluff ledges. Harry suggests we document this unusual event on film. We proceed to Twin Falls where the ice is most dramatic. The falls are frozen over the entire forty-foot drop and obstruct the trail. Harry slips twice, once nearly over the cliff.

February 6, 1989

Day two of ice-column documentation: Yellow Rock Falls. Between faulted blocks of sandstone, lies a raccoon, deceased. Black Vultures perched above are startled and flee with a dramatic "whooshing" wing beat. Equally startled, my heart duplicates the sound. I am disturbing their meal. The raccoon is disemboweled, and only a few morsels of the carcass remain.

February 8, 1989

Petit Jean is Arkansas' oldest state park; and like Devil's Den was constructed by the CCC. Its superintendent's position is vacant, and the department has asked Wally to apply. He announces that he will do so. Petit Jean is the department's flagship and (as all rangers recognize) a place of honor to serve. The list of superlative sites and stories is lengthy and sufficient to keep an interpreter occupied for an entire career.

February 11, 1989

While making trail repairs, a group of visitors stop and ask if I would lead them into Devil's Den. Preferring interpretation over manual labor, I honor their request. It is the first cave tour to lead since my days with the National Park Service in the lava tubes of Craters of the Moon.

February 22, 1989

Annual bat survey begins. The park harbors two endangered species, the Indiana Bat and the Ozark Big-eared Bat, the latter is the rarest in North America. Less than three thousand are known. The team is assembled, and includes Dr. Harvey, Mark Clippinger from Beaver Lake State Park, Fred Bagley from the U.S. Forest Service, Brent, Harry, and me. The weather is clear with 29 degrees, but the windchill dips near zero. No one complains. With rope and rappelling harness, I descend two caves which have never been surveyed. Neither prove productive. The overall survey yields four Ozark Big-eared Bats. For the team, the count is disappointing; but for me, the sight of an endangered species is worth the effort.

March 2, 1989

An unusually large flock of robins are congregating around mile one of Butterfield Trail. I estimate at least 200-300 while hiking the downhill portion from Arkansas Highway 74. The American Robin is a permanent resident of the Ozarks and Lee Creek Valley. Their presence here does not signal the vernal equinox or spring migration as many might believe. Probably similar to other species, birds migrate based on hormonal changes triggered by ever-lengthening daylight. They get the urge.

March 3, 1989

Last Tuesday Wally announced his pending transfer to Petit Jean State Park. This evening at 6:30 p.m. a bon voyage dinner commences. Friends, neighbors, the entire staff, and a few loyal visitors have come to wish him well. Wally served as naturalist for 10 years starting in 1974, and then served as superintendent until today. To everything there is a season, and like the many superintendents before him, his term has come to an end. Solomon wrote, "*There is no remembrance of former things.*" There will come a day when this is true; however, the importance lies not so much in the remembering, but in having done something worthy of it. The land will speak of his achievements in whispered breezes for years to come.

March 4, 1989

A winter storm rolls in, first with thunder and lightning, then hail. Hail turns to sleet, and cabin guests begin bailing for home. I find this odd. There is no better place to be stranded than in this valley, miles from worry or tedious plans. Channel Five – our one and only TV station – is predicting four to twelve inches of snow.

March 5, 1989

I wake to find the local meteorologist finally got it right. Three to four inches are on the ground, and it continues to snow. The National Association for Interpretation workshop begins tonight in Tulsa, and Harry and I plan to go. As snow accumulates Harry realizes he should stay home with the family. I have my heart set on going, and at 5 p.m. I ignore warnings to remain. Six inches of snow in the valley means eight on the ridge. It takes nearly an hour to drive to Winslow. US Highway 71 is congested with stranded vehicles, adding to the tribulation. I press on and reach Alma at 7:30 p.m. just before state police close the highway. With a cup of coffee in a crowded McDonald's, I wait to rendezvous with Keith Hobbs from Village Creek State Park. He arrives an hour later with his own horror story. Together, we travel the deserted highway to Tulsa, following ruts carved by an eighteen-wheeler. Monday, 2 a.m., we arrive.

March 11, 1989

A visitor requests assistance pulling his van from the mud. The van is located off Washington County Road 61 in the Ozark National Forest. Keith Wells (park technician) and I head to the scene in the Chevy 4x4. Keith feels sure we can retrieve it. Ordinarily, stranded motorists outside the park are advised to call a wrecker. Whenever visitors get stuck, run out of gas, lock their keys in the car, or forget a hose, fuse, bulb, etc., they hope the park rangers will take care of them. In most cases we do. The van is sucked from the mire with little effort.

The superintendent vacancy at Devil's Den State Park is being advertised, and a few candidates have come to investigate the park. Jessee Cox, assistant superintendent from Bull Shoals State Park, pays us a visit. He is young, yet older than I, and single. He is due for a promotion and will probably get the job. Susan and I invite him to supper and discuss the park's future as we see it.

March 12, 1989

With the day off, Susan and I hike to Quail Valley. It has become one of my favorite areas. I explore the bluffs and crevices below Vista Point, while Susan waits above. I discover a cave which begs to be entered, but near the entrance I am mobbed persistently by an Eastern Phoebe. Against a ledge, a nest of mud reveals her reason for attempting to run me off. My curiosity to explore exceeds my regrets to disturb. In penance, I honor her home with the name Phoebe's Cave.

While examining the bluff shelter of Quail Valley, Susan and I find a passage beneath a faulted block to Hidden Valley. Neither are truly separate nor technically a valley. Much like the park's crevice area, a portion of the bluff has slipped creating this ravine and fracture caves beyond. We relax by the falls, eat lunch, and stretch for a nap.

The roaring water lulls me to the brink of deep REM second phase. I dream the falls have dried and it deeply disturbs me. I wake from the torpid slumber in a state of anxiety to inform Susan that the waterfalls are gone. She laughs. Instantly the roar of the falls returns; however, it occurs to me there is truth in the dream. How long can this tiny intermittent stream send water over ledges? The moment is fleeting, and by midsummer hikers will not share in my present experience.

March 22, 1989

Since Wally's departure to Petit Jean, Tim has served as interim superintendent. Harry and I meet with him to discuss projects and upcoming events. Both Tim and Brent have applied for the vacancy.

March 23, 1989

Living this far from town can be a hardship for a spouse, especially one with a college degree and nowhere to apply it. Statistics reveal that divorce among park rangers is high for these reasons. Susan enjoys the isolation as much as I but would like to apply herself to something meaningful. Although overqualified, and despite the minimum wage, she accepts a receptionist position at the visitor center.

March 25, 1989

Our long-time friends, Paul and Tracy Frick from Kansas City are down to visit. I take Paul to the quarries in his Suzuki Samurai for a little four-wheeling. At sunset we tour the lake by paddleboat and reflect on the present quality of life. Susan and Tracy sit beside the falls and share the latest news, which is hard to get in this remote forest canyon.

March 28, 1989

One of the more exhausting aspects of this job is to present a nature program to six classes of second graders, one class at a time. I have a lot of respect for teachers. At the end of the day, my throat is sore, and I am fighting a splitting headache. Today, I am traveling to Bentonville to show and tell wildlife of Northwest Arkansas. It is National Wildlife Month, and the school librarian has the children lined up in the hall waiting to listen to the ranger. Little do they know, seventeen years ago I attended school here. Little did I know then, I would be back. I try to imagine myself at their age. What is it that I would like to hear? What were my perceptions of wildlife then, and which needed a little myth-busting?

April 1, 1989

Over 170 competitors register to participate in the upcoming Ozark Mountain Bike Festival, the first of its kind in Arkansas State Parks. Tim and Wally proposed the event last summer, and then asked the department to send them to Crested Butte, Colorado to gain ideas from the Fat Tire Festival held there annually. Tim has planned a mountain bike limbo, slow race, observed trials, hill climb, guided trail rides, and a bike toss. An Arkansas Mountain Bike Championship is scheduled for the fall and will include cross country and criterion races.

April 5, 1989

A spear point is found near Lee Creek by a backpacker. He presents it at the visitor center and inquires as to its authenticity. Tim is our authority on such matters, so I yield to him. He believes it is from the Woodland Indian period and may be one thousand to two thousand years old. The hiker wishes to keep the artifact, but this is a violation of federal law since it was found in the Ozark National Forest. I congratulate him on his luck and persuade him to place the artifact in our exhibit case until we receive further instructions from the Forest Service.

Unfortunately, when an artifact is removed or relocated, its scientific value decreases. Greater knowledge is obtained by studying the artifact (*in situ*) in its original location. I wonder if this visitor considers the man (or woman?) who once shaped the point, fastened it to Giant Cane (*Arundinaria gigantea*) which grows tall and strong along the banks of Lee Creek, and threw it with the accuracy to kill, perhaps with the aid of an atlatl. Does he think of himself as a kindred spirit in a shared humanity, or does he see only the ancient tool that may impress his friends? How long before this piece of chert gets tossed into some forgotten shoe box?

Canada Geese, Brown-headed Cowbirds and a Little Blue Heron make their first appearance for the year. I check them off my list, hoping to beat last year's record of the total number of species found.

April 6, 1989

I have come down with a case of spring fever, caused in no small part by a cloudless sky, the incessant chirping of robins and the powerful scent of new growth. The annual wildflower weekend starts Saturday, so I must determine what is blooming. The Yellow Rock Trail reveals Eastern Redbud (*Cercis canadensis*), Bird-foot Violet (*Viola pedata*), both white and yellow Trout Lily (*Erythronium albidum* and *Americanum*), and Spring Beauty (*Claytonia virginica*). I eat one of each, but decide violets and redbuds taste best. The greatest floral diversity is on Devil's Den Trail below Twin Falls. I find Large-flowered Bellwort (*Uvularia grandiflora*) and Dutchman's Breeches (*Dicentra cucullaria*) in bloom but eat neither.

April 7, 1989

Grade school classes visit the park daily, but once again I am on the road to other area schools. I present a career orientation program for 8th graders on what park interpreters do, and how to become one. It was at their age that I decided to be a forest ranger or mountain man, whichever required less responsibility. They look at me in this silly hat and call me "Smokey", "Ranger Rick", and "Joe Ranger". They have no idea what a park interpreter does, so I break them in slowly. "What does a ranger do?" I ask. "They pick up trash and take care of wildlife", one boy answers. Wildlife take care of themselves. Rangers make sure visitors let them continue. The interpreter is the park's scientist and teacher. It is an exciting job, I tell them. One of the boys asks how much an interpreter makes. I pause and then reluctantly answer. Subsequently, all possible converts to the profession are lost. Many years will pass before they realize that money is less important than quality of life. Some may never learn.

April 8, 1989

A crew from channel 29/40 has arrived to cover the wildflower weekend event. I thrive on speaking to large crowds, but TV cameras are intimidating. Good public speaking requires give and take with the audience. Hundreds (thousands?) of people are watching via the airwaves, but there is no way to receive viewer feedback.

The weekend could be considered a success if judged by attendance alone, but the hike is a disaster. It is impossible to stop and discuss a wildflower with fifty people. All crowd around to see one specimen yet crush the remaining colony.

April 12, 1989

Once again, I am in front of the camera. This time there is no speaking part. Susan and I participate in the production of a state park commercial. We play the part of tourists browsing through the gift shop, riding a paddle boat, and checking into a cabin. While we are on the boat, Tim stands on the dock waving to us like a good little ranger. Arkansas State Parks and Tourism has some of the best photographers anywhere. Nearly every image is perfectly staged to entice the out-of-state tourist into visiting the Natural State in all of its glory. To be fair, this is how the game is played, and there isn't a marketing firm in the country that would rely solely on candid shots for their brochures or portfolio images.

April 17, 1989

Blue-winged Teal break from migration to rest on the lake. From the paddle boat, two drakes and a hen are counted.

April 18, 1989

It is a good day for adventure. I have picked a route off the southeast side of Holt Ridge to explore. The daypack is stuffed with lunch, pen, notebook, binoculars, and camera. I park the Trooper at benchmark 1,438 in section 35 and walk down the abandoned road which parallels what I call Quarry Creek. Brent calls it B&W Creek, named by him and Wally. These trivial designations mean nothing to the deer that I just flush from its banks. Rock Doves also see me, and dart from my approach.

I examine the bluff from where they have flown and determine it worthy of inspection. Boulders lie in crumbled mazes below the sandstone bluff. Here, as in Quail Valley and Imp's Leap Ravine, the bluff has collapsed creating crevices and a few insignificant caves.

Continuing along the road, I hear familiar sounds of a hidden waterfall. It is too distant to be the one at Quail Valley. Curiosity unleashed; I scoot down a thirty-foot shale bluff to creek's edge. The current has cut away the shale midstream, and glides smoothly across bedrock. Twenty yards further, water plunges to a blue-green pool sufficiently deep for swimming, but a little too cold.

I follow the stream to its confluence with Blackburn. Bravely fording the big creek, I hike an adjacent ATV trail. The trail leads to Rock Hole and Bluff Camp. Many wildflowers are in bloom, but oddly I have encountered few wildlife since the start. Near the confluence of Blackburn and Lee, the ATV path becomes a full-fledged 4x4 road. The road veers south, leading me ever further from my vehicle. Off trail, I bushwhack through Common Greenbrier (*Smilax rotundifolium*), and Vernal Witch-hazel (*Hamamelis vernalis*) back to Blackburn, crossing it near Junction Camp. Joining Butterfield Trail, I begin the assault on Holt Ridge. After losing elevation all morning, I now must gain it back.

Brent and Harry were here a month ago rerouting the trail around private property. The new route is scenic, weaving among huge boulders high on the ridge. The trail cuts to the base of a twenty-foot bluff, and then, with no other option, continues up through a waterfall. Above the falls, the view into Lee Creek Valley is impressive, but in a few weeks, foliage will obscure it. Finally, the sounds of wildlife; I hear a Barred Owl and Wild Turkeys around mile marker ten.

April 19, 1989

The University of Arkansas Recreation Department has asked me to conduct a backpacking class. This evening, I will speak to twenty-five students about proper equipment to bring and places to go. The biggest mistake beginners make is overestimating their needs. I once witnessed a young man carrying an entire roll of toilet paper, five pairs of underwear, and a book on wilderness survival. Too much food and clothing find their way into an already overstuffed pack. I advise the class to travel light, prepare for rain, and bring whatever it takes to sleep well. A good night's sleep can make or break a trip. We then spend the next hour pulling out gadgets and gear to discuss what might be considered essential and what is convenient or a luxury.

April 21, 1989

After work, Susan and I take a stroll along Lee Creek Trail to the walk-in campground. She is interested in wildflowers, so I quiz her on the names as we encounter them. She enjoys this time of year when I speak Latin (which sounds romantic). More migratory birds have arrived. We hear the flutelike call of the Wood Thrush and "weeeep" of the Great-crested Flycatcher. A Sandpiper flushes as we approach the quarry pond. It is either a Spotted or Solitary, but I cannot be sure.

April 23, 1989

The temperature reaches a record 92 degrees, and recent overnight lows have been in the seventies.

April 25, 1989

Several members of the Oklahoma City Audubon chapter are here for their traditional and annual week of birding. I am introduced to John Newell, their leader, and he invites me to tag along with the club. This is my first spring birding trip in the Ozarks, so I am taking advantage of John's expertise. Among the many bird species ticked off the checklist, my favorites are the American Redstart, Kentucky Warbler, and Northern Oriole due to plumage color and call. John is completely focused on the task at hand, but I am distracted by the diversity of wildflowers. Fire Pink (*Silene virginica*), Wild Geranium (*Geranium maculatum*), and Wild Strawberries (*Fragaria virginiana*) are in bloom today.

April 27, 1989

School groups continue to visit the park for the end of season picnic. Harry and I divide the students into two groups. My group finds an Eastern Hognose Snake and there is pandemonium. The girls are screaming, and the boys are threatening to kill it – each playing out their stereotypical roles. The snake now has every child's full attention. My job now is to harness the charisma of this creature and enlighten these students. But what is most important for them to consider and remember? I focus on these three truths: (1) The snake has no intention of doing us harm. (2) There is nothing macho in killing a hognose snake, and (3) All living things have been given life by the Creator and therefore have the inherent right to exist and to be.

To my knowledge, no one has ever been bitten by a hognose. I ask them to stand aside and watch the snake go through its defense routine. When threatened it puffs its head, giving it the dangerous look of an adder (the locals call it puff adder or spreading adder). This behavior is like a playground bully trying to look bigger and tougher than he knows he is. After puffing, the hognose will strike, not to bite, but to scare. Failing this, tactics reverse. It rolls briefly as if writhing in pain, then lies motionless. The act is exactly the advice given to people in grizzly country in an unfortunate encounter. If the prey appears dead, the predatory will often lose interest. Furthermore, predators prefer to initiate the kill. It is instinct. The theory goes that, if the prey dies of its own accord, it may not be safe to eat. The children watch with fascination. I have given them an alternative perspective on the value of a snake, and I have won the interpretive moment.

April 28, 1989

The waiting is over. Jessee calls from Bull Shoals to tell us he has been hired as park superintendent of Devil's Den.

May 2, 1989

To assist Jessee with orientation, I take him four wheeling along park boundaries, to the overlook, and to Holt farm. Later, he and Tim arrive for supper, and we discuss park issues and goals.

May 22, 1989

For the third day in a row, thunderstorms slam the valley like a bowler's strike. This time they arrive at 5 a.m. knocking out power to the valley—a frequent occurrence during these intense storms. Several trees are down.

The sky finally clears around noon, and I head for Yellow Rock. Every intermittent stream is a raging torrent. The roar of water conceals my footsteps allowing me to observe a Red Fox (*Vulpes vulpes*). He does not see me but appears intent on eating a Blue Jay. Perhaps the water's roar also concealed his approach to the bird. A camera hangs around my neck but reaching for it may alert the fox to my presence. Slowly I position the camera, focus, and shoot. Nothing happens! I forgot to advance the film. Instantly the fox locates me and vanishes in one leap down the ravine. Seeing a fox in broad daylight is an incredible experience. Photographing one is beyond my talent and equipment.

May 23, 1989

My good friend, Dan Sharon, arrives from Fayetteville to enjoy a little hiking and photography. We venture to the caves to document the inside of Devil's Den. This is my first attempt at flash photography, so Dan gives an impromptu lesson. The trick is balancing the F-stop aperture with the distance of the subject.

Shooting too close with a low F-stop will cause the flash to overexpose the film, even in total darkness. Shooting too far away, even with a low F-stop, will result in under exposure. And then there is this whole ISO thing! Finally, trying to focus while holding a flashlight compounds the problem. I am sure in time I will find the right combination, but for now I have several rolls of film with which to experiment.

May 24, 1989

Starting today, the park is in the cigarettes business. The vending machine is unloaded next to the public bathrooms. Several employees as well as visitors smoke based on the thousands of butts I have collected along the trails. I am against selling cigarettes at Devil's Den. Parks are places where mental and physical health are promoted, encouraged, and rewarded. Parks are for clean air, clear minds, and free spirits. Smoking pollutes the air, clouds the mind, and restricts the physical abilities of the visitor, if not now, certainly later. Selling cigarettes is no service to visitors if they leave the park worse than when they came.

The Arkansas Department of Parks and Tourism is being pressured to make its agency self-supporting. In turn, each park is being pressured by the central office to increase its revenue. Unfortunately, this whole cigarette enterprise is about politics and the appearance of running state agencies like private businesses. The problem is, as soon as a state agency runs like a business, the private sector cries foul against unfair competition. Parks have advantages like free tourism marketing, leveraging large material contracts, and less pressure to make quarterly profits. I agree with the notion that a system of parks working together can become self-sustaining with some units being profitable and some costing the system yet too important not to be a state park. Society benefits when it sees the value of a park first before counting the cost. Parks (collectively the park system) should be a nonprofit enterprise that looks for ways to protect important areas without bankrupting the system.

Some desperado is banging on the cigarette vending machine, trying to get the pack to fall off the hook. "No, I do not have the key, and the next nearest tobacco outlet is thirteen miles away," I answer, trying to sound as helpful as possible.

May 26, 1989

Campers can be cutthroats on holiday weekends. One of my duties is to enforce park regulations. Some of these were designed to create a fair process of acquiring campsites. One regulation says that you must be ready to occupy your site immediately. Its purpose is to prevent the locals from coming on Thursday and reserving a site which they have no intention of using until Friday when sites are at a premium. All but 18 sites are first-come, first-serve. This means that the first one who comes to camp gets the site, not the first one to throw out a lawn chair (not even the first one to pay!). The policy is nearly impossible to enforce. It is difficult to distinguish between a person violating the policy and one who is returning to town for groceries or camp supplies.

I explain this policy to a camper waiting to register, and I ask if she is ready to camp?" She pauses, then responds, "Why of course." I suspect she is a "dropper" a person who drops a lawn chair on the site and leaves). We'll get her later. If she fails to occupy the site by 10 p.m., another regulation permits us to remove the lawn chair (tent, trailer etc.), reopen the site, and keep her money. She knows this but takes her chances. They all do. In the meantime, honest campers must wait for us to enforce the rule. Visitors with high integrity coming from out of the area feel that the only way to get a campsite is to compromise their integrity and play the game.

May 27, 1989

The vacation season officially begins. Summer is here, the park is full, and interpretive programs begin in earnest. Harry and I have been looking forward to the daily softball game. We provide equipment, choose teams, and serve as pitchers. The 4 p.m. game has been a tradition for the past 15 years. Even CCC enrollees played ball here in 1937. Their team, the "Devil's Angels", played area high schools and other CCC camps. I am successful in scoring a triple on both turns at bat. This has all the signs of being a good season.

An unbelievable 168 visitors attend my evening presentation, "Waterfalls of Arkansas."

May 28, 1989

A Kentucky Warbler is playing hide and seek with me below Twin Falls. "Kerr teek, kerr teek, kerr teek" attracts my attention. I suspect she is nesting nearby and that I am invading her territory. If I remain, she may eventually reveal her nest, probably near the ground. It is a battle of wills. She fights the urge to return, yet I am willing to wait as long as necessary. Surely, I can be more stubborn than a warbler. My theory proves correct. After scolding me for twenty minutes, she decides that either I am no longer a threat, or the need to return to the nest can no longer be postponed. Perhaps she has completely forgotten me. All the same, she reveals the nest. I am surprised to find it one foot from the trail and less than six inches off the ground in the tangled fork of a Spice Bush (*Lindera benzoin*). Thousands of visitors will walk within inches never knowing what they have missed.

June 2, 1989

The Summer Missionaries arrive today. Jay and John are college students who will be living in the park all summer. Their mission is to conduct a Sunday worship service at the amphitheater and "Day Camp," a daily fun activity for children. The missionaries are sponsored by Baptist Student Unions on college campuses and by Southern Baptist Churches. They are paid a stipend and a small expense account. Considering many students will earn a few thousand dollars over the summer, Jay and John should be commended for their dedication. It wasn't that long ago, during the summer of 1984, that I served a similar Baptist mission in Panquitch Lake, Utah. It was then and there that I realized preaching in Forest Service campgrounds wasn't all that different than interpreting in state park amphitheaters. That summer was the second time I ever saw real mountains.

June 4, 1989

While pretending to be Batman, a boy falls and sprains his arm. I provide first aid and encourage his mother to consult a doctor. The mother says he was jumping from one boulder to the next pretending to fly when suddenly he got a dose of reality.

June 9, 1989

I am experimenting with new programs this season, and today I put one to the test. Devil's Den is no ordinary state park. It attracts many college-aged visitors who desire adventure. They come to hike, bike, spelunk, rappel, and ride horses. I plan a four-mile/four-hour guided hike to Quail Valley. The schedule suggests bringing water and lunch. Fourteen visitors come ready for adventure. Among them are George and Karen Stowe-Rains, a couple Susan and I recently met. George and I have planned several adventures, one scheduled for tomorrow.

The four-mile hike is successful, and we are rewarded with the discovery of several new crevices.

June 10, 1989

After work, Karen shuttles George and me to Lake Fort Smith State Park. We plan to backpack 18 of the 165-mile Ozark Highlands Trail. Lake Fort Smith is the official trail head, 15 miles southeast of Devil's Den. Someday I would like to see this trail and the Butterfield connect.

June 15, 1989

Touring the cave and crevice area is the most popular interpretive activity that we offer. Despite the published tour description and physical requirements, many arrive unprepared. A family of four plan to share one flashlight. A lady arrives in flip-flops, and another in a dress. Over 40 visitors have assembled, and I lead them into the cave. By the time those in back enter, the group in front reaches the end. There is little room to pass each other in the cave, and any attempt to interpret becomes laughable. I am impressed with the camaraderie, each helping one another up and down the ledges. Communicating with the entire group is impossible so I climb onto a ledge and watch the commotion. After a few minutes, individuals begin asking where their guide has gone. In jest, they speculate that I am probably lost. I am lost in the moment, contemplating how quickly a dark and gloomy cave can be transformed into a wonderful and friendly place. Thirty minutes ago, we entered as strangers, but now we are bonding in this shared adventure.

Once again, I get to play the role of good ranger. A wallet is recovered much to the owner's relief. Through camping records, I can track him down and return it. I had a similar experience during the summer of 1986 while working at Craters of the Moon National Monument. A visitor had travelled nearly an entire day before realizing that he had left his jacket and vacation money of approximately $109 at the trail head of last night's guided hike. I happened to be the one on duty when the man called. I promised him that I would look for it. I located the items easy-enough, and called the man to inform him that the items went out with the day's mail to his home address. He was so overwhelmed and relieved that he took the time to write to the park superintendent and Secretary of the Interior!

June 17, 1989

A local Troop has volunteered to remove the trash from Devil's Den Cave. Litter has accumulated for years and is an odorous, depressing site. I assist them with the cleanup and discover a few items I would rather not touch. We find dozens of empty beer cans—one unopened, and two full of urine.

We find used condoms. Ironically, one theory on the origin of the name "Devil's Den" involves an unmarried couple who had sex here. They mysteriously disappeared into the cave, never to be seen or heard from again. The devil took them. The tale was told and retold by many parents to their sons and daughters in an attempt to discourage fornication.

An inventory of cave litter includes the following: cans, bottles, broken glass, candy bar wrappers, candles, batteries, flashlights, cigarettes, canteen, rope, condoms, underwear, shoe, shirt, Band-Aids, coins, twigs, branches, lighter, trail brochure, unidentifiable food items, toilet paper, and human feces. Caves bring out the best in people.

June 21, 1989

Alan Gresham, an old acquaintance from college, is hired as Trail Crew Supervisor. He and his wife will be moving to the park soon which will bring our valley population to 13, including three dogs. There are twenty miles of trails to maintain, and many are in poor condition. It will be good to have a crew working full-time.

June 27, 1989

Over the past two weeks, heavy rains have transformed Lee Creek into milk-chocolate, but now the creek returns to its normal cool-mint coloration. The water level is average and perfect for fishing. My brother-in-law, Charlie Bullard, and I plan to spend the day fishing from Cedar Grove upstream to the horse camp. Years ago, we spent a day fishing Sugar Creek in Bella Vista and have since preferred creeks to lakes. Fishing from shore or boat does not have the same primal experience as actually getting in the current with the adversary. The fish move from pool to pool, and we are right in there with them fighting brush, rapids, snakes, and underwater cliffs.

There are some courtesies to consider when creek-fishing with companions. Since every hole potentially holds success, the leader must restrain from fishing it out before his partner gets an opportunity to lay a lure in its deep recesses. If he gets too far ahead, he will spook the fish downstream where his partner is. One solution is to move ahead at about the same speed, designating sides of the creek or alternating holes. Equipment used in this style of fishing is basic. I prefer a telescoping rod and ultralight reel strung with two-pound test.

We are well-acquainted with our prey. There are only a few game species that fare well in upland Ozark streams. Green Sunfish (Centrarchidae: *Lepomis cyanellus*) are most common, thus most often caught. Many amateurs call them perch, but they are members of the sunfish family. Green Sunfish tolerate warm, low-oxygenated water. They have large mouths and appetites to match. Once, I caught one on a bare hook. "Greens" rarely exceed seven inches but are heavy-bodied fighters.

Longear Sunfish (Centrarchidae: *Lepomis megalotis*) are smaller by comparison, flat-sided, and have smaller mouths. With skin of brilliant orange and blue, they are by far the most colorful game fish in the Ozarks. One might expect to find them in more tropical streams. "Longears" are fighters but not so easily caught.

The "trout" of warm waters is the Smallmouth Bass (Centrarchidae: *Micropterus dolomieu*). Like trout in western streams, they are prized above all others, are good eating and fight until exhausted. In Lee Creek, these "brownies" rarely exceed twelve inches, and are more often caught in the 8-10 inch range.

At Sugar Creek we take our oath on beetle-spins or plastic grub worms, but today (especially here on Lee Creek), I fish one lure exclusively, the Rebel Crawdad. It floats until slowly retrieved, bringing it to the desired depth. I have two rules for creek fishing: (1) cast where you can see the fish, and (2) use a lure you can watch. Half the fun is watching native fish lunge after fake tackle. A cast is made from mid-creek to the bank. The lure is left motionless for three seconds, then given a quick, light jerk. I retrieve the lure slowly with an occasional twitch. If after covering eight feet, no fish have taken interest, I quickly retrieve the lure and recast. Casting upstream to a pool below a set of rapids is often productive. Here the Smallmouth Bass are lurking.

After roasting for several hours in the sun, we call it quits. My total count reaches 15 with a couple "brownies" to my credit. Charlie catches less, but it is I who has the home court advantage. Back at the cabin, our wives ask, "Where are the fish?" Charlie and I rarely keep them. Most are too small to eat. More importantly, we fish, not for trophies, but for the experience. There are more rewards in a few hours of fishing than in a month of work. We share thoughts and dreams. We watch Green Herons hunt and water snakes on the prowl. We hear Ovenbirds screaming "Teacher, Teacher, Teacher!". We smell algae-covered rocks and the unforgettable fragrance of fish slime on hands and clothing. We feel the water rush around our ankles and tiny minnows nipping leg hairs. We are one with the creek, the neotropical birds, and of course fish.

June 29, 1989

Usually, Harry and I are pleased if we can get all the bases covered for the afternoon softball game. Because many have come for the extended holiday week, there is no shortage of potential team members today, ranging in age from 5-65. For the sake of safety, we divide the players into two groups – those 5-12 years old and those 13 and over. After every kid has had the chance to hit the ball at least once, the kids' game is declared over.

Now it's time for the serious game, which over the years has created rivalries among the returning visitors like James Hauser, a friend of Harry's from Kansas City. James is one of those guys who always gets picked early in the lineup due to his size and strength. At his first time up to bat, James sends the ball across the road, hitting Bob Horn's trailer. Bob is also from Kansas City and forgives James for his uncontrollable power. Bob knows the risk, but figures no one else can hit the ball that far, and besides, does not want to give up the best campsite for viewing the game.

The rules of the game are complex. Most importantly, the park will not be held liable for injuries and/or damages during the game.

It takes a while to learn Devil's Den softball rules: (1) bunting, stealing base, sliding, diving or tagging are not allowed, except when the out is forced, the runner may be tagged, (2) If a ball hits a tree in fair territory it is an automatic double unless caught from the tree for an out, (3) If a ball hits the cherry tree down third base it is foul even if the offending branch is hanging in fair territory, (4) Any ball hit on the bathhouse roof can be caught for an out, (5) Any ball hitting the bat house hanging on the electric pole is an out, (6) runners are not required to tag bases because they are not tied down, but must simply run around them (exceptions include when trying to beat out a throw or when waiting to advance), (7) All runners return to the previous base when the pitcher touches or catches the ball, (8) If the pitcher catches the hit, the play is dead and no base runners can advance, (9) If the pitcher makes the playoff the ground, he must get rid of the ball and receive it again before play is dead, (10) the most any team can score in one inning is ten runs, and finally (11) Woman always get picked first, and never strike out. It is the one chauvinistic rule that is never disputed. All these rules were established over the years to prevent injuries and to allow for an abnormal playing field. It also encourages the whole family to play since no one knows the rules better than any other.

June 30, 1989

4:45 a.m., a camper calls to report a couple of teenagers in a white pickup knocking over a Coke machine. I stumble out of bed, throw on my uniform and head out for a look. I cannot find the kids but instead I encounter a drunk driver near the county road. I persuade him in my best, yet drowsy composure, to park in an unoccupied campsite until sober.

July 1, 1989

Every odd year, on the Saturday before July 4th weekend, alumni of CCC company 3795 hold a reunion. These men are the living legacy of Devil's Den State Park. To honor them, Jessee, Tim, Brent, Harry, and I serve their evening meal. There are several men in attendance, but fewer than last year, probably more than next. Most are in their 70's; but turn 18 as they relive memories of their days in the CCC.

July 3, 1989

A more recent tradition than the CCC reunion and far less constructive is the one I am being drawn into today. It seems a couple of families from Texas camp here each year around the fourth. At night they load up in the back of a pickup and string toilet paper around employee residences. Apparently, the tradition is too old to break, but I try anyway. Everyone's cabin has been hit but mine, primarily due to the vigilant watch of my dog, Bridger, who barks when they approach. Unsuccessful tonight, the Texans are sure to be back tomorrow.

July 4, 1989

Devil's Den Games begin! One of the greatest park traditions is the annual Fourth of July games which include sack races, watermelon seed spit, egg toss, horseshoes, softball throw, cow chip throw and crosscut saw competition. Many in attendance participate each year such as Donny Landon (local and frequent champion). Among returning competitors are members of the Texas toilet paper gang. They are upset with me for last night's foiled attempt. The TP gang consists of family members and relatives ranging in age from 10-60. The gang leader is a gray-haired grandmother. One of the young kids attempts to hit me with an egg after the egg-toss competition but is no match for my quick pitching arm. I return volley hitting him square between the shoulders. He incorrectly assumed a good ranger would not fight back. Upon returning home I find that my house was toilet-papered during the games. I have been double-crossed by George and Brent who have clearly sided with the enemy.

July 7, 1989

One of the more rewarding experiences of a park interpreter is speaking to a conservation organization. There are many of these in the area, including the Ozark Society, Sierra Club, Native Plant Society and Ozark Highlands Trail Association. Tonight, I am speaking to the Northwest Arkansas Audubon Society. It is a great opportunity to meet others in the conservation cause and share new ideas.

July 8, 1989

Thanks to Harry, I now know where Farmer's Cave is located. Likely the valley's largest geologic feature in the Pitkin Limestone formation, the cave is classified as a solution cave caused by acidic water dissolving the rock and creating underground passages. Farmer's Cave greatly contrasts to the sandstone caves on Devil's Den Trail. My brother, Doug, and I return and explore several passages. I am excited to discover its extent, and to see a Cave Salamander.

July 9, 1989

Visitors do have the best intentions, but sometimes they are frustrating. Two young men bring a fawn to the office and request that we raise it. They say it was abandoned in the crevice area. Tim explains that the fawn should have been left alone. The mother was surely nearby. The deer's best hope for survival is to locate it back to where the mother was last seen. The young men are tired, embarrassed and show no desire to return the fawn. Tim and George carry it back to its origin, an exhausting mile round-trip.

July 11, 1989

Today's softball injuries include abrasions and wounded pride. I lose the game by hitting a pop fly for the final out. The more embarrassing play, as captured on video, went as follows: Harry's second cousin is on third base. I am the pitcher. The ball is hit to me on the ground, and I advance to make the tag. The runner at third charges ahead and we collide at home. From the video it appears I plowed the young boy in a brutal effort to make the out. The boy, determined to score, becomes a runaway freight-train. I am left with the injury and he with the run.

July 16, 1989

One advantage of living in the woods is the lack of yard work. The woods, in their wild and wonderful state, encroach to the very walls of the cabin. I like it this way. Susan prefers landscape. After much foot-dragging, I yield to her desire and go for the lawn mower and weeder. Back at the cabin, I proceed to civilize the forest. Amid the oil, smoke, and dust, I discover the remains of a rare and medicinal plant, Golden Seal. Nearby is the foliage of Dutchman's Breeches. Both species are past their bloom and far from appropriate habitat. Later, I discover Tim had transplanted them a few years ago. Both species grow naturally along Devil's Den Trail, and to my knowledge, nowhere else in the park.

July 24, 1989

Alan, George, and I return to Farmer's Cave armed to the teeth with various scientific instruments and equipment. Today's mission is to map the cave and proceed farther than Doug and I a couple of weeks ago. Alan and George explore while I sketch passages and photograph features. George crawls down a pit and back into a small tunnel. "Eight inches wide, three feet high," he yells. To our knowledge, no one has previously named any of the rooms or features. I assume the task. Chandelier Room, The Epiglottis, Garage, Saddle Room, The Pentagon, Drinking Room, and Key Room are named today. The cave has few dramatic features or speleothems. What stalactites there were have been vandalized. Still, some small formations occur such as popcorn, flowstone, soda straws, and draperies. We encounter one Cave Salamander, two Slimy Salamanders, one Eastern Pipistrelle, Cave Crickets and, oddly, acorns which are sprouting. Their presence tells of a fluctuating creek level and of another opening.

Winding through a low passage, we come to three junctions. One to our left concludes in a small room. The one to the right is very narrow and assigned to George. Alan and I proceed through the middle one. It requires belly-crawling inches at a time. After 10 feet, the room opens considerably. Our voices echo across 50 feet of darkness. The ceiling is at least 12 feet high. I call it "The Garage". The room appears large enough to park an 18-wheeler. George is hollering from his passage. He is on the other side of the wall, but a 10-foot climb will bring him into "The Garage." I peer down the hole and he confirms that he can see my light. The passage is tight and curves to my ledge at an awkward angle. George presses on. After several groans he maneuvers into the light. I lower a rope to him, but he cannot find the footing needed to position himself into the hole. After several minutes, he wears out and abandons the passage.

Passages diverge in all directions from "The Garage." We proceed left to another room with many passages—five to be exact. At the entrance to "The Pentagon" there is a wall consisting of mud and gravel. We climb it and find a passage with potential. It is low and wide, terminating into a 10-foot slide. Each room is connected by a small passage. We enter one to find an empty six-pack of Busch Beer. I note on my map "The Drinking Room." In the next I find a post office key belonging to a box in the Chicago suburbs. "Key Room" is the last place to sit with any comfort. From here we enter, single file. Before terminating into a passage only a bat could navigate, I discover the best drapery formations in the cave.

Back at the "Garage," we attempt one more passage. This one begins with a 12-foot mud bank and a low squeeze against the ceiling. Once through the squeeze we find ourselves on a saddle of compacted mud. Passages drop away from both sides. We explore briefly then exit. The "Saddle Room" may prove to be the staging ground for the cave's next big discovery.

July 25, 1989

Although it contradicts my philosophy on fostering independence, I look forward to assisting visitors with keys locked in a car. What a terrible feeling it is to realize you are miles from town, the spare key is in Shreveport, Dallas or wherever, and you can't even find a coat hanger. Ranger to the rescue! I bring the jimmy stick (a flat metal bar) and other assorted tools and begin. First, I try with the stick down the door panel, sometimes finding instant success. Secondly, if visible and within reach, I go for the keys directly with a coat hanger through a crack in the window. Once, I even hooked on to keys in the ignition by maneuvering a coat hanger specially designed on site. Locksmiths charge $50 or more to come to Devil's Den, especially on Sundays. Who can blame them. The ranger can save the visitor money and prevent wasted hours and heartache.

Again, humiliation at the softball game. Up to bat five times, I proceed to pop out three. My team loses.

July 29, 1989

Twenty-five people attend the morning hike to Yellow Rock. All goes well until the group encounters a snake. There is the usual panic by some, but I quickly control the moment. No matter what an interpreter is discussing at the time, be it geology, history, or wildflowers, discussion ceases when a snake is spotted. If the interpreter continues to ignore the snake, he talks to a deaf audience. It is a Black Racer. Non-poisonous, I tell them to their relief. To see the characteristics of a non-poisonous snake, I catch and hold it close for their inspection. The snake is trapped between us and the bluff. I approach slowly. Distracting with my left hand, I grab it behind the neck with my right. It squirms and wraps its body around my arm, defecating spontaneously. It is in no pain but likely a great deal of stress. Everyone gathers around to see this mysterious serpent. I point out the round pupil which in almost all snakes is a non-poisonous trait. Its head is somewhat round and scales under the tail are in two rows, unlike pit-vipers.

All are caught in the moment. Young children are jockeying for a position to see and feel its dry, scaly skin. Adults are watching and sharing snake stories of their own. I feel as all teachers must, the glory of revealing something valuable. In all the spectacle, no one considers the snake's predicament. A few seconds ago, it was basking in the heat. With little warning, it was snatched by the throat and groped by a dozen oily fingers. We are looking at the snake but fail to notice its head working through my grip. Suddenly, it reaches around and bites my thumb. Instinctively I drop it. Everyone jumps back and reacts as when we first encountered the snake. Seconds later it is gone. Standing under the bluff, blood dripping from my finger, I realize they are all staring at me. I have transformed from expert into victim in less than a minute. The way to recapture the audience, I suspect, is to make light of the incident. "I'm pretty sure it was non-poisonous," I tell them.

August 3, 1989

Traditions are occasionally meant to be broken. I schedule a softball game for 7 p.m. which apparently makes all the difference in my performance. I score two home runs and win the game.

August 5, 1989

Attempting to increase visitation in August, I plan a special event which begins today. We needed something catchy like "Buzzard Days" to attract attention while at the same time offering a unique educational experience. [Note: Buzzards do not occur in North America, and the word itself is slang for Turkey Vulture and Black

Vulture]. Lake Catherine State Park celebrates Possumfest, Crowley's Ridge State Park celebrates Mosquitofest, and some other park (I forget which) celebrates armadillos. Lee Creek Valley does have an inordinate number of Turkey Vultures, so it seems appropriate. Many confuse them with eagles and find vultures to be filthy. Vultures keep themselves quite clean even though they tunnel into maggot-infested roadkill and urinate on their own legs to regulate their temperature. A Vulture's head is naked which helps to kill maggots by exposing them to the hot sun. I imagine how blood-soaked head feathers could lead to an itchy scalp. Buzzard Days consist of a morning hike to Yellow Rock, slide program entitled "Raiders of the Roadkill", Buzzard Burger special at the restaurant and vulture-calling contest. Oddly, we see no vultures at Yellow Rock; however, we do interrupt a wedding in progress. Hopefully, no one will tell the bride her special day is for the birds. The vulture-calling contest is held at the amphitheater. Contestants are judged by accuracy of the call and appearance. Two come dressed for the occasion. Several in the audience attempt the call, imitating crows, hawks, blue jays, and owls. Only at the conclusion of the contest do I reveal that vultures do not have a call. They may wheeze, snort, hiss, or make a coughing sound, but overall, they are silent. Kelly, a young girl from Kansas City, is declared the winner by applause.

August 6, 1989

Ranger duties call. A young boy has fallen into one of the crevices and may be paralyzed. He is extricated from the crevice and transported in a private vehicle to emergency care in Fayetteville.

The phone rings again. This time an RV has stalled on the road to camp area "A". I hook a rope to the Trooper and tow the RV into a campsite. The immediate problem is quickly resolved.

August 20,1989

Occasionally, several employees will have the same scheduled day off. Jessee, George, I, and others pile in the Trooper and head down Holt Road in search of adventure. Our main objective is to do a little rock climbing. At Quail Valley, we establish a rappel, and everyone takes a turn. After lunch the ropes are moved to another part of the bluff for belay-climbing. I top-rope George as he attacks the 60-footer.

I have always loved to climb. For a few years I did so without the safety of ropes, giving very little thought to the enormous risk. Fortunately, my wake-up call came early in my climbing career. Once, Paul and I were free soloing an unnamed route on White Rock Mountain. About 30-40 feet up, he reached for a nonexistent handhold and fell suddenly. Miraculously, he grabbed a treetop which bent over gently as he fell, practically sitting him down with not so much as a scratch. The incident was over as quickly as it began. We were both a bit shaken and speechless. I still had more than half the climb above me to complete.

This climb is different. I am wearing a Chouinard climbing harness, secured with a locking biner and rescue-8 to 150 feet of Blue-water climbing rope. On belay is George who, having depended on me for this added layer of safety, will return the courtesy.

The first eight feet of the route is a cinch. After this, handholds become less obvious. Ledges are plentiful, but each comes with an overhanging cliff. Forty feet up, I work my way across the ledge to a crack. If I slip here, I will undoubtedly swing several feet before the belay will catch (the pendulum effect). With adrenaline and determination, I crawl onto the ledge. With a good foothold, there is no fear in looking down. Everyone is looking up, making fun of my technique (a primitive form of encouragement). Sweat, sand, dust and insects begin to annoy me. Concentrating on the final push, I examine an overhanging ledge chest high. Here I must completely trust George to keep a tight belay. I swing my left leg high looking for a hold. After three tries I find one, and now reach with my right hand. On three, I pull on the rope with my left until I can reach the top with my right.

Standing on the bluff above the oaks, a sense of accomplishment rushes over me. I search for some divine understanding of what I have just done and why. I am left with only these simple truths: A risk successfully taken renews the human spirit. Unspoken pride fuels the next risk. The brave practice death.

August 21, 1989

Climbing continues, but this time "on the clock." I have suggested the park allow rappelling in a designated area as opposed to prohibiting it altogether. The question is where? Most would prefer Yellow Rock, but conflicts would result. Hikers should not be expected to step over ropes to see the view, and climbers would be endangered if they did. After rappelling several routes, none seem exactly right. Finally, I choose a faulted block known as "Devil's Teapot". It stands 50 feet high and 100 feet from the main bluff. Yellow Rock Trail runs beneath, providing access for climbers and spectators. Devil's Teapot contains a deep fracture called Wild Dog Crevice, named years ago when Brent discovered a stray dog giving birth near the entrance. The Devil's Teapot seems to be suitable for both climbing and rappelling. If the rest of the staff agrees on the location, I will begin writing the proposal.

August 23, 1989

Susan's father paid us a surprise visit yesterday. Today, I take him four-wheeling to one of my favorite places. One mile north of camp area "A", the Outlaw Trail forks to the right. Several years ago, horse rides were given here. The trail name was attributed by the outfitters. A quarter mile down the Outlaw Trail, we take a spur trail to the creek. Lee Creek is dry except for pools, exposing a flat bed of limestone in the Hale Formation. This section is over one hundred feet wide and three hundred feet long terminating with an abrupt slope. The bedrock is so full of crinoids, horned corals, and other fossils that I give it the name "Fossil Flats."

August 31, 1989

Only ten visitors attend the evening program. Except for Labor Day weekend, the season is over. There are few campers, which explains tonight's low turnout. During my presentation on wilderness, the discussion turns to pollution and litter. A man in the audience insinuates that kids today are the ones littering the highways. I want to tell him that teenagers are not to blame any more than old men are; and that throwing an aluminum can in the ditch is no worse than throwing one in the garbage where its next stop is the landfill. At least the one in the ditch may yet be collected and recycled. There is a certain hypocrisy about sending aluminum cans, and glass bottles to the landfill yet cursing a litter bug. Furthermore, I have read no study that indicates younger drivers are more likely to part with their gum, orange peelings, or fast-food containers than adults. The problem is much larger, runs deeper, and is older than this man suggests.

September 5, 1989

The summer season ended yesterday, but tonight we celebrate the fact. All employees and family members assemble at the pool for food, spirits, and fun. Tim and George bet who would be first to paddle around the island and back. It is a tight race, but Tim looks as if he has something to prove. Everyone is either swimming or being thrown in the pool. Finally, Jessee is caught off guard and thrown into the algae-crusted lake. Somehow, I escape the big dunk.

September 12, 1989

After nine months of exploration, I have yet to reconnoiter Ellis Creek, which flows into the southwest corner of the park. I set out to remedy this oversight. The Isuzu Trooper and daypack are loaded with the usual maps and equipment. Ellis Creek cuts through limestone of the Pitkin and Hale Formation; however, most of the headwater cuts through Brentwood Limestone of the Bloyd Formation. The geology is fascinating. Solution caves, sink holes, faults, bluffs, waterfalls, and limestone flats are all present. At the first creek crossing, I park the Trooper and proceed on foot up the dry creek bed. A light drizzle begins, making the rocks slippery. Gravel gives way to a small pool. Green Sunfish and Smallmouth Bass dart from my approach. The pool is guarded to the east by a thirty-five-foot shale bluff. Skirting around to the west, I continue upstream to the next pool and a crumbled stone wall. Overhead, crows mob a Broad-winged Hawk. Birds are everywhere. I can hear jays, chickadees, and a nuthatch. Beaver-chewed twigs line the pool's edge, but (*Castor canadensis*) himself is not seen. To the left, a small intermittent stream exits an intriguing hollow.

At first the hollow rises gently, then becomes more rugged as boulders choke the ravine. I take to the high bank and climb to a bench (Elevation 1,380). The bench is flat and wide with a gentle rise to the left and south-facing bluff to the right. From the bluff I can see Ellis Valley and Holt Ridge. Greenbrier, aromatic sumac, and huckleberry weave an impenetrable snare. A horsefly attacks unrelentingly. I run to escape the annoyance but nearly collide face first into a spider web. I stop just in time, but the fly has seen it too late and crashes headlong into the sticky silk. I step back, catch my breath, and watch the spider seize its prey. One bite and the buzzing ceases. Ironic that I, prey of the horsefly, emerge unscathed, while it dies in the clutches of another predator.

"...the race is not to the swift, nor the battle to the strong, nor bread to the wise, nor riches to the intelligent, nor favor to those with knowledge, but time and chance happen to them all." Ecclesiastes 9:11

I snap a few photographs and descend to the creek. Cardinal Flowers (*Lobelia cardinalis*) are in full bloom along the banks of Ellis. An Eastern Screech-Owl makes his presence known, or perhaps mine.

September 14, 1989

The word is out. Mountain biking is a popular park activity, and there is no time like the present to participate. I borrow one of the rental bikes and follow George up the fire road. Fifteen minutes later, I discover my muscular ineptness. My butt hurts, my legs are burning, and twice I find myself sailing over the handlebars. Injuries include scratches, bruises, flat tire and broken rear reflector. No matter how glamorous biking may look, I would rather strap on a 30-pound pack and hike Hell's Half Mile. I must remember to ask Tim or George what it is about mountain biking that they find most appealing. Is it the speed or the access to places in the park that are closed to automobiles? Is it the adrenalin production that can be so addictive? Or is it the tight curves and quick twists encountered at high speed. Clearly, mountain bikes are the wrong conveyance for wildflower watching or skipping rocks across a glass-like pool.

September 16, 1989

The Boyds invite Tim and me to a party at their Lee Creek cabin. It will take half an hour of four-wheeling to get there—all the more reason to go. Upon arrival we meet several others who have braved the trip. There are plenty of refreshments and conversation. I meet Tom McKinny, president of Sierra Club's Ozark Chapter, and others who care deeply about protecting and preserving the valley. We talk of buying as much land here as possible to protect it from logging or further development. Looking north from Yellow Rock, one can see the entire watershed of Lee Creek. It is a grand, unspoiled view, one of the last in the western Ozarks. Most of the land is private, yet how long will it remain unexploited? What will the next generation see from Yellow Rock?

September 17, 1989

On morning rounds, I am appalled at the number of campers attempting to leave without registering. Perhaps they do not realize there is a fee. They think the ranger collects at the site, and if they pack in a hurry they can slip out before meeting with one, I meet them. Camping on public land should be inexpensive where amenities are few or nil. When electricity, plumbing, toilet paper, and park security are involved, visitors must pay for the service. The average Arkansas resident pays only eight pennies a year in general state taxes for Devil's Den State Park. That buys the camper a quarter-roll of toilet paper. Skipping out on fees requires no elaborate heist, and it is easy to rationalize. (How many times have I heard the excuse: We came in really late last night" or "We just got in." In their rationalizing, they have not stayed long enough to warrant having to pay, but the result is underfunded park operations, vandalism, and fewer services. Eventually, parks would not be worth visiting, or at the very least the park experience impacted.

October 2, 1989

Not everyone is sold on the rappelling site (August 21). I continue to lobby the case and write the mountaineering proposal. Harry has never rappelled. Today is as good as any to learn. We climb Devil's Teapot and discuss the trade-offs: environmental degradation verses recreational opportunity. Harry watches as I demonstrate a rappel. With little encouragement, Harry walks to the ledge, looks down, leans out and steps. In this first step, the rappeler's courage is determined. It is the least stable. Harry proceeds without hesitation. After three steps he relaxes and enjoys the thrill.

October 3, 1989

I return to Devil's Teapot and Wild Dog Crevice to explore this minor cave. George is always ready for adventure and accompanies me. The entrance requires a low crawl but opens shortly enough to stand. The crack is one to two feet wide, but the ceiling varies from three feet to more than thirty feet high. The passage angles downward, terminating in a small room. A series of ledges allow us to climb to a second level of the same fracture. The upper passage extends nearly the length of the crevice but terminates near the entrance. There is a 10-foot drop to the floor; I dare not jump. With George waiting behind me, I must make the decision for both of us. We chimney down the fracture by wedging our bodies against the jagged sandstone walls.

Harry informed me of another cave somewhere in the vicinity. big-eared bats have been documented in Yellow Rock Crevice (another misnamed, fracture cave). If Devil's Teapot is designated a mountaineering site, we must research this cave and determine the impact, if any, it will have on the endangered species. Scouting around, I find the crevice in question. Inside, two large cave passages diverge. We choose one to the right and discover a huge room. Except for Farmer's Cave, this may be the largest underground room in the valley. On Inspection, I locate a bat hanging from the ceiling. George takes a closer look and confirms – big ears. Cave Orb Weavers are too numerous to count. Vandalism and litter are not yet present. Perhaps its well-hidden entrance and distance from the crevice area across the valley have saved it from exploitation. The question now is how long it will remain pristine if mountaineering is permitted. I am starting to feel conflicted. I have been advocating for this recreational activity, but I am also a sworn protector of what little remains of the park wildness. This is the struggle that most park professionals experience: striking a balance between the development of facilities (and recreational opportunities) and maintaining/restoring the natural, wild, and free.

October 4, 1989

Once Harry learns of the sighting, we return to confirm it. The bat is still there. There is only one, and historically, few big-eared bats have ever been found in Yellow Rock Crevice. We speculate as to the impact mountaineering would have on the bat's population, but there is no way to know for sure. The mountaineering proposal is complete. With consensus, we send it to higher powers. How far will it go?

October 7, 1989

The Arkansas Herpetological Society is conducting their fall meeting in the park. I wish I could spend the weekend with them flipping logs for snakes, salamanders, and such, but another commitment prevents me. I am leading my first backpacking trip on Butterfield Trail.

Over 30 attend the 12th annual environmental backpack workshop. Harry leads a dozen. James Wilborn, college student and seasonal interpreter, has volunteered to assist with my group, and has taken the sweep position. The group consists of men and women of all ages and backgrounds including a schoolteacher from Oklahoma, a fire chief from Kansas City, and others from as far away as Dallas and Wichita.

After shuttling to Holt Road, we begin the two-day, 12-mile hike. We stop every quarter mile to rest, check gear, snack, and interpret the outstanding trail features. Lunch is held at Quail Valley.

With only three miles before camp, we linger at Quail Valley, exploring bluffs and crevices. I lead a group of 10 into a large crevice to view spiders. While exploring, a member of the group slips on the talus shale. The fall results in a nasty bruise to his back, and he is in severe pain. I propose a plan of extrication that would involve James and another hiker returning to the trailhead with the injured man, but he refuses to abandon the hike. After allowing him time to catch his breath, we proceed to the creek. He struggles with his pack but is determined to continue.

At the bottom of the hill the Butterfield intersects an old pioneer road. The trail follows the road to the right, but I lead a portion of the group to the left to see the Francis Marion Mannon homesite. Francis was the son of Moses Mannon who helped settle Lee Creek Valley in the 1840's. Francis moved to Blackburn Valley after serving in the Civil War. Moses had 11 children, and Francis in turn had 13 with the help of three wives. Francis was not a polygamist. Women commonly died giving birth in those days. Men remarried as much for love as for necessity. Women played a crucial role in raising children and running the farm. The group is fascinated with the 14-foot chimney which stands in the woods like an ancient monument.

I march the backpackers two miles without a break. We take 15 minutes at Rock Hole to soak tired feet on the banks of Blackburn Creek. A mile later Bluff Camp is reached, tents are erected, wood gathered, and supper prepared. I spread the sleeping bag, lean back against a mature hickory, and observe the others. A young boy named Jim is running around the fire catching Fence Lizards. I ask him not to harass the wildlife, but minutes later I catch him throwing one into the flames. "Lizard killer!" I shout. Jim takes it as a title of honor.

After supper, we gather around the fire, play word games, and watch James fix banana-boats. As the night wears on, some retire to their tents. Those who stay share personal beliefs on the environment, politics, and religion. Strangers we were a few hours ago, but now we are revealing our innermost beliefs and feelings. I stoke the fire one last time, lie back, and face the stars. Tents are useful when seeking shelter from rain and insects or for privacy, none which are concerning to me this night.

October 8, 1989

One by one backpackers emerge from their tents and huddle by the fire. I quickly consume my breakfast of instant oatmill, but others prepare elaborate servings of bacon, eggs, biscuits, and fried potatoes. Yesterday I intentionally packed light on food, betting that many of the beginners would overestimate their appetite. Once they realize their folly, they will offer the leftovers to anyone. I take my share to help them honor the tradition of offering the guide "first fruits" of the first cooked meal on the trail.

With breakfast consumed and gear loaded, we begin the six-mile return hike. At Junction Camp, we meet Harry's group, which got a late start. At Hell's Half Mile we take our final break. Some are too tired to hike the spur to Holt Ridge Vista, and instead settle for a mediocre view while waiting for our return. The hike concludes with a group photo from the suspension bridge around 1 p.m.

Upon return, I am called to respond to an accident in the crevice area. With emergency gear, I make haste to Devil's Den Cave, and there I find a young boy with a badly cut head. The parents are in such a state of shock, they refuse to let me examine the injury. Instead, they race to their car and the hospital. Although trained in medical first response, I cannot help them if they refuse it.

October 9, 1989

There is much to learn concerning local history. I am told that Robert Winn is one of the authorities. A native of Winslow, Robert now lives in Fayetteville and has invited me to his house for conversation. We look at old photos, call a few of his friends to confirm stories, and share personal experiences. He shows me his library and private journals in which I take great interest. After six hours of conversation, I depart for home with 10 times the knowledge I came with, including several names of other local historians. I am also more convinced that a gold mine of history is being lost in Lee Creek Valley.

October 18, 1989

It is 6 a.m. and TV Channel Five is broadcasting their morning show live from the park restaurant. The park was chosen as a location to feature fall foliage and Ozarks travel. Jessee, Tim, and George are interviewed along with Jean Crone, a good friend of the park.

October 24, 1989

Several days ago, Susan and I traded with Debbie an old, black-and-white TV for a half-day horseback ride. I believe we are getting a better deal. The sun blazes through a turquoise sky, and autumn foliage is at its peak. Debbie, Susan, and I strike out for old Arkansas Highway 170 and take a trail high above the east ridge of Ellis Creek. We pass beside MacDonald homesite. Folks say he sold moonshine to CCC boys. Only a clearing where the house stood, and a hand-dug well remain. The trail continues up Hurricane Ridge. The effects of the 1912 tornado are still evident near the top. After completing the one-hour loop, we cross the highway and head down Yellow Rock Trail. The bank is steep, and I worry about falling off the horse. The animal is strong, but I lean back in the saddle just the same.

We reach the horse camp around noon. Debbie disperses sandwiches, chips, and cokes. After lunch Susan poses for a few pictures on horseback for a future slide program I am producing. We continue along the Holt Ridge Horse Trail. Near the creek, Susan and I dismount and attempt to walk the horses down steep limestone ledges. They refuse to go and let us know with a buck and a whine. Debbie hollers and they behave; however, I am not anxious to remount. We cross the creek without difficulty. For a quarter mile the horse trail follows the Butterfield downstream, affording great views of Lee Creek. The ride concludes back at West Mountain Stables.

October 25, 1989

Following work, George and I take black-and-white photos of the crevice area to submit to Gurney's Guide to American Caves. I bring along rappelling gear and flashlight to explore Imp's Leap Crevice. George has not previously visited the crevice, and I have only poked around the opening. Inside, a passage leads to a 10-foot ledge and cave. At the lowest end of the room, the passage narrows. George pushes through and announces the presence of a big-eared bat. Once again, we meet with this elusive endangered species.

October 26, 1989

At 11:30 p.m., Brent wakes me to assist him with a disturbance in the walk-in campground. He handles most problem campers alone, but here the assistance of the Washington County sheriff's department would be a long time in coming should the need arise. We trade the police sedan for the park's 4x4 pick-up to cross Lee Creek and into the camp. On Brent's request, I wait by the truck radio while he confronts the rowdy group. Several teenagers are whooping and hollering like drunken fur trappers at a Rocky Mountain rendezvous. Containers of alcohol lie scattered. A giant bonfire launches missiles into the night with no intended target. A lecture about park rules and a stern warning would have no effect, so Brent expels them from the park.

October 28, 1989

I am more patient with kids having a good time than with campers abusing the park resource. On my way to the evening program, I find a truck parked at the very edge of the lake. It is amazing that even an SUV could reach this location. With tent erected and campfire blazing, they sit on the bank, fishing. How does anyone have the audacity to ignore so many regulations designed to protect the resource? They have driven through the middle of a picnic area, parked on the grass, camped in an undesignated area, built a campfire outside of a grill, disturbed a historic structure, and fished without a license? People claim to be ignorant of the rules, but are they? "There wasn't a sign," they often say. If you erect a sign, they will claim that they did not see it. If they do see it, they will remove it, pitch it in the woods, and make the claim anyway.

October 29, 1989

Frequently, visitors ask where park rangers go on vacation. Harry and I are preparing to answer that question. At the conclusion of the annual fall colors weekend, we set out for a seven-day trip to Canyonlands National Park. Living and working constantly in a park requires one to seek an even greater wilderness experience to find rejuvenation. Visiting another developed park such as Devil's Den would only distract me from the outdoor experience I seek. I need the primitive, the remote, the time and opportunity to get lost and find myself by accident a day or two later. Give me silence plus a raven, A cold sunrise and a Townsend's Solitaire. That's where this "park ranger" goes.

November 10, 1989

The staff at nearby Withrow Springs State Park is short-handed this weekend. With Susan out of town, I gladly accept the reassignment. It will give me a chance to write a bird checklist for Devil's Den. My only duties these next three days will be to answer phones and conduct late night patrols. A large, empty house is provided. I have brought Bridger, a good book on John C. Fremont, and park bird records to occupy my time.

November 18, 1989

While working the front desk, a frantic woman reports an injury at Devil's Den Cave. I get as much information from her as I can, then head to the scene. Upon arrival I meet a group at the cave entrance. It turns out, a Boy Scout troop is practicing extrication procedures. I don't know whether to be relieved or furious, having run a quarter mile for nothing.

December 1, 1989

The past couple of days I have uncovered several theories on the origin of the name "Devil's Den". The popular theory claims outlaws hid here after the Civil War. The media has even suggested Jessee James hid in the cave, but then, nearly every tour cave from Texas to Missouri has claimed this. So far, no evidence has surfaced giving credence to this theory. Pearl Starr, daughter of the infamous outlaw Belle Starr, once owned a home in Winslow; but that is as close as outlaws came, excluding moonshiners. Folklorist Ernie Dean suggested the park got its name when early pioneers heard the devil's roar in two caves. Most agree the park takes its name from the cave, but no one agrees on when or why.

An historian once wrote that superstitious pioneers associated caves with the devil. This much must be true. The whole park is filled with devil placenames. The whole country is filled with devil placenames: Devil's Tower, Devil's Postpile, Devil's Lake, Devil's Backbone, Devil's Slide, Twin Falls of the Devil's Fork, and a thousand other places. Beyond superstition, however, is our need to name unique or bizarre natural features after the devil or God. Hells Canyon, Angel's Landing, Bright Angel's Point, Garden of the Gods, Valley of the Gods and many more grace U.S. maps.

The park is named after Devil's Den Cave, which received its name most likely after 1875 and before 1933. It was named by someone who felt an overwhelming need to give this earthly orifice some recognition. He could have named it "Bob's Cave" or whatever, but "devil" attracts attention. The cave wasn't named by a committee. One person did so, and from there it spread to renown. One final thought, "Devil's Den" does not appear in print anywhere before the arrival of the CCC. Old timers tell me it has been called Devil's Den since before their arrival, which puts the date back to at least the 1920's. Only God knows for sure, and perhaps the devil keeps it secret.

December 2, 1989

Arkansas State Parks has offered a bid on 160 acres at the park's northern boundary known as the Buxton Property. A man named Buxton once owned the land and operated a sawmill there. By default, the cutover land reverted to the Bank of Prairie Grove who has been trying to sell it ever since. Today, a land assessor and I visit the property to determine its real value. Regardless of his assessment, it is priceless. Someday Lee Creek Valley will be the last woodland oasis in the middle of two major cities – Fayetteville and Fort Smith. Already, plans are under way to construct a four-lane interstate connecting the two. It is imperative that the Department purchase this property.

December 6, 1989

The trail crew uncovers a hidden crevice while moving a huge boulder on Devil's Den Trail. Upon hearing the news, I grab rappelling gear and head out with Tim to investigate. Apparently, the boulder was placed there by the CCC to serve as a covering and walkway. So much erosion has occurred since then, the boulder has become an obstacle. I lower the rope and descend with the excitement one must feel when opening a time capsule. The hole leads to Right-Angle Crevice but is too narrow to explore. To our disappointment, no big discoveries are made, and we decide to replace the boulder.

December 10, 1989

A couple of months ago, Robert Winn told me about a Civil War skirmish that took place in upper Lee Creek Valley. The site is called U.S. Hollow. A Union scouting party hid in sandstone alcoves on a south-facing bluff. Confederate troops were camping in the area, so the scouts hid in the bluff shelters for several days. Topographical maps do not list a U.S. Hollow, but based on the area's description, Wattle Hollow must be the place. Locals say "Wattle" should read "Waddle", named after a man who settled the area. Whatever the spelling, it is worthy of investigation.

Jessee, George and I drive beyond Jim's cabin to the Old Bethlehem Church site. I show them the cemetery and foundation before continuing upstream on foot. The occasional remnants of a wagon road can be traced, but most of the hike requires bushwacking. At the mouth of the hollow, we jump the intermittent stream and climb to the bluffs. These south-facing bluffs range in height from 15 feet to 40 or more. Sandstone ledges crumble to the touch. Several alcoves are present. I climb into a small opening leading to a large room. Three people could rest here comfortably and remain hidden. Each alcove we come to is larger than the last. Some could easily shelter a dozen men. We look for evidence proving this to be a Civil War hideout but find none. Still, I am convinced we have found U.S. Hollow.

December 14, 1989

According to statistics Harry and I keep at the front desk, over 800 people registered to hike the Butterfield Trail this year. A few dozen states are represented, but as expected most are from Fayetteville and Arkansas in general.

December 16, 1989

Very cold! The lake is frozen to a depth of six inches. Against better judgment, Harry and I walk on the ice. We take pictures for posterity and historical record. Rarely does the lake freeze this thick. Harry walks the entire length, but as I venture beyond the safety of shore the ice grunts, groans, and cracks. I tiptoe back as if doing so lessens the weight.

December 21, 1989

The temperature drops to 17 degrees with a windchill in the negative. Brent conducts an outdoor safety meeting. The plan is to practice search and rescue (SAR) and treat a victim for hypothermia. George volunteers to be the pretended victim and hides in the crevice area. We search for him in various directions, but by the time we find him, he is no longer pretending. All of us are nearly hypothermic.

December 23, 1989

The temperature drops to negative three Fahrenheit. This may be the coldest temperature recorded in the park for the past several decades.

December 24, 1989

The temperature slowly climbs back up to 18 degrees. The lake is still frozen, and several visitors venture out. One is ice skating. I take a few photographs to document what might be a first in the history of the park.

Chapter 4: Becoming an Expert

January 5, 1990

I have heard stories of people getting stuck in a passage between Right Angle Crevice and Devil's Den Cave. One account tells of a Springdale High School student who was trapped for seven hours, Labor Day Weekend, 1987. Park rangers and EMS personnel tried everything in the effort to remove him, even soaking him with vegetable oil. Finally, near complete physical exhaustion, the young man was extricated using air bags. About one of every one hundred people attempting this passage succeeds. Harry, George, and I are determined to add our names to the list.

We enter Devil's Den and proceed to the main junction. After climbing an eight-foot wall, three passages diverge: one low, one high and another to the left. It is this left passage we enter. Thirty feet beyond, a narrow, well-hidden passage branches left again. Most never see it.

Harry leads the way, then George and me. It is so narrow; I cannot see Harry for George. The walls are five feet high, but only inches wide. At one point the walls constrict waist high like an hourglass. To crawl under is impossible. Climbing over is awkward, but there are no other options. One by one we conquer the hourglass.

Harry studies the next leg of passage and questions our advance. I know I cannot go back. He has reached Devil's Corkscrew, a passage requiring a miserable, twisting crawl. The walls are a foot apart, and the ceiling is 16 inches from the mud-packed floor. Moaning and groaning, he rotates his body into the opening an inch at a time. Once through, we hear a triumphant yell. "It opens ...we've made it!"

He is only partially correct. He's made it. George is next, but not anxious. Squirming, he reaches the entrance to the Corkscrew. After several minutes of kicking, he fails to gain an inch. Having waited for what seems an eternity, I begin to experience claustrophobia. I tell George he must try again for my sake if not for his. Harry's report from the front is encouraging. George finds renewed strength, succeeds, and joins him in the larger passage.

Claustrophobia clutches me with its bony fingers. A chill runs down my back as I contemplate aloneness. If muscles become tense or if I rush the passage, I will become stuck. I close my eyes, take slow deliberate breaths, and imagine a spoonful of chocolate pudding oozing down my throat. I must become pudding in this sandstone esophagus. If I gain only an inch at a time, it will be like savoring the flavor before swallowing.

Jagged edges tear at my flannel shirt and snag my belt buckle, effectively halting momentum. My arms reach ahead but become pinned by the walls. Only my toes move freely, pushing off the floor inch by inch. Finally, fingers reach the opening and search for handholds. With what little upper body strength is left, I dislodge myself and erupt from the opening like an exploding mud pot in Yellowstone.

Harry and George have moved on, assuming correctly that I would be all right. I am alone, but standing, and proud to be alive. The next obstacle is a razor-sharp ledge above an unknown depth. I sit, dangle my feet off the ledge, and search for the floor. I cannot see it but proceed anyway. After sliding four feet the walls untuck my shirt. Twelve inches farther, the shirt rides over my chest exposing skin to the cold, muddy wall; and still no *terra firma*. Just before the flannel hangs me by the neck, I reach it. After a series of consecutively smaller rooms, light from Right Angle Crevice is seen. One by one we exit, praising the sun and swearing never to do it again.

January 10, 1990

I spent yesterday in town researching the old Mount Olive School that existed near the park from 1880 to 1938. After a visit to Robert Winn's, and a little research at Shiloh Museum, I learn that there were two school buildings. One, a log structure built in 1880, was destroyed by fire around 1915. Some say the Dotson twins (Otis and Otto), torched it to avoid class. The second was a framed structure used until 1938 when the district consolidated with Blackburn. For a time, the building was occupied by a local named Cye Hickey, and later, dismantled completely.

When I first began my quest to locate the school, I was told it stood on the highest point, often called Possum Knob. In fact, many still refer to the school as Possum Knob College. A previous search yielded no success. Not until paying close attention to its legal description do I realize the buildings were located somewhere downhill.

Harry and I, determined to settle the issue, set out for Mount Olive. Within 15 minutes I stumble onto what appears to be a foundation. Kicking leaves away, we uncover a perfect arrangement of stones 16 x 20 feet. It is a triumphant moment! Once thought to be gone forever, we now put Mount Olive back on the map.

Anxious to share the discovery, I lead Tim and Alan back to the site. After the tour, discussion turns to other known ruins in the vicinity. Tim shows us Moonshine Cave, a half mile downhill. Interpreters led visitors here in the 1970's, but this is my first visit. It is not a cave in the strict sense, but a bluff shelter walled-in for storage. In 1905 the landowner, John Johnston, commissioned Dad Hallet to construct the wall. When the Johnstons moved to Wagnor, Oklahoma in 1919, it was quickly occupied by moonshiners, hence the current name. Since the 1933 repeal of prohibition, the shelter has been occupied by drifters, hippies, and hunters. Tim explains that the bluff shelter was first used by Late Archaic or Early Woodland Indians, based on evidence retrieved in 1978, by the Arkansas Archeological Survey. The Survey also found a pig's tooth, suggesting its use as a hog pen.

We find the shelter vandalized. Beer cans and shotgun shells lie scattered. A recent campfire has charred the wall. We pick up what litter we can, vowing to return and restore the structure.

January 13, 1990

The first annual winter backpacking trip begins this morning. I have planned this event for months despite skepticism of its success. I was told no one would attend a hike in the middle of winter. The thermometer reads 19 degrees, but thirty-eight bravely attend. Brent takes the first dozen; I lead the rest.

We begin at Mount Olive, continue down to Vista Point, and tour Phoebe's Cave. Inside, passages fork in three directions. Two double-back, but one is too small for me. The middle crack leads deeper into the bluff but soon becomes impassable. Phoebe's Cave offers little more than a brief diversion from the trail and a home for its namesake. The hike continues to Quail Valley, Mannon homesite, Rock Hole and Bluff Camp. By sunset, the temperature reaches a comfortable 45 degrees, but still a white man's fire is built. A cool night is predicted. By 10 p.m. everyone has abandoned the blaze for sleeping bags. I lie awake, watching a full moon rise and fall over the ridges. Barred Owls call through an enchanted forest.

January 14, 1990

I wake at 6:30 a.m. to find the campfire rekindled. A few comrades huddle around the fire cursing their poorly insulated bags. I have slept well but can remember trips when I haven't. I shivered at 2 a.m. and begged for a sun that refused to rise. I sip hot chocolate with stale donuts and reflect on past miseries. We break camp and rendezvous with the first group at Anna. After touring Camp Meeting Cemetery, we divide the group once more for the return hike. Some are too exhausted to tackle Holt Ridge, so Brent guides the weary along the banks of Lee. I lead the assault on Holt Ridge. We both reach the park around 2:30 p.m. under a clear sky and 60 degrees.

January 17, 1990

Intermittent and ephemeral streams are finally flowing again after two inches of rain fell yesterday and one inch today. Lee Creek has been parched and desiccated for the past eight months.

January 19, 1990

All the creeks are at flood stage due to another three inches of rain since morning. White caps in the current reveal the river's rage. George and Alan shuttle a canoe to the north end of camp area "A" then launch into the class-III rapids. Harry and I prepare to photograph the event. Seconds later, George and Alan whiz by, hanging on for dear life. We run alongside watching, praying. At breakneck speed the canoe heads directly for a log completely blocking the channel. An attempt to beach the canoe is made too late. Both go headlong into rapids as the canoe wraps the log. George quickly surfaces, but Alan is swept downstream before grabbing a branch. Silently, they withdraw from the flood, drenched and freezing. With great struggle, the canoe is winched ashore. Alan and George show signs of hypothermia. For a moment we all stand on the road at the edge of the crested waters, dazed, dumbfounded and adrenalin depleted.

January 21, 1990

The weather is clear and 56 degrees, too nice to spend in the cabin. Harry shuttles George and I to Mayfield where we begin a reconnaissance of lower Lee Creek Valley. With gear secured, we ford the stream and follow it along the southeast bank, exploring each bluff, rapid, and pool. We come to a hand-dug well filled with last week's rain. Uphill, a rock cellar is discovered, but little else of this 19th Century homesite is evident.

Once more we cross Lee Creek, searching for the long-lost Queen of Sheba School. Along an ATV path, we find a stone wall and foundation, but are not convinced that this is it. Exhausted, we find a comfortable rock and eat lunch by an intermittent waterfall.

Conversation turns to future explorations, but eventually gives way to the soothing sound of water and human silence.

After lunch, we hike to the Trooper and drive to Lee Creek Community in search of El Horrendo, the class-IV rapid south of Silver Bridge. We ask directions from locals who apparently prefer to keep it secret. No matter, the location is nearby, and requires only a few minutes of trial and error. To get to the falls, we drive a mile of open field thick with Broom Sage. Near the creek the field gives way to woods and swamp. Here the road serpentines through a dozen mud holes which the Trooper adequately negotiates. The road ends at creek's edge. Upstream the roar of water is heard—-El Horrendo! Camera in hand, I run along the bank to the base of this terrible rapid. It is one of the two worst (best?) on Lee Creek. At flood stage a canoe can shoot the ledges but will snag at low flow. In either case the odds of disaster would be worth calculating.

January 22, 1990

This evening an Eastern Screech-Owl in gray phase perches outside the cabin. I walk slowly toward the eerie call, coming within six feet. He refuses to fly. I am no threat to him. Perhaps with the same ability that dogs use to detect human fear, the owl senses my respect.

January 23, 1990

It is hard to explain my passion for historical research since my greatest knowledge lies with the natural sciences. Inevitably the two are linked – cultural and natural history. It seems I cannot interpret the landscape without understanding how it has been altered by man. Likewise, I cannot appreciate the lifestyle of my predecessors without considering how the environment shaped them. To learn more about the park during the 1950's and 60's, I consult Ray Stroud, retired park superintendent now living in Strickler.

Having never met Ray, I am pleased to be granted an interview. I have heard many stories about him and expect a difficult interview.

Ray greets me at the door of his self-constructed cabin. He is a thin man, weathered by the years and cigarettes. He has a rough edge to him, but clearly a heart of gold. Once introductions are dispensed, I ask permission to record our discussion for the park's oral history collection. For over three hours he freely speaks. As facilitator, I interrupt only briefly to clarify an answer, direct a question, and change the tapes. During his tenure as superintendent, he has been assaulted, shot at, and duped by bank robbers. I listen quietly as Ray recalls the memories.

" .... These people came up the park and wanted to know if I would go down and pull them out. They came up [county road] *220 ... They said they ran their pickup off, got it stuck on a rock down there. "Yea, I can pull you out".* [Visitor:] *"We ain't got no money." I went down there and .... brand new Ford pickup. I hooked the chain on that ole Jeep, I jerked it around a few times I got it off the rock. They followed me back up to the park. Ol' boy said, "I'd sure like to go swimming" "wished I had the money".* [Ray Stroud:] *"Aw shoot, go swimming"... (you know, in the afternoon right along closing time). So, they had quite a time around there, two men and a blond-headed woman. And my wife's stepdad was working for me at the time running the snack bar. And he was watching the news—the ten o'clock news that night. And "Ray!", he said, "Come here!", ... "Your girlfriend, your blond-headed girlfriend, is on television." I go down there and look. These guys robbed a bank, stole a pickup, got up there and hung up the pickup. I pulled them out, took care of 'em, let 'em go swimming, even fed 'em a sandwich, even let 'em have five gallons of gas to get back to Fort Smith .... It was around six o'clock when they left the park. And this was on the ten o'clock news that they already had 'em. They caught 'em with that pickup ....*

"Tell me about the people that shot at you" I ask Ray. *"Actually, I don't know who they were ... kind of a long distance." "Hunters or local trouble?"*

Well, part of 'em was hunter and one of 'em, I don't know. He's out of Oklahoma I reckon. But I think I stumbled into a dope deal .... I was going down running my campgrounds, you know. This was after closing in the fall ... I went down by 'E' area and started round through there [and] heard something. BING! I knew it was gunshots but driving around along in the truck [I] didn't pay too much attention. I already made the first circle and started the second, so I stopped the truck and rolled down my window. And about that time, I heard one go over. And I heard too many of them go over. I knew what that was. I had no gun or nothing with me. So, I just went out of that campground. [I] went all the way back up 'ere and got my pistol and throwed it in the seat of the truck and got back up 'ere. And they's just come out of that campground and headed up on this side. I couldn't tell how many of 'em there was. And they came out and turned off this road up 'ere at Zinnamon. And from 'ere and them dirt roads, and the way I was driving, and the dust they was foggin'—what roads I was on I don't know, but I wound up in Oklahoma. I never did ketch 'em. When I got to Oklahoma, I still had that .038 layin' in the seat beside of me. Evidently, Oklahoma Highway Patrol seen this chase going. And I had no red light or no radios or nothin'. But they seen somethin' goin' on so they blocked the road. And this ole boy came to the road block and he just went right down off interstate 40 and right out across the field in that car and got away from all of us. I pulled up 'ere and told 'em. And the ol' boy said "You're kinda out of your country, ain't ya?" I said I didn't realize it, you know, not realizin' I was clear in Oklahoma. That first [bullet] went through the tailgate of my truck.

"Ray, it seems you've been shot at more than anyone in state park history. Tell me about another close call."

I started to the mailbox one day, it was during deer season, and Rosalee was hangin' out clothes out there on the clothesline, right there at the end of the shop. She said, "I don't know what in the world that was!" Then I heard a rifle shot, looked 'ere and that sheet had a little black hole in it. And I shoved her up against the building and I said git in the house. And I started for my truck and PING!, PING!, PING! again. And I got right up there past second turn. And I met a little ole doe deer comin' down that hill with her tongue hangin' out. I mean she was movin' it on. Course, I was movin' it on too. They's shootin' right down over the office. I kept goin', and I got the ole boy at the top of the hill. I said, "Didn't you git that deer you's shootin' at?" "Naw", he says, "I didn't get it", he says, "Thank it wuz a doe anyway". I said, "what kind of a rifle you got?" Stuck it out, he says, "Oh, it's my dad's bolt action, nice lookin' rifle, nice scope on it". He handed it to me, and I walked over to a big ole rock and I went to work. I got done, I said, "You damn nar shot me while ago and my wife!" I said, "Now I'm Ray Stroud ... I have no right to tear your rifle up", (you know we wadn't even law enforcement officers at the time). I said, "I had no right to tear your damn rifle up, but there the damn thing is.

[In those days, Ray was about the only enforcement in the park. If there was trouble, he had to deal with it the best he could. Such was the case when he confronted some fellows down at the pavilion during an evening dance. Alcohol was not permitted, and he made sure folks knew it.] Ray continues ...

In fact, the last ol' boy I hit was over a can of beer. I told them they couldn't have their beer in the dinning room ... One ol' boy said "I'm sorry Ray, I knew better", and [then] took it over and put it in the trash can, just dropped it in there. The other ol' boy said, "I'd like to see the son-of-a-bitch make me git rid of my beer." I followed him over there and he went across the dance floor. I pecked him on the shoulder. I said, "I told you, you're not supposed to drink that here". "Either dump it out, take [it] back to the car... leave the park and then drink it." And he was a big ol' boy. "I want you to try to pour it out" [he said,] trying to act drunk. He had a great big belt buckle on ...that big around ...standin' kinda rared back. An all of a sudden I knew exactly where I wanted to pour that beer. So I took it and that's where I put it. He stood there rared back and let me pour every drop of it. I even shook the can, and sat it down. He standed there wavin' his arms, tellin' me what all he was gonna do. I thought, well, might as well hit him once, cause I'm gonna git a good one anyway. Hit him right in the mouth—and man he went down. I was more surprised than he was because, I mean, I put him on the ground.

Ray continues telling stories of the old days at Devil's Den long after the cassettes are filled. I leave knowing I have not heard the half of it. Which stories were embellished for my benefit, and which were verbatim, I may never know; but it matters little. I have experienced another character in the drama that defines the Lee Creek Valley.

January 29, 1990

A hiker reports a doe stuck in the upper crevice area. Alan and others join me out at the scene to find her deep within "J" Cave. Apparently, she fell into Big-ear Crevice while attempting to cross. She miraculously survives the fall but continues to complicate her situation by crawling in the wrong direction. For a half an hour we push and pull until finally wrestling her to the surface. She is emaciated, in shock and unable to stand. We comfort her but come to the realization that she will not survive. To wait longer would be painful for her and unbearable to watch. With his own gun, Alan fires twice to her head. It is small comfort to know that a wake of vultures will eat well tomorrow.

February 5, 1990

Spring fever spreads through the cabin. Susan and I take the mountain bikes out to cure the illness. We ride through camp area "A" and up the fire road, pausing briefly at the Dotson and Hale homesites. Swearing to turn around at any moment, we continue further north to Lee Creek crossing. The turquoise water slips gently over rounded sandstone pebbles. Except during winter, it is unusual for the creek to be running here. Typically, the water disappears 100 yards upstream and resurfaces some distance below. We do not attempt to cross although enticed. We have already ridden further than intended. On the return, we face the same slick rocks and mud holes which now seem more hazardous. The tires skid and slide across the bedrock. With each slip I fail to remove my feet from the clips in time to balance. Susan's experience is similar, but unlike me, she manages to stay upright. Mountain biking may be fun, but not painless.

February 6, 1990

Vigilance is the key to preventing vandalism. Whenever a situation appears suspicious it is investigated. On his way home from work, George passes Devil's Den Trail head. It is nearly dark, yet he observes hikers carrying liquor. Concerned, George comes by the cabin and the two of us pursue them. Leaning against the old tree at the entrance we find a fifth of Jack Daniels. Obviously, they are in the cave. With flashlights in hand, we enter. A hundred feet beyond, we stop and listen for voices. "Let's cut off the flashlights and wait for their return", I whisper. They come within 15 feet before we hit the switch and scare the mischief out of them. "Park Rangers! ... we'd like to have a word with you", I shout. Like stray cattle we herd them from the cave and begin the interrogation. All are under 21 as expected, and most have been drinking. Brent arrives on the scene and gives them the third degree before giving them the boot.

Had we not pursued the gang, no doubt one of us would have discovered graffiti in the cave, litter on the trail, a campfire built at the entrance, or live trees hacked for firewood. Alcohol rarely raises a teenager's environmental consciousness. Looking back on my own adolescence, I testify from experience.

February 7, 1990

Historical discoveries are sometime made in the most serendipitous manner. Keith Wells drives the fire road while I discuss improvements needed to protect the park's historic sites. As we pass the Dotson homesite, he notices a blue object several feet uphill. I think nothing of it, but we stop to look. It turns out to be a tea kettle; however, it rests adjacent to remains of a log structure. Some of the wood has not yet rotted. From its size, we speculate it was a shed. Very few historical sites in the valley still have wood remaining. Inspired by this finding, we canvass the entire area, and locate a barn foundation and CCC dump.

February 16, 1990

Once again, the team assembles for the annual bat survey. Several caves are searched, but only eight bats are counted, a modest improvement over last year.

February 27, 1990

The day of reckoning has come. Representatives from the Central Office and two professional climbers arrive to discuss our mountaineering proposal. Each of us climb and rappel Devil's Teapot. It is apparent from the start they are not in favor of the proposal. I suspect they are going through the motions for our benefit. The real decision rests with the director who may have already decided.

The two professional climbers work the face of Devil's Teapot. It is a challenging ascent. Near the top, a few jagged rocks are loose and pose a potential threat to the inexperienced. It is these rocks which persuade the climbers not to recommend the site. There are two other obstacles to the proposal. One is liability. Once again, the threat of a lawsuit rears its ugly head. If climbing is permitted and injuries occur, the department fears litigation. I do not profess to know the laws surrounding tort claims and disclaims. I realize some absurd suits are won, but common sense should dictate individual responsibility when recreating in natural settings.

Possibly, another obstacle to the proposal is the attitude professional climbers have toward rappelling. Many rock climbers believe that rappelers are reckless amateurs. Almost anyone can afford to buy the equipment and learn to rappel. Granted, climbing requires a greater skill and specialized gear, but even professional climbers rappel following an ascent. I suppose the more people participate in a sport, the less elite that sport becomes. Regardless of the ideology, that would be a poor excuse for disapproving the proposal. Many become interested in climbing because they have been introduced to rappelling. It teaches use of equipment, determination, and courage. Rappelling introduces an exciting sport to scouts, church youth groups and inner-city kids. Devil's Den could help facilitate these by permitting regulated mountaineering somewhere in this spacious park.

To be sure, the issue cannot be about resource damage. Mountaineering would to a degree degrade the bluff, but much less than campsites, roads, and other facilities in the name of recreation. Some degree of trade-off with natural resources is inevitable when providing outdoor recreation.

March 3, 1990

Sunny and 67 degrees. The park is crawling with visitors. Not surprising, an injury occurs in the cave. I provide first aid to a young boy who discovered the "Guillotine," a razor-sharp rock hanging from the ceiling in Devil's Den. It often causes head injuries because spelunkers are looking down at precisely the moment they need to be looking up while in this passage. The first rule in spelunking is don't lose your head.

March 12, 1990

Serviceberry (*Amelanchier arborea*) is blooming along the bluffs of Arkansas Highway 170. Its dainty, white blossoms are frequently mistaken for plum (*Prunus americana*), another member of the rose family which blooms a few weeks later. Serviceberry is named for the tradition of using the flowering twigs to decorate church sanctuaries or grave sites. This tree also goes by the names Sarvis and Shadbush. "Sarvis" is a Southern way of saying "service." Shadbush refers to the bloom coinciding with the shad run, which means great fishing.

Pussy's-toes (*Antennaria plantaginafolia*) and Bird's-foot Violet are blooming on Yellow Rock Trail. Susan, Bridger, and I spend the afternoon strolling through the humid forest. Despite the clouds, the mercury rises to an unseasonable 84 degrees.

March 13, 1990

Our management meeting is interrupted this morning by a missing person's report. Yesterday a mountain biker was riding with friends along Holt Ridge and became separated. He was not properly dressed to spend the night, and worse, he is diabetic. Realizing the urgency, we alert all staff and initiate a search. George and Jessee bike the trails inaccessible by vehicle. Alan sets out on the five-wheeler, and Harry, Tim, and I alternate driving the 4x4 and hiking sections of trail. At the office, Brent coordinates efforts with the US Forest Service, Washington County Sheriff's Department, and the Arkansas State Forestry Commission. As each sector is cleared, Brent marks the map. After nearly two hours of searching, we speculate the biker is somewhere along Lee Creek, perhaps as far south as Crawford County. Finally, James Adney, park maintenance supervisor, locates the man sitting on the east bank of Lee Creek two miles south of the park.

March 15, 1990

Ken Eastin, Arkansas Trails Coordinator, arrives from Little Rock to inspect our crew's accomplishments. Tim and I accompany him on Devil's Den Trail. As the conversation turns to water bars, berms and screes, my mind fades to visions of trout lilies poking through fresh, spring soil. A well-built trail not only serves to provide access but is a means in which to protect fragile areas.

April 7, 1990

Wildflower Weekend coincides with the blooming of False Garlic (*Nothoscordum bivalve*), Rose Verbena (*Glandularia canadensis*), and Prairie Blue-eyed Grass (*Sisyrinchium campestre*).

I meet a man from India while leading a walk on Lee Creek Trail. Cultural diversity is rare in these parts, so I waste no time meeting him. His business brought him to Fort Smith, and while there, colleagues recommended he visit Devil's Den. There is something very innocent about this wealthy, middle-aged Indian. As we walk the trails and cross creeks in search of flowers, he becomes a young boy, caught in the splendor of the season. Dress shoes and all, he wades into the cool waters of Lee. Shoes are replaceable; he knows he may never walk this way again.

April 8, 1990

While leading a walk to the crevice area, Harry and I come upon a fresh campfire built at the entrance to Devil's Den. Harry continues with the group, while I lay in wait for the scofflaw who built the fire and left beer cans scattered. No one exits the cave. Later, Tim and I question teenagers in campsite 30. We feel sure they are the culprits but lack the evidence to prove it.

April 11, 1990

After an exhausting day of interpretation with 425 first and second graders, I reward myself with a little woodland solitude. The limestone bluff along Lee Creek and the park's southern boundary, is sacred. I wander aimlessly among the boulders and glades, listening to the soothing rush of water. Sphagnum Moss (*Sphagnum sp.*), Hairy Lip Fern (*Cheilanthes lanosa*), and Prickly Pear (*Opuntia humifusa*) grow in an odd association along the forest floor. Just beyond, abandoned fields stretch between the ridges.

An hour later I find myself at the abandoned trailer of Thomas Leon "Buddy" Mayfield. Buddy died some years back, and everything here at his vacation home was left to decay. I approach but get the eerie feeling that I am being watched. "*Hello?*" Only silence answers. I knock and the door swings. Curiosity is a demon. I enter and find the trailer, dark, musty, and rat-infested. I try not to touch anything. Directly across from the door is the bathroom. A robe hangs nearby.

A single toothbrush rests in the holder. The tub is rusty, and the curtain torn. To the right of the front door is one of two bedrooms. A bed, covered with Brown Recluse exoskeletons, occupies the room, and blood stains the sheet. A few items of clothing hang in the closet as if placed there yesterday. I walk away, glancing back to see if I am being followed. *"Buddy? Is that You?"*

April 12, 1990

It seems like good fishing weather, but for some reason the fish do not agree. On reflection, I am always trying to rush nature into the next season. In any case, it is good just to be back in the rapids.

A black bear has been hanging around Brent's house the past couple of nights, apparently attracted to dog food on the porch. I drive to Brent's place, but the bear is nowhere to be seen. A half hour later Brent calls. The bear is back. Susan and I return, park the car next to the old Zinnamon Church, and carefully sneak to the house. The bear is around back, curiously sniffing dog food and honey. The Arkansas Game and Fish Commission has placed a trap in Brent's yard in hopes of collecting the three-year-old male and moving him to a remote location. I stand at the window, watching. It is my first sighting in the wild, if it is accurate to say a bear on the porch is "in the wild." We watch for nearly 40 minutes, but he is too smart for the trap. We retreat to the car with one eye back to the bear.

April 13, 1990

Brent informs me that the bear has finally entered the trap and will be released in upper Lee Creek Valley this morning.

April 15, 1990

Zinnamon Church is conducting a sunrise service at Yellow Rock. I can imagine no better place to worship on Easter morning. By 7 a.m. the sun has crested the ridge, although the service is scheduled for 8 a.m. Upon arrival, I find two teenagers who spent the night around a campfire. They are inebriated yet continue to drink. One pretends to fall off the bluff, and probably will. I am out of uniform and decide to say nothing for the moment. Suddenly, one of the boys crunches his beer can and throws it over the bluff. I had hoped to leave the job behind for a few hours but can tolerate them no longer. I introduce myself as the ranger and lecture them on proper behavior at Devil's Den. They leave without further aggravation. I prefer to worship in the retreat of nature, even this wild and remote sanctuary has been violated.

April 16, 1990

Beautiful day, 81 degrees. There! Right there I have broken my word to never call something beautiful, for nothing was ever made more so by labeling it thus. *"A rose by any other name..."*

While hiking Vista Point Horse Trail, I encounter several new flowers. Most attracting my attention are those on the steep slope of Holt Ridge Vista. Post Oak (*Quercus stellata*) and Eastern Red Cedar (*Juniperus virginiana*) give way to grass-covered sandstone ledges. Wild Hyacinth (*Camassea scilloides*), Yellow Star Grass (*Hypoxis hirsuta*), and Long-bracted Wild Indigo (*Amorpha fruticosa*) add color to the glade.

Voices are heard a short distance away, and I am surprised to see that it is Harry and Brent collecting Columbine for transplanting. They are below an overhang, yet on a ledge high above the ground. The only safe passage to them is down a steep crevice. As I make my way to the secret ledge, I wonder, is this how the Puebloan people felt as they moved up and down and across the face of sandstone cliffs? I find Harry and Brent hard at work, and equally surprised to see me. On the way out, Brent reveals a colony of Palmer's Saxifrage, an uncommon but attractive flower.

A thunderstorm rages through the valley this evening. Lightning is constant.

April 17, 1990

According to the gauge, last night's storm dumped 3.65 inches.

April 18, 1990

Most park interpreters talk to literally 20,000 visitors annually, possibly more. This translates into 100,000 people to whom I have spoken face to face since the beginning of my career. With some I have carried on lengthy conversations, or perhaps walked side by side on some extended tour. I have shared my thoughts and feelings with them, and they with me. Most never return – a once in a lifetime encounter. A few are seen year after year until they are more family than customer. Today, a couple from Michigan visits the park. From his voice, I would know him anywhere. He and his wife were among the first visitors to receive an interpretive presentation from me. About every other year they end up visiting the park at which I am currently working – and purely by coincidence. After a lengthy "catch me up on your life" conversation, they slip into the night to parts unknown. I feel certain we will see one another again no matter where this work/adventure leads.

April 19, 1990

The bear at Brent's house last week was shot yesterday by a woman attempting to scare it. She thought the gun was loaded with birdshot, but was, in fact, loaded with buckshot. If only it would have strayed to cabin four, I would have gladly shared the woods – his woods.

April 21, 1990

The first Annual Spring Backpack trip begins! James Wilborn has returned to assist me and the group I am leading. Tim takes the other. After a six-mile hike, we make camp at Rock Hole. Blackburn Creek is running above normal; however, with plenty of sun and 81 degrees, no one can resist a swim. Yesterday's rain brought another two inches, but the sediment has already settled.

April 22, 1990

There can be no better way to celebrate the 20th anniversary of Earth Day than by waking up in the woods to Black-and-white Warblers, Yellow-throated Vireos, and Red-bellied Woodpeckers.

On days like this nature affirms my choice of professions. On the return hike, we pose for a momentous picture at Holt Ridge Vista holding a homemade Earth Day flag, crafted by James.

April 23, 1990

Today is spent on the back patio of the cabin reading The Journals of Lewis and Clark. Occasionally I am distracted by Summer Tanagers, Ruby-throated Hummingbirds, and a Great-crested Flycatcher that have recently discovered our bird garden. Susan is busy preparing a feast of grilled chicken with mushrooms, potato salad, and French bread. After dinner I teach her how to identify several new birds by sound. It is a long-term goal of mine to convert her to the avocation of birding. So far she is sticking with the program.

April 24, 1990

The soil around the patio has suffered greatly from the numerous rains this spring. I decide to build a retaining wall from a pile of stone nearby. This pile seems to be the remains of rock used in the cabin's construction. With wheelbarrow and sweat, I move the stones from one side of the yard to the other to construct the wall. As each rock is removed, salamanders, centipedes, and worms are exposed but quickly make their escape. At some point during the project, I am bit by a Brown Recluse. I have heard of the awful ulcers that develop around the bite, so I take immediate action. A colleague once suggested applying Epsom salt and a hot, wet rag to the wound. I can find no Epsom salt, so I use table salt instead. For several hours I sit with this concoction pressed to my shin.

April 25, 1990

I continue with yesterday's treatment as often as possible.

April 26, 1990

Treatment continues, and it appears the wound is healing. Physicians may scoff at the remedy, but I believe the worst is over.

April 27, 1990

The Guillotine claims yet another victim. I provide first aid to a New Orleans girl who suffers a nasty gash in the head while spelunking in Devil's Den.

April 28, 1990

Members of the Tulsa Audubon Society are visiting. I join them on Lee Creek Trail and quickly concede that they are better birders than I. They direct my attention to a Blue-winged Warbler, and I quickly add it to my life list. Also in the park is Mike Mlodinow, a local writer and ornithologist. With so many experts roaming the park, several new sightings should be recorded.

May 2, 1990

At 1:30 p.m. two men report a strange sight down at Cedar Grove. They observed a man in a car either asleep or worse. Jessee, Tim and I respond. As we approach the scene, we notice a hose connecting the exhaust pipe to the driver's window. Tim prepares to give CPR, but instantly realizes the futility. The man is dead (blue-green dead), probably has been for several hours. In the front seat lies a bottle of whiskey, and cassettes tapes lie scattered on the floor. From the driver's license, I determine he is exactly my age. What could have troubled this man so much as to take his own life? I speculated about his misfortunes while waiting for the coroner. We lift the stiff and bloating body into a black zippered bag. From darkness to darkness, there is no escape for him. If only the hopeless man could see the futility of a long-term solution for a short-term problem. His was not a good death.

Hours later, I still feel as if death soils my hands. It cannot be washed away. By evening the park rain gauge marks 4.15 inches.

May 3, 1990

Another inch of rain is recorded this morning, causing the water to crest the dam's third level. The CCC Dam across Lee Creek, aptly named Lake Devil, is built to allow for three main levels of water over the dam, as controlled by a wheel gate. When water flows over the second level, we take notice and monitor for flash-flooding. At the third level, flooding is inevitable. After that, the creek is a raging torrent and has (or will) cause facility damage, especially in camp area "A" upstream.

May 5, 1990

Nine visitors with binoculars assemble at Lee Creek Trail for an "early bird" walk. The ninth annual birdwatch weekend begins. While most campers are still sleeping or preparing breakfast, we stroll the camping loop in search of Wilson's Warblers and Northern Orioles. Rose-breasted Grosbeaks are heard along the fire road. Their call is like a squeaky door hinge. I'm hearing rumors that Painted Buntings are being seen. I would like to add that colorful yet elusive species to my life list. I offer $5 to anyone who can lead me to it. Karen Garrett, a frequent visitor from Rogers, has spotted one near the bluffs across from camping area "B". We return to the scene and hack our way through thick brush to the base of the bluff. I wait, watch, and listen, but the bird is no longer there.

May 6, 1990

Day two of birdwatch weekend, 13 visitors attend the morning hike. Turkey Vultures perch with outstretched wings, attempting to dry from last night's rain, and perhaps to bake a few parasites. Swainson's Thrushes are spotted but few other "good" birds are seen. [Note: A good bird is one that is rarely seen, or few in number, or anatomically appealing such as a Scissor-tailed Flycatcher, Scarlet Tanager, or Painted Bunting]. When conducting a count or survey where one of the goals is to list as many species observed as possible, then a bird species value is just as important as the next. A Painted Bunting is just as important to the list as an LGB (Little Gray Bird).The two-day count comes to sixty-four bird species and one Speckled Kingsnake.

May 10, 1990

Every few weeks vandals scrape off the paint on Devil's Den Trail signs or uproot the station markers altogether. At Twin Falls, I sit on a milk crate – my back to the cliff – and begin to repaint the sign. The trail slopes, causing the crate to rest uneven. I lose my balance. In the tumble and literally kick the bucket and splatter paint all over me. The crate and I come to rest just inches from the cliff.

May 13, 1990

This afternoon I hike the fire road in preparation for next week's history tour. Near Hale homesite, I find another hand-dug well. There are three associated with this site. A greater number of ruins will make the hike more interesting. Continuing to Fossil Flats, I discover that the creek is too high to cross without getting soaked. I remove my apparel for the crossing but quickly decide that a swim in the soothing rapids is a better objective.

May 14, 1990

On the five-wheeler loaded with tools, I return to the homesites to clear brush from the foundations. Tim follows on mountain bike. The history tours are just five days away, and there is much work to be done. We spend the better part of the afternoon working at Dotson homesite.

On the return, I lose steering control of the five-wheeler when the front wheel slips into a rut. I am unable to steer it out. Seconds later the rut leaves the road, and the wheeler follows. Both man and machine lunge suddenly over the edge. I hear myself cry, "*Oh God!*" Miraculously the machine becomes pinned between two trees and is suspended over the embankment. Just before the handlebars slam against the oak, I withdraw my fingers from the grip. My body is thrown to the forest below. Instinctively, I roll to avoid being crushed by the machine. Strangely, it does not fall, but instead remains wedged above with the engine running. I summon the courage to climb back up and turn it off. Minutes later Tim crests the hill on mountain bike and finds me sitting in the road. "What's the deal?"

he says before realizing the situation. I point to the wheeler. "Are you alright?" he says in disbelief. "I'm a little shaken ... bruised my knee a little ... that's all." Tim pedals to the office to get Jessee and the 4X4. On their return, we attach the winch and extricate the wheeler. "You were damn lucky," they say. Luck was never a factor. God spared my life for his purposes and mercy.

May 15, 1990

Fishing is especially good this morning. Three smallmouth, two long-ears and ten greens devour my lure.

May 20, 1990

Paul and Tracy Frick are here for a visit. Susan, Bridger, and I guide them to Fossil Flats to wade in the rapids. While climbing a waterfall Bridger slips on the moss and falls seven feet to the creek. He survives without a scratch but gives me quite a scare. We name the site appropriately, "Bridger Falls." Minutes later, another accident leads to the naming of Shin-cut Bluff. While fording the creek upstream, Paul steps in a hole and lacerates his shin. There is almost always a backstory to geographic placenames.

May 23, 1990

The public's expectations never cease to amaze. An irate camper demands his money back because kids in a nearby campsite kept him awake last night. I explain to him that we could have corrected the problem, had he given us a call. I apologize to him on behalf of the inconsiderate campers but explain that a refund under this circumstance is unwarranted. On other occasions, I have heard visitors request a refund when it rains. Rain, like rowdy kids, is a part of life (indeed, part of the park experience!). We may be inconvenienced, but we cannot expect to be compensated. A few hours later a Texas woman barges in to protest that a group of kids are playing football in the campground. Having traveled a great distance to find solitude, she is in no mood for screaming children and flying pigskins. It is daytime, quiet hours are no longer in effect, and the kids have as much right to recreate here as she. They are scheduled to leave shortly, so I request that she be patient a little longer. She is upset to the point of tears, cursing me, Arkansas State Parks, and the governor. An Arkansas woman standing nearby, responds: "If you don't like it, go back to Texas." Tim approaches the counter, and I step between the women to prevent a fight. If only Devil's Den could be all things to all people, life would be good. Park management is people management, plain and simple.

May 24, 1990

There must be something in the air. Once again, I find myself defusing hostilities. A middle-aged man demands a discount on the camping fee. I explain which discounts are offered by the Department, including the Golden Age Passport. He presents a Golden Access Card and claims to have gotten discounts at other parks. The question is which park, federal or state, Oklahoma, or Texas etc. Each state honors different discounts, and a federal park may offer a different one than a state park in the same state. What is the purpose of a discount? Parks are not solely for amusement. If we are to continue protecting outstanding examples of natural and cultural history, we must pay the price, not squabble over a few bucks. Arkansas, like many other states, uses the discount as a marketing tool, to keep campsites full in low occupancy seasons, or to increase volume in less-visited parks.

May 26, 1990

With eyes closed, I can tell it is Memorial Day weekend. Several groups of visitors are fighting over sites, reserving non reservable sites, cutting down live trees, skipping out on fees, and generally acting like a two-year-old at a food fight. The response from the park is "All-hands-on-deck!"

June 8, 1990

For several months now, Harry has been preparing for a new special event called Bat-O-Rama. Tonight, the event begins with a guest speaker from the US Forest Service. Over 130 attend the program to learn about these mysterious and beneficial creatures. Everyone gets what Harry hopes will be an annual Bat-O-Rama collector's button.

June 9, 1990

Bat-O-Rama continues with tours into Devil's Den and Devil's Ice Box. Between Tim, Harry, and I, more than a hundred visitors are led into the caves.

June 16, 1990

The temperature climbs into the 90's. On three separate occasions I ask visitors to observe the "No Swimming" signs posted around the lake. Next to spelunking, swimming is the most traditional form of recreation in the valley. With the completion of the dam in 1937, the lake became the best swimming hole for over twenty miles. The project included a diving tower and beach at the southeast corner. In those days, no one seemed to mind swimming in the source of their potable water. In the 1960's a concrete pool was built, and the lake closed to swimming to protect this drinking water supply.

June 19, 1990

Rains of late spring washed away steppingstones at Lee Creek Trail crossing. To replace them, and to offer a cool activity for campers, I schedule a dam building workshop. Despite the 95-degree heat and park full of people, only Rusty, the summer missionary, comes to help.

June 20, 1990

I suspect that yesterday's dam program failed due to the hint of labor. Today's interpretive program, a wade/hike to the natural bridges, attracts 48 visitors.

June 24, 1990

The past couple of days, a research team from the University of California at Santa Barbara has been studying plant communities adjacent to the park. Plots randomly selected by computer have brought them to this area. I volunteer to spend the day assisting them with the identification of woody plants. What joy it is to be in the company of men and women who can translate and recognize a *Quercus-Carya* Forest when they see one.

July 2, 1990

Charlie has returned to participate in our annual fishing trip. Susan shuttles us to Cedar Grove so that we may fish our way upstream. By noon my count reaches 18. Most are greens but a few Smallmouth Bass and Longear Sunfish are caught. Charlie's catch is 17, but he has been gaining on me all morning. While removing a hook from a Green Sunfish, Charlie punctures his finger beyond the barb. For 15 minutes he struggles with the lure but cannot remove the hook. We walk a mile to the visitor center to utilize surgical tools, but still, we are unsuccessful. Four hours later, the hook is removed by a physician at Washington Regional Hospital's emergency room. As Charlie fades in and out from the pain, he mumbles to the surgeon, "Save the lure; it's a good one."

July 3, 1990

Having recovered from the infamous fishhook incident, Charlie is ready, once again, to hit the creek. We drive south to fish at the confluence of Fall Creek. We come to a deep, blue pool. A three-pound largemouth surfaces, followed by a 15-pound carp. They rise and fall like great whales in search of air. It is futile to fish in the pool. The Rebel Crawdad was not made for such depths. We continue to a gravel shoal and rapids. The fishing is poor, but the scenery exceptional. By noon I am exhausted. Charlie continues to work upstream. I lay my clothes on the rocks to dry and soak my sunburned body in a shaded pool.

July 14, 1990

The first annual summer backpack trip begins this morning. A dozen adventurers hike Butterfield Trail to Blackburn Creek. We follow the dry creek bed downstream to Junction Camp pausing periodically to swim and fish the holes. At camp, we pursue our own interests: swimming, reading, and sleeping. While looking for a place to relieve himself, Rick Hembree discovers a Timber Rattlesnake. Just before squatting, he notices the ground moving under him.

Nonchalantly, Rick reports the sighting. We joke about the potential "*em-bare-ass-ment*" of being bit on the bum. He leads us back to the sight where the snake remains. It is my first wild sighting of a Timber Rattlesnake.

After several days of 90-100 degrees, the climate chooses this weekend to change. The high reaches only 73 with an overnight low of 56. Expecting normal hot July weather, George, Dan, and I had packed light to save on weight. We traded the heavy sleeping bags for sheets and wore only shorts and T-shirts. We toss and turn all night on the verge of hypothermia. Morning finally comes, and we huddle around a fire to rejuvenate. From the experience Dan and I devise a new proverb for backpackers, "Pack light, freeze at a night." Harry says I have the best luck when it comes to backpacking weather. While this may be true it comes with the misfortunes of not heeding the old Boy Scout motto, "always be prepared."

July 25, 1990

State parks director Richard Davies is here to see the Buxton property which was recently purchased by the department. He has determined its value on paper but would like to see firsthand what we got for the money. We take the Trooper up the fire road, stopping at various points of interest, including lands north of the park which are still for sale. The entire Buxton tract was offered to the Department, but only enough funds for half were available. It begins to rain, turning roads to ruts. Near the old sawmill, the Trooper bogs in the mire discouraging our visit to that site.

July 27, 1990

While unlocking the visitor center this morning, I notice the Red Milk Snake George caught on July 4th is missing from its cage. Searching, I find it curled under the counter, and taking sympathy, I let it go. The Timber Rattlesnake in the adjacent cage also begs for freedom. It has bloodied its nose against the Plexiglas.

July 28, 1990

A copperhead is discovered in the woodbin, and word spreads among the visitors. Several rush over to offer their assistance in the kill. They are disappointed to hear that I plan to carry it to woods and set it free. "How come you don't kill those things", one man asks, "they could kill someone!" The comment does not deserve a response, but I am obligated to give one. "So do bears, bees, black widows and hundreds of other creatures. If I were to kill everything that has the potential to kill me, it would be a lonely world indeed." I'm not sure that's what the author was thinking when *"...God saw everything that he made, and behold, it was very good..."* (Genesis 1:31).

July 31, 1990

Nature plays a trick on a turtle and me this afternoon. The interpretive tour of Lee Creek yields more than the usual wildlife sightings. One of the children captures a Three-toed Box Turtle. I interpret the reason for which the turtle is named. On close inspection, however, we discover the turtle does have three toes on the hind feet, but four on the left front and five on the right. We name the new-to- science reptile *Terrapene ambiguous-digitatum.*

August 5, 1990

Natural resource inventory continues. Today's blooms include Hoary Vervain (*Verbena stricta*), Three-seeded Mercury (*Acalypha rhomboidei*), Croton (*Croton*

capitatus), Flowering Spurge (*Euphorbia corollata*), and Seedbox (*Ludwigia alternifolia*). August blooms, except for Cardinal Flower, lack inspiration. This evening, I drive to the overlook and gaze at the full moon. Naked branches of a large dead oak stand silent in silhouette. To the untrained eye, upper Lee Creek valley is mostly an uninhabited Oak/hickory forest, but to the naturalist it is a continual cradle of life.

August 8, 1990

An Eastern Screech Owl attempts to out-perform me tonight. It continues to disrupt my program at the amphitheater to the point where I must yield to the owl. Owls, like snakes, will steal the show every time.

August 9, 1990

Today's blooms include Elephant's Foot (*Elephantopus carolinianus*), Ground Nut (*Apios americana*), Bush Clover (*Lespedeza hirta*), and Monkey Flower (*Mimulus alatus*). You can tell a lot about a plant just by its name. All four are named after their most obvious feature, but only the last one has an attractive bloom. Elephant's Foot refers to the leaf; Ground Nut suggests its fruit; Bush Clover might identify the fluffy inflorescence but might just as well refer to the abundant foliage. Monkey Flower joins the ranks of Cardinal Flowers as some of the showiest of late summer.

August 21, 1990

I have received a lot of strange requests over the years, but this one I get this afternoon beats all. A visitor from Missouri asks if he can milk the venom from the snakes on display. The cages need cleaning anyway, so permission is granted. We take them into the A/V room and lock the door. The man has brought a video camera to record the event. I stand back and observe. He reaches into the cage and grabs the copperhead. This species is usually docile, and on rare occasions I have held one. He slowly massages the fangs over a 35 mm film canister to release the venom. The Timber Rattlesnake is next. It is harder to control and nearly breaks loose from the man's grip. It never occurs to me to ask what he plans to do with the venom. Then again, I am not sure I want to know.

September 2, 1990

Another season concludes. It has been a rather long and hot summer. Every day last week reached or exceeded 100 degrees. To escape the heat and crowds, Susan and I leave immediately after work for an extended trip to Glacier National Park and cool Montana breezes. Our plan is to stop at dozens of state and national parks, attend interpretive programs, study their interpretive exhibits, and take note of the kinds of items they offer for resale.

September 30, 1990

On busy weekends, it is routine to walk the trails, talk with visitors and collect litter. Ahead on Devil's Den Trail is a young man that should be carefully monitored – the kind that flouts societal norms. I follow behind him a few hundred yards. Suddenly he stops, looks around, tosses a can of hot cheap beer, then unzips to relieve himself in Right Angle Crevice. I walk up behind, catching him in the act. He is so wasted and ignorant that my lecture has no effect. The smell of urine permeates the air. I hate weekends.

October 1, 1990

On morning rounds to Arkansas Highway 74, I discover a Ford Bronco parked on the roadside. Tim, Jessee and I search the woods for the driver. I hear turkey calls and search in that direction. I discover a fully camouflaged hunter. Although the park is surrounded by National Forest open to hunting, Devil's Den is designated a wildlife sanctuary. We escort the hunter back to the vehicle and wait for the Arkansas Game and Fish officer to arrive. The young man believes he was hunting in the National Forest. His story is convincing, but I pity his ignorance. His vehicle is parked next to a "no hunting" sign and just inside the park entrance. The officer arrives and issues a citation amounting to $160.

Hunting is not allowed in state parks for several reasons, one of which is for the safety of other visitors. There must be some place where wildlife truly find refuge, where they can be observed, studied, and left to their own devices without constant pursuit from man. I have no qualms with hunters, and on occasion have participated in this ancient rite; however, it is of great benefit to both man and beast to set aside some lands for the exclusion of hunting.

October 6, 1990

The fall backpacking trip runs smoothly until Junction Camp is reached. Nearby we encounter locals shooting beer cans floating down the creek. I inform them of the danger of shooting near camp, especially with so many children present. Secondly, sinking cans in the creek is littering, illegal on any public land; but these are rednecks, and talk is cheap. The fact that we outnumber them three to one is likely the only reason they stop.

October 7, 1990

Day two of the backpack trip brings disaster. Morning finds us lingering inside our tents to avoid the thunderstorms. Harry and Dan failed to heed the backpacking proverb and left their tents at home. Now they are huddling under tarps which are ineffective shelters against the deluge. By 8:30 a.m. they and a few others strike for home. The rest of us remain until the worst of the storm has ended. On the return, we are nearly stampeded by dirt bikes and shot by bow hunters. The woods are not what they used to be.

October 11, 1990

In 1837, John Hudspeth mapped much of this valley for the US General Land Office. His map shows a small farm near the confluence of Ellis Creek and Lee. Ellis Creek is named after the man who settled here. I hope to find evidence proving the exact location of his homesite. The forest is a tangled mass of briars, cedars, and saplings. Every step is hindered by the vegetation, but I am determined to find a well, stone wall or some artifact revealing the site. An hour later I have nothing to show for my effort and reluctantly, I admit defeat. It will take an archeologist and proper digging to make a convincing discovery. Exploring north of the county road, I find the crumbled remains of rough-hewed logs. It is the third homesite in the valley with wood remaining. Beside the structure, a yucca grows, looking very much out of place.

October 14, 1990

Someone tried to break into cabin one last night, according to the occupants. The noise woke them in time to see a man fleeing the scene. This morning, I investigate. The screen on the south window is broken. I think of the many times I have left Susan alone at night. Our cabin is just a hundred yards away. Crime continues to grow even here in our secluded valley.

In search of other historical sites, I hike along the old wagon road north of Twin Falls. This road was the first into the valley from the east and was the main route between Lee Creek and Blackburn community. The road's west side is supported by a rock retaining wall, now crumbled in numerous places. Steep bluffs rise in the east exhibiting fantastic waterfalls. The road eventually crosses Butterfield Hiking Trail near the one-mile post, after which, the road becomes negligible. What was it like 130 years ago to bounce along in a wagon while descending to the wild and mysterious Lee? What were the impressions of these early settlers when passing Twin Falls and the giant bluffs of the crevice area. I can only conclude from the words of John Hudspeth's map: *"Remarkable Precipice."*

October 22, 1990

White-throated Sparrows and Yellow-bellied Sapsuckers have arrived for the winter. They have probably been here for a few weeks already.

October 25, 1990

Aerial photos show a huge bluff east of Vista Point. Topographical maps confirm the elevation to exceed 40 feet. If I am to know the area intimately, I must investigate this bluff. Just beyond the Civil War graves, I leave the trail and strike south. At the southern end of the bench, I head east along the bluff which increases in height. At its grandest point, the bluff ends abruptly. I step out from the Post Oak (*Quercus stellata*) and Farkleberry (*Vaccinium aboreum*) to a grand vista of Blackburn Valley. The crag and vista are too significant to go unnamed. "Blackburn's Bluff" is appropriate, and I think old Blackburn would have been pleased. Now that the feature has a name, hikers will undoubtedly include it on their route. Man's need to name a thing is only surpassed by his curiosity to see a thing that is named.

November 13, 1990

Most people have sympathy for dogs lost and alone, especially a puppy. Someone has abandoned one. Tim has taken care of it these past few days, hoping it will be claimed. No one does. Stray dogs are found in the park about once a month. Sometimes beagles are separated from hunters, and some are wild, but most are strays dumped by irresponsible owners. Most strays die a slow painful death filled with hunger, ticks, and mange. If they venture into the wrong neighborhood, they are shot. Such is the problem in parks. Taking dogs to the animal shelter cost $3. Tim chips in the money to pay the disposal fee for this dog, but too many are abandoned here.

We cannot keep paying out of pocket, and Department funds cannot be used for this purpose. A dog with no identification is kept for a few days, then it is disposed. No one likes the duty, but it has been forced upon us.

November 15, 1990

Brent says the only place to find Venus'-hair Fern (*Adiatum capillus-veneris*) is under Devil's Racetrack. Old park maps show the racetrack to be the stretch of bluffs running east-northeast from Highway 170 Overlook. Starting here, I walk Yellow Rock Trail until I find a way down the bluffs. Once below, I explore cliff shelters and search for ferns. A layer of calcareous sandstone is exposed and supports a half dozen Venus'-hair Ferns. Around the corner, I encounter a Rock Dove drinking from a mossy boulder. My presence startles the bird, but it remains. I watch as it laps the droplets splashed from a small waterfall. It tolerates me. I speak softly to assure it no harm. The dove glances between sips. Slowly, I walk to within three feet and kneel beside the dove. After a lengthy one-sided conversation, I depart, but turn back to see it fly away. The poet in me searches for meaning in this chance encounter. We are all spiritual beings and long for connection to the creation.

November 21, 1990

The switchbacks along Arkansas Highway 74 are treacherous under the best of conditions. Add rain, darkness and an exhausted driver and the road becomes a death trap. Nine hairpin curves require the driver's full attention down the 600-foot descent. At 6 p.m. I respond to a wreck on hairpin number three. A Truck loaded with antiques misjudges the corner, hit the brakes, and slid into the steep ravine. Neither the driver nor passenger are injured, but the antiques will have to be sold for parts.

November 23, 1990

Anyone who spends less than a year in the park cannot claim to have explored it all. As I approach the end of my second year in the valley, I still have much to see. I have always wondered where water from Twin Falls originates. Apparently, others have as well. A small footpath leads around the bluff and above the falls. I climb the ravine until it terminates at an insignificant seep. Walking the bench south-southwest, I come upon the remains of a foundation. Too small for a house, I suspect it was a shed. The land is so rocky and steep, the only thing a farmer could brag about here is the view. On the next bench I find three stone terraces. I cannot imagine there ever being any soil worth saving. The bench swings east and out to a knoll. On top, I find a three-sided stone pen. Who built this structure, and for what reason? I can only speculate. It is by far the most intact stone wall in the entire Lee Creek drainage.

November 28, 1990

Historical sites reveal themselves to me one by one. Some are obvious, others barely detectable. In the 1930's the CCC constructed over five miles of hiking trails and dozens more for equestrian use. Over the past 50-60 years sections of these have been closed and nearly lost to present knowledge. Three abandoned sections are found on Devil's Den Trail. In the late 1970's changes were made to reduce the length while creating a single loop. An abandoned stretch of Yellow Rock Trail is only now rediscovered as I walk below the bluff north of the highway bridge. I follow it to its connection with the present trail near the first switchback. I feel the urge to restore this section, but it would serve no purpose other than nostalgia. As a naturalist my first instincts should be to restore the original habitat.

December 2, 1990

As if the trip to Glacier National Park with Susan was not sufficient rejuvenation, Harry and I head for Big Bend National Park to spend a few silent nights in the Chisos Mountains. Pat and Susan dislike the timing. The big earthquake along the New Madrid Fault is predicted to occur tomorrow or the day after.

December 12, 1990

For several days I have been working on a comprehensive map of the valley. Much of the information conforms to current topographical maps, but trails and historical sites are added. Susan and I drive to Holt Farm to check a few details. Once again, I face my nemesis – the steep, boulder choked hill near the county line. We succeed, but not without sacrifices to the Trooper. The map is the important thing.

December 15, 1990

Not all Boy Scout Troops are the same. Many have contributed considerable time and effort cleaning the park, restoring trails and structures, and planting trees; but some troops (like the one I encounter today) are a liability. Three scouts cut live trees to make hiking sticks while the leader plucks ferns. If he is not conservation-minded, one can hardly expect the boys to be. It is a sad day when I must lecture what should be an exemplary group of visitors.

December 21, 1990

The high for the day reaches forty degrees which occurred this morning. The temperature has fallen ever since. By afternoon, sleet begins, and out-of-park employees break for home. The Devil's Den Christmas Party planned for tonight promises to be a smaller attendance.

December 23, 1990

The temperature sinks to ten degrees. Fresh snow covers Friday's ice.

December 26, 1990

Snow and ice have yet to melt. I assist a visitor by pulling his car from the ditch. Over the course of the day, I manage to get both park vehicles stuck. Keith comes to my rescue, and I return the favor by helping him spread chat on Arkansas Highway 74 for his safe return home.

December 28, 1990

A new phone system is being installed today. Now I must dial twenty-six numbers to place a personal, long-distance call. I had trouble hitting all the right buttons when there were only eleven. Progress may be inevitable, but it's often inconvenient.

December 30, 1990

The hill to the upper cabin loop is steep and narrow. With the existing ice, it is treacherous. Guests arriving late to cabin two get stuck halfway uphill. Going back means sliding into the ditch. I position the 4x4 in a culvert above and winch the car to the front door of the cabin. "Now that's service!" the man says.

Chapter 5: Settled

January 5, 1991

Midnight, a man calls from the park pay phone to say his wife has been kidnapped and is being held in one of the rental cabins. I dress quickly and meet him at the visitor center. In case of foul play, I wake Jessee and Brent, and ask them to meet there. After checking registrations and vehicles licenses, we find no evidence to support his claim. "She might not be here. I just came on a hunch", he says. Back in bed, I lie awake for hours contemplating scenarios of what could have been.

January 7, 1991

Ice on the ridge this morning prevents most from entering the valley. Little business is expected. Other than cabin guests exchanging towels, I doubt we'll see another visitor. On the way to the office, I accidentally lock the keys inside the patrol vehicle with the ignition on. Because the phone lines are down, I drive the Trooper to Brent's house to see if he has spare keys. He does not. Meanwhile the Trooper overheats, and it is nearly an hour before my return. Fortunately, Tim manages to unlock the car with a coat hanger and turns off the ignition.

January 8, 1991

Petit Jean is hailed as Arkansas' flagship park. The land was offered to the National Park Service, but they declined it. Steven Mather, then Director of the NPS, suggested that the land be used as a state park, and in 1923 that is exactly what resulted. Five documents in our files suggest Devil's Den was established prior, in the year 1916. My exposure of these has caused concern in the department since it predates Petit Jean. Today, I am asked to produce the papers to be scrutinized. All the documents are from reputable sources such as graduate theses, but it turns out each is based on the previous of which the first was in error. In 1916 the National Park

Service was established, and this may be the source of confusion. Overwhelming evidence shows Devil's Den to have been selected as a state park in 1933 between May and September. Construction began on October 20, 1933. Devil's Den will have to settle for being one of the first four.

January 11, 1991

Rain yesterday, and near freezing temperatures today have led to a dozen cancellations for tomorrow's winter backpacking trip.

January 12, 1991

Fifteen resolute and fearless backpackers embrace the freezing drizzle to hike the Butterfield Trail, including my trusted assistant, James. As we approach Quail Valley, we discover two young couples camping under the bluff. One of the young ladies, unaware of our approach, drops her drawers to relieve herself on the trail and within fifteen feet of the primary water source. I shout to inform her of our presence, but it is too late. Her humiliation is regrettable; however, the incident serves as a teachable moment for my group. We discuss backcountry ethics and the principles *of Leave No Trace.*

We had planned to eat lunch at Quail Valley but seem to have lost our appetite. At Rock Hole, we scavenge for wood and struggle to build a fire. The wood is wet, and no one has the patience to build it properly. James tries to start the blaze by spilling white gas over the embers. The flames instantly jump onto the bottle, igniting his glove and coat. Instinctively he drops the bottle which creates a ground fire. He then runs in circles trying to put himself out, creating more fires. Finally, he drops to the ground, and we extinguish the burning clothes. Once James is safe, we begin to put out the other conflagrations. If the situation was not so serious it would have been hilarious. Everything burned but the wood. For the rest of the trip, we show him no mercy. Whenever one of us gets cold we ask James to come and stoke the fire...and don't forget the bottle!

January 13, 1991

The overnight low dips to 20 degrees. Frost covers the inside of the tent, and I discover all the cold spots in my sleeping bag. Both fuel bottle and water filter freeze. At daybreak the group huddles around a sorry excuse for a fire, tolerating smoke for the warmth it brings. If nothing else, camping in such weather builds character.

January 19, 1991

A visitor reports seeing smoke from the upper crevice area. Keith and I investigate. We locate a campfire and gear, but no camper. I walk to the edge of Imp's Leap Ravine and shout. A young man echoes back. He approaches and I ask what possessed him to camp here. There is no correct answer, only the "I didn't see a sign" defense. He claims he does not know it is illegal to camp in undesignated areas or that cutting live trees for firewood is not permitted because he personally did not see a sign in the woods telling him it was forbidden here. I have him extinguish the fire and spread leaves and other debris to disguise his impact. Keith and I help him pack and escort him from the park. It is the visitor's responsibility to know the rules of the park, which are posted on bulletin boards, brochures, and available for the asking from any employee, especially at the visitor center.

During morning rounds, I spot a Greater Roadrunner crossing Arkansas Highway 170, and while home at lunch I observe a Brown Creeper outside my window. Both sightings are unusual.

February 23, 1991

Sunny and 64 degrees. A warm breeze with a hint of spring lures me to Lee Creek Trail. I spook a deer near the walk-in campground. A bouncing white flag is seen briefly. At the quarry pond a Great Blue Heron takes flight. Seven-foot wings slowly rise and fall until the forest canopy is gained. I continue to Fossil Flats and Bridger Falls. Across the intermittent stream a narrow ridge stair-steps to a calcareous bluff. I reconnoiter the shelters and ledges and find a coyote skull. Placing it on the end of a stick, I position it at the entrance to a shelter now called Coyote Bluff. Descending the narrow ridge, I locate Hairy Lip Fern (*Cheilanthes lanosa*) and several veins of Baldwin Coal in the Woolsey Member. Nearby, a Five-lined Skink makes a pre-spring appearance. Such

discoveries reward my appetite to explore.

February 28, 1991

Tim, Bill Gatewood (a former department employee), and I walk the fields south of the horse camp in search of archeological artifacts exposed at the surface. It is a pedestrian survey conducted to confirm the presence of prehistoric human activity. Bill and Tim find several lithic flakes in the old roadbed. After learning what to look for, I assist in the search and find several as well. These stone chips or flakes are remnants of flint-knapping, the process of making points and primitive tools. The lithic debris could have been transported here by Lee Creek floods, or as Tim and Bill believe, left by a prehistoric encampment. No other great discovery is made; although, a few days ago visitors displayed their findings from Cedar Grove which included potsherds. We continue up Ellis Creek Road. More flakes are found as well as several bottles circa 1950. Over time the bottles have become miniature terrariums for moss and Ebony Spleenwort (*Asplenium platyneuron*).

March 2, 1991

On morning rounds, I meet a camper who says he worked here as a lifeguard back in '57 or '58. He recounts the park's appearance before the pool was built, back when the lake had a swimming beach and diving platform. The CCC built a wooden platform which was replaced by a concrete structure. Now both are gone. A wealth of history is stored in the minds of previous employees. I should think a reunion would be a great way to tap into those resources.

March 7, 1991

Lindel Center, owner of West Mountain Trail Rides and Stables, offers a complimentary horseback ride for park employees this evening. There is a mutual benefit between the park and the stables. Many come to Devil's Den because they believe the park offers horseback riding. The park offers only horse trails and equestrian campgrounds. We send business to Lendel, and he in turn provides the type of recreation many visitors seek. I have traveled this trail before, but not in late winter. Through the defoliated forest, I can plainly see three pine plantations previously unknown to me. These stands represent the closest clearcuts to the park made by the U.S. Forest Service; even these are decades old.

March 9, 1991

On routine patrol, I catch a group of college kids rappelling off Imp's Leap. They are, of course, ignorant of regulations regarding this activity. Even if the mountaineering proposal had been approved, it would not have included this delicate area. I escort them off the trail, and suggest they use the bluffs of Quail Valley, which is under the jurisdiction of the U.S. Forest Service and a place where the activity is perfectly acceptable.

Around 8 p.m., I respond to a wreck near Ellis Creek bridge. A spring break party is being held at Cedar Grove. In all the coming and going a truck rear-ends a Ford Pinto. The car is totaled, and injuries are sustained. The driver of the truck is intoxicated and transported to county jail. Cedar Grove serves as the party place in Washington and Crawford County. The location is remote and neither county has the manpower to patrol it regularly. Since the Grove is in the National Forest, they can be sure no one from that agency will hassle them after 5 p.m. The only way into the Grove from Washington County is through the middle of Devil's Den State Park; therefore, we are left to deal with every imaginable problem.

March 11, 1991

Flags are flying at half-mast today in honor of soldiers killed in the Gulf War. Three flags are flown from the visitor center pole:

American, Arkansas, and one donated by Woodsmen of the World with the park's name in red letters on white cloth.

March 12, 1991

The park staff gathers at Jessee's house to clean and landscape the yard as a gift to him and his new wife, Sandi. There is much work to do before their return from the honeymoon. While raking, Brent unearths two Ozark Zigzag Salamanders. Work ceases while we watched the little amphibians squirm away to the woodpile.

March 16, 1991

Since mid-January, I have closely observed the first bloom of each wildflower species. Every day I walk a different trail to stay abreast of the floral activity. Pussy's Toes, Grape Hyacinth, Spice Bush, and Bloodroot are in bloom. Redbud is about three days away.

March 19, 1991

James Vaughn and Doug Robertson with Boston Mountain Grotto have agreed to survey Farmer's Cave. The map I made with George and Alan last summer was, at best, a crude sketch. Jim's map will be an accurate assessment. With tape measure, compass, and clinometer, Jim and Doug take readings from Ellis Creek bridge to the entrance of Farmer's Cave. The entrance elevation is exactly 990 feet above sea level. While they record tedious measurements, I scout the creek bank for wildflowers. I am distracted by water flowing into the creek from under a bluff. This must be the exit of the stream in Farmer's Cave. The passage is too flooded to explore, but there are other ways to verify my theory. The survey continues into the cave. We count 38 Pipistrelles, 37 crickets and two Slimy Salamanders in the first 240 feet of passage.

The survey cannot be completed in one day, but we do make time to investigate the woods for other caves. I locate a sinkhole about a hundred yards up the road. Jim and I enter the small hole to discover a medium-sized room filled with litter dating back to the 1940's. Upstream of the natural bridges, I locate a potential cave, but the opening is choked with alluvium. Entry will require excavation. Below the limestone shelf, a spring emerges. Our hopes run high for future discoveries.

March 20, 1991

Jessee returns from the honeymoon, bringing his wife, and her two daughters: Courtney and Cayce. Our valley community grows from 11 to population 14 (five males and nine females).

March 21, 1991

After closing the visitor center, it is routine to take keys to the cabins for late arriving guests. Today, it is my turn. During the rounds I am caught in the worst hailstorm in recent history. I run from vehicle to cabin dodging golf ball-size hail. One hit could knock a man flat, but miraculously I am spared. Driving the loop, I notice guests have thrown blankets from the cabins over their vehicles. I watch the wind blow the blankets into the street where they become soaked with mud and ripped by hail. I cannot blame the guests for trying to protect their cars, but I fear they have not given thought to the cost they have placed on the park. New blankets exceed the rental price of the cabin. My own vehicle suffers damage, but the hail dents only give the Trooper character. These, along with the other bumps and scratches, serve as makeshift journals of bygone adventures and stories I will later tell.

March 22, 1991

I confirm a colony of Palmer's Saxifrage (*Saxifraga palmeri*) on a ledge below Right-Angle Crevice. Nearby, the first Black-and-white Warbler of spring dances around a fallen log.

March 23, 1991

The past couple of days Harry has been renovating the old CCC trail in Imp's Leap Ravine. While the trail will not be promoted, interpretive hikes are planned. I hike the trail to see the results of his labor. It is amazing to see the number of old steps that for many decades were lost to the leaves. Along the way a plump Fox Sparrow appears unexpectedly from a crevice. I have not seen one in years and am glad to add it to my Devil's Den list.

March 25, 1991

Standing in front of the visitor center talking to campers, I hear an unfamiliar bird singing from the top of the Sugar Maple. I suspect it is a neotropical migrant and run for the binoculars. After a lengthy observation, I am convinced it is a Yellow-throated Vireo. Records show this to be the earliest sighting in Northwest Arkansas.

March 26, 1991

The search for new blooms continues. Brent informs me of a pear tree in bloom in camping area "E". It is an old one, most likely planted before the campground was established. From there I walk to the glade east of the horse camp. Beside a colony of False Garlic, I find human feces. There are no restrooms in the horse camp so campers either walk a quarter mile to the toilets in area "E" or use the cat method of burial. We have pleaded for funds to build restrooms here, but so far it is cost prohibitive. Whatever the price, it is less than the cost of an E. coli, Giardia, or Cholera outbreak or the continued presence of feces and toilet paper scattered in this rare plant community.

March 29, 1991

Snow falls for an hour this morning to remind us that spring can be unpredictable and is transitional in a month of its own choosing.

April 1, 1991

Jessee notifies Harry and I that he is being required to terminate Pat and Susan's employment. After a year of faithful service, the department leaders decide that they are in violation of the governor's policy on nepotism. This is an unfortunate decision. Both positions are hard to fill. Their employment was won by merit, and there is no supervisor/subordinate conflict. I believe there is more at play here than what we are being told.

April 5, 1991

The trail crew program ends, but not for lack of work. Several miles of trails still need repair. Alan and his family will be moving tomorrow, decreasing our valley population to 11.

April 6, 1991

This afternoon a young man walks into the visitor center to register for a campsite. He has no driver's license, no license plate, and no other form of identification. On a hunch, Brent reports the man's name to the county sheriff and learns he is a wanted felon. Suspecting trouble, the man flees to his car and speeds from the park. Brent pursues. The chase ends at a sheriff's roadblock in West Fork.

April 10, 1991

Jeanne Crone, local resident, and frequent visitor has spoken about the spectacular falls in the Blackburn Valley and has offered to guide me there. Dan Sharon and I have set aside the day to see Periwinkle and Winslow Falls. We pick Jeanne up at her mountain top home in Winslow and drive to the trail head.

Periwinkle Falls is a three-mile round-trip hike into the headwaters of Blackburn Creek. Scenes here remind me of special places on the Buffalo River. Dan sets the tripod and positions for the best picture. Jeanne and I wander downstream in search of floral rarities. After the hike, we drive to Signal Hill, eat lunch in Collier Cemetery, and tour the old Boston stage station. Jeanne points to holes in the rough-hewn logs which are said to have been made by gunfire during a Civil War skirmish. We continue across a wide field to a ravine hiding Winslow Fall.

Winslow Fall is nearly 100 feet and situated in a hollow just north of Periwinkle. The fall has been a favorite destination for residents and visitors since the resort era of the 1880's. Dan and I walk the bluff, searching for the perfect photographic angle. Wild Hyacinth and Yellow Star Grass adorn the sandstone glade. Once the pictures are taken, the best way to experience a waterfall is to lie nearby and dream. With eyes closed, I watch a yellow leaf dislodge from the bank upstream. Softly, it floats past violets dancing in the breeze. The leaf is swept into an eddy, shaded by oak and Farkleberry. Round and round it pinwheels, breaking loose at last by a surge of current. Seconds later it is swept over, tumbling slowly, and catching the sun. A humid and forceful wind, created by the powerful waterfall, carries the leaf. It lands as gentle as a feather on moss-covered rocks. There it will remain until spring floods. Its journey ends not in my lifetime.

April 11, 1991

This morning on my way to work I open the door and nearly step on an American Coot. Apparently last night's storm blew the bird off course. It must have spent the night nestled between the doorstep and wall.

April 13, 1991

My luck with weather during special events expires. The 10th annual wildflower weekend begins today, but rain confines us to the audio/visual room. Carl Hunter, author of Arkansas Wildflowers, is our guest this evening. Wet visitors crowd the room to experience his slides and stories.

April 15, 1991

Two years and four months have passed. Finally, Brent trusts me enough to reveal the location of the park's Ginseng colony. Ginseng root is prized among Asian cultures. The root is harvested from eastern deciduous forests and sold at a considerable profit. Because of this, Ginseng is rare. Only about a half dozen plants are found inside the park.

April 17, 1991

There are many secrets in these hills. I discover another while hiking a drainage north of Cedar Grove. A small intermittent stream cuts through shale, forming long slides and miniature falls. Occasionally the tangled brush gives way to glades of Wild Hyacinth and False Garlic. I count over 70 plant species in this drainage. A quarter mile upstream the ravine divides. I search the left and find a steep north-facing bank covered with Christmas Ferns (*Polystichum acrosticoides*) and Jack-in-the-pulpits (*Arisaema atrorubens*). The other ravine is longer and far more interesting. Narrow at first, it expands to reveal three converging waterfalls. Gray clouds gather, and a soft sprinkle begins. High on the east bank, a bluff shelter looms. I claw at the slippery bank to reach the dry sanctuary and wait for clouds to pass. A small Pipistrelle clings to the roof. Nearby, crickets sleep. As rain drips from the overhang, I envision a prehistoric man, sitting on this very rock, flint-knapping. His small fire crackles and pops beneath a roasted rabbit. The coals sizzle from the drippings while smoke rises and stains the ceiling. He ceremoniously inhales the fragrance of cooked lagomorph, ponders the scene before him of ferns and waterfalls, and wonders how long this rain will last.

April 18, 1991

I spot a House Wren amongst the briers and Winged Elms (*Ulmus alata*) at the north end of area "A". This somewhat common wren has eluded me for years, but this afternoon I finally add him to my life list.

April 20, 1991

The second annual spring backpacking trip begins with a hike to Holt Ridge Vista. I lead the group under the bluff where I had seen Palmer's Saxifrage (*Saxifraga palmeri*) this time last year. Orange Puccoon (*Lithospermum canescens*) blooms on the glade above. The hike continues to the lower quarry, Quail Valley, Phoebe's Cave, and the old graves along Vista Point Horse Trail.

We shed our packs at a small intermittent stream. Old maps call this Falls Hollow, not to be confused with Falls Hollow in the headwaters of Blackburn. A small eight-foot fall is visible from the trail, but others must exist downstream. I invite the group on a short reconnaissance, but only four come. We work our way down ledges, frequently crossing the stream. We halt abruptly at the edge of a 25-foot bluff. Faulted blocks of sandstone rise like monuments from the forest floor. The waterfall conceals a shelter of extraordinary depth. The opening exceeds a width of 40 feet and depth of over 50, although the height is less than five. Incredibly, it seems we are the first to find it. No footprints are found on the soft, dry shale. I would not be surprised, however, to see the bare print of ancient man. If he knew of this place, he surely would have slept here.

We set up camp on Mount Olive atop fresh shoots of Broomsedge (*Andropogon virginicus*) and under the shade of Post Oaks. The first Whip-poor-will of spring announces his arrival. The clouds depart around 7:30 p.m. in time to make the evening even cooler.

April 21, 1991

Morning and breakfast come early (6:30 a.m.). While others wash pots and pans, I chase an Ovenbird and other spring arrivals such as Summer Tanager and Kentucky Warbler.

The hike continues to Moonshine Cave. I am delighted to find a small colony of Shooting Star (*Dodecatheon media*) which has yet to be confirmed within park boundaries. Wild Hyacinths, too, are abundant.

Lunch is eaten at Bridger Falls. A light drizzle sets in, and some group members opt to shorten the trip. The rest of us continue to Hale and Dotson homesites, reaching trail's end around 2:00 p.m.

April 22, 1991

After chasing *"teacher, Teacher! TEACHER!"* for several years, I finally see the bird that makes this call. Ovenbirds are among the most vocal of spring but are very shy. Near the sewer treatment plant, I observe one as well as a Nashville Warbler. White-throated Sparrows persist. They had better hurry north. They do not belong here in breeding season.

April 30, 1991

To date, much of the history of Lee Creek Valley has come from tax, census, homestead, and marriage records, historical society publications, and old photos. All these resources pale in comparison with the opportunity before me. Lewis Henry ("Hank"), Harold, Irene, and Martha Sue ("Susan"), (all great grandchildren of Moses Mannon) have come to have a firsthand look at their roots.

Moses Mannon moved to Cane Hill, Arkansas from Tennessee in 1828. Eleven years later he moved his family to Lee Creek Valley along with John Eaton and the Hiram Taylor family. Moses cleared and farmed the land below Yellow Rock until his death in 1848. He was buried in the Mannon-Taylor-Eaton Cemetery near the junction of Butterfield and Lee Creek Trail. Francis Marion Mannon, was the ninth child of Moses and Mary, born April 19, 1836 (the year Arkansas was granted statehood). Francis married Malinda Taylor, the girl next door, and together had two children. Malinda passed away during the Civil War. After her death in 1862, Francis enlisted in the Union (Co. D 1st Cav.) and quickly saw action in the battles of Wilson's Creek and Prairie Grove. In 1863 he married Malinda's sister Margaret who died five years later giving birth to their second child (his fourth). Francis married a third time to Susan Ford. Together they had nine children. Francis outlived all his wives and four of his thirteen children. He was buried at Blackburn Cemetery in 1899.

The grandchildren are most interested in visiting his homesite, where the chimney still stands and jonquils bloom. We take the Trooper beyond the upper quarry to the intersection with Butterfield Trail. From here, a two-mile round-trip hike awaits, but they are determined. On the bluffs above Quail Valley, Harold tires, and we proceed without him. Hank, Susan, Glen (Irene's husband), and I stand beside the chimney Francis built in 1870. Hank recounts stories of his youth. A century dissolves into a fragment of time. I have visited this place many times, but only now feel its richness. In the voices of his grandchildren, this old chimney comes to life.

May 1, 1991

As the birds arrive so do the birders. Not to be out scooped, Susan and I take out a paddle boat out and stalk a Northern Waterthrush, adding yet another bird to my list. The Northern and Louisiana Waterthrushes can be difficult to distinguish. The former is seen here only on migration. On the other hand, the Louisiana Waterthrush will nest along these banks. Birding continues along Woody Plant Trail and at Mayfield. Prairie Warblers seem especially abundant this year.

May 4, 1991

To celebrate the 10th annual birder weekend, I have invited my mentor from Tulsa's Oxley Nature Center to speak. Bob Jennings is an exceptional birder. To increase his life list, he frequently jets to exotic places for new sightings. I have enticed him to come to Devil's Den this year by offering him a weekend at a cabin and the best warbler viewing west of the Mississippi. On the morning walk, he helps the group locate over 40 species of birds, including a rare look at a Chestnut-sided Warbler.

May 5, 1991

John Newell locates a Cerulean Warbler and leads Karen Garrett and I up Yellow Rock Trail for a look. It is the one bird Bob had hoped to see. Unfortunately, he left for home an hour ago.

May 12, 1991

As I lock the office doors, I notice two fellows standing by the phone. "Can I help you before I close?", I ask innocently. They look at me like a poacher eyes a buck. The first asks if the restaurant is open. I tell him it opens Memorial Day Weekend.

The second man asks, "Is the swimming pool open?" "It, too, opens Memorial Day Weekend", I answer. Following this, I'm asked if the store is open. "I'm sorry, it closed at 4:00 p.m." "Why are the cabin fireplaces locked?", they ask. "We lock them on May 1st by policy to prevent waste of energy. In the past, some people used the fireplace and air conditioner at the same time", I say. Both proceed to dump their frustrations on me for all the closed facilities. I might as well be tied to the flagpole and whipped for all the department's sins. I am psychologically exhausted. As a public servant abuse is expected. Response in-kind is not an option. I rationalize, empathize, and whole-heartedly apologize.

May 13, 1991

Two phone calls this evening are worthy of note. A lady from Texas calls to ask my opinion of her vacation plans to Arkansas. For 45 minutes we discuss destinations in the Natural State based on her schedule and route. She apologizes for taking up so much of my time, but the time was both enjoyable and well spent.

The second call comes from Fayetteville around 9 p.m. A giggling, teenage girl asks if there are any boys in the park. Since the park closes in an hour, I advise her not to drive all the way just to find out.

May 17, 1991

An old man reports losing his buddy in the woods down Washington County Road 61. Jessee and I interview the man and initiate a search. After four unproductive hours, we suspect the story is false. Several phone calls later, we locate his friend in Springdale who says he was neither lost nor at Devil's Den. He tells us that the old man is known to be mentally unbalanced. County deputies, arriving to assist in the search, end up taking the man back to town.

May 26, 1991

Another summer season commences. So many attend the softball game that three teams by necessity are created. Teams rotate in and out every half inning.

May 27, 1991

A busy Memorial Day Weekend comes to a peaceful conclusion. In the evening, I escape to my special place along the bluffs of Mayfield Glade. Upstream, a pair of beavers glide gracefully across the tranquil pool. Small ripples reflect the last of a setting sun. A water snake swims toward the beavers unaware of their presence. It comes within 10 feet and stops suddenly. In the brief pause, I watch the snake contemplate its options. It turns left to swim around them, but then thinks better of it. In a quick dash the snake retreats. The beavers act indifferent.

Casually I stroll the glade, photographing small features which capture my attention: Widow's Cross (*Sedum puchellum*), Sandwort (*Arenaria patula*), and lichen. I return to my lawn chair-perch above the creek. Chirping frogs, the faint gurgle of the creek, and Chuck-will's-widow melodies give way to the silence of pen and paper. I attempt a few lines of poetry to capture the splendor of the moment, and to erase the stress of yet another holiday weekend in the trenches.

PARVIFLORA
Before it bloomed in crystal vases
Beauty hid in secret places
Walk with me down obscure traces
Lost as one, in open spaces.
The sun is setting as it should.
Casting fire upon the wood
Cirrus clouds form eastern faces
While breezes dance in grassy laces
Blanket spread, two hearts are resting
Unaware of birds there nesting
Passions flame until aurora
'Midst the scarlet parviflora
May 30, 1991

Susan and I christen our new 16- foot Dagger canoe, the S.S. Nuttall. The name is given to honor the English botanist, Thomas Nuttall, who paddled up the Arkansas River in 1819 discovering many plant species common to the valley. It is he who first published the name Lee Creek in his journal entry of May 23. We launch at the north end of the Lake and circle the island in search of turtles and Jewelweed (*Impatiens capensis*).

June 1, 1991

Six attend my program on how to fish Lee Creek. After a brief equipment demonstration and discussion on proper identification I lead them to the water. The moment is at hand, and talk is cheap. If I fail to catch one now, I will lose credibility. So long as he is in uniform the interpreter is viewed as expert, but many a visitor is quick to spot a fake. Hooking a Green Sunfish is not so much a matter of skill as it is knowing what makes the fish react. If there are any in this pool, I will catch one simply because the fish cannot help itself. It is the fish that validates my expertise. I must only lay the right lure in its proximity. They watch as I retrieved my first unsuccessful cast. I try again, this time putting the lure within inches of the opposite bank. Wham! The lure is dragged below, and the fight is on. Once the point is illustrated I yield the creek to others using the same techniques a young boy immediately catches a bluegill the rest are charged with excitement and race each other to the next hole. It occurs to me I have failed to cover the ethics portion of the lesson.

Leaving the group, I spot an albino catfish rising to the surface near the Bluffs albino catfish were stocked in the lake upstream nineteen years ago. I can only speculate as to the origin of this one.

June 4, 1991

Heath and Winfred (summer missionaries) arrived today, increasing our valley population to thirteen. Heath promises to be a competitive softball player.

June 7, 1991

Yellow False Foxglove (*Areolaria flava*), Motherwort (*Leonurus cardiaca*), Hairy Petunia (*Ruellia humilis*), and Woolly Mullein (*Verbascum thapsus*) are in bloom. I collect a new specimen of tick trefoil. Pouring over my collection of field guides and taxonomic keys, I look for the perfect match. Based on its range, blooming, habitat, and distinctively shaped leaflets, it can only be (*Desmodium glutinosum*), bringing the number of *Desmodium sp.* to ten within park boundaries.

With all the recent blooms, plants are foremost on my mind, and serve as the primary theme for this morning's interpretive walk. Plants may seem boring to the average visitor, but it may be due to their lack of understanding or poor presentation of the subject by the interpreter. I will not allow these visitors to be bored. Plants are the oldest, largest, and most numerous living organisms on earth. How can anyone not take interest? Those who do often focus entirely on the flower. True, the flower symbolizes beauty, fragrance, and youth; however, much is missed if the entire plant is not considered. Despite the flower's showiness, it is often the leaf which gives the plant its name. Lance-leaf Coreopsis, Birds-foot Violet and Spiderwort are a few examples. It is also true in many cases that the leaf, not the flower, is most fragrant. Examples include Aromatic Sumac, Leaf-cup and Calamint.

Identification is not interpretation, but the name is much of the story. Why for instance is Widow's Cross called such? Why is Jack-in-the-pulpit and not the reverend or preacher? Queen Anne's Lace and Dutchman's Breeches are easy names to interpret, but Joe-pye Weed, Rattlesnake Master and Lady's Thumb are less obvious. Even more interesting yet obscure is the meaning of some scientific names. On the face of it, visitors may not care to know that Asclepias is the genus of milkweeds, but what if they also learned that Asclepias was also the Greek god of healing? Would that spark an interest in the backstory? Which is more interesting, Bloodroot or Sanguinaria – meaning bloodthirsty savage? So many visitors to nature fail to see the characters beyond the calyx or corolla.

June 12, 1991

Softball games continue to improve as the attendance increases. Over 50 visitors are present; Almost half have come to watch. I hit two home runs but win only the consolation game.

June 21, 1991

The park is in full swing. Campgrounds are near capacity each night, and day-use facilities overflow. The pool is especially crowded. No less than 75, including Susan and my sister's family, pack in and around the little concrete water hole. Amidst the screaming and splashing, lifeguards fail to notice a small boy who has sunk to the bottom. Michael, my eight-year-old nephew, happens to scan the bottom of the pool with his new goggles and sees the boy. He realizes something is wrong. The boy's eyes are open but there is no response. He swims down and pulls the boy to the surface. Others observant of the situation, rush to pull the boy out. An off-duty doctor and nurse begin CPR while Susan phones EMS. The boy is revived, thus avoiding the first drowning death at Devil's Den in recent history.

June 30, 1991

This evening at the park laundry, I meet Castle Goldman from California. Castle served here in the late 1930s with the CCC. He shares a 1938 photo of himself pointing to a cross engraved on one of the rocks near the bridge abutments. The cross designates the rock which rolled over and killed Eddie Cornelius a CCC enrollee during the wall's construction. Intrigued, I accompany him to the site to see if the cross is still visible. With flashlights in hand, we search. Over 50 years of wind, rain, and ice fail to erase this memorial. We find a small three-inch cross etched in the corner of a large sandstone boulder.

July 4, 1991

For fifteen years the annual Devil's Den games have been held in the picnic area below the pavilion. This year I convince the staff to make some changes, and this morning the games begin in camp area "E". Harry organizes the horseshoe pitching tournament. Heath and Winfred plan the kids' games, while Jessee and I prepare for the softball tournament. This year the egg toss was dropped from the agenda much to the protest of some. Men and women are divided into four teams, and the softball tournament begins. Harry, Tim, and Jessee umpire the game while I keep score, announce the batters, and joke with the crowd. The playoff game begins at 7 p.m. By 8 p.m. spectators begin lining up behind Tim who cranks homemade ice cream. After the ice cream is consumed and the games are concluded campers retire to their sites. Fourteen hours of continuous activity leaves Harry, Tim, Jessee, Brent, and I longing for a day off, but tomorrow work resumes. Holidays are for normal people with normal jobs.

July 5, 1991

Around 2 p.m. a visitor reports that a member of her party is suffering from heat exhaustion somewhere near Upper Quarry. With a medical bag and a jug of water I hop in the 4X4. On the way, I request additional details. She says her girlfriend and family were hiking to Quail Valley. On the return, the girlfriend collapsed and could walk no further. She instructed her to rest while help is summoned. Driving into the Upper Quarry we meet the victim walking down the road. She is dressed in a black sweater, dark jeans, and cowboy boots; she is overweight and has no water. With the temperature and humidity pushing the upper 90s, she is a walking heat stroke. I give her water, place a cool rag on her neck, and transport her back to the visitor center.

July 7, 1991

With a few exceptions, summer attracts the most demanding impatient campers while winter attracts the friendliest. Bob and

Sherry Horn from Kansas City are two of those exceptions. I first met Bob on one of the park-sponsored backpacking trips. Tonight, Susan and I are invited to their campsite for supper. An interpreter never turns down free food. After supper and conversation, Susan and I stroll down the road to the Soule's campsite. Jay and Carol are from Wichita and like Bob and Sherry have been coming to Devil's Den for nearly two decades. Both have a lot of family memories tied to the park. Carol serves the dessert as we sit around the campfire discussing park history and interesting bird sightings.

July 9, 1991

The Sheltons arrive for a few days of camping. Dennis, Kathy, and the boys are from Tulsa; When they come, they make up half the softball team. An interpreter's social life is almost exclusively linked to visitors. Once a bond is created, it is rarely broken. The Sheltons, like the Horns and Soules, will remain forever a part of my Devil's Den experience.

July 22,1991

A bear is reported around 7:30 p.m. on Arkansas Highway 74, but I am unable to confirm the sighting. It is probable that black bears are moving west from White Rock Mountain, but I am hesitant to add it to our official records.

Temperatures have been hovering around the upper 90s for eighteen days, but finally it reaches 101 degrees.

July 26, 1991

A trace of rain is recorded this afternoon. Nearly half an inch has fallen over the past couple of days. It is the first significant rain since mid-June, and the first time the high temperature has remained in the 70s since June 5. It is a perfect day for a hike. I take advantage of it by leading a group of thirty-four on Lee Creek Trail. We observe two deer and discover Biennial Gaura (*Oenothera gaura*) and Monkeyflower (*Mimulus alatus*) in bloom.

August 1, 1991

Jim Vaughn is back to complete the survey of Farmer's Cave. Heath and I assist in the effort. I pull tape and take clinometer readings with Heath while Jim records numbers and sketches passages. Our main objective is to complete the map north of the Garage. First, we survey the series of passages connecting the Drinking Room, Key Room, and beyond. After lunch, we continue by mapping south-southeast of the Garage. Forty feet beyond the Saddle Room, the passage narrows, and the ceiling constricts. I find it impossible to proceed, but Jim is more experienced and eager. In less than a foot of height and two of width, Jim pushes on. After a miserable crawl of 15 feet, he finds room on the other side to sit. Heath follows successfully. Claustrophobia affects all normal people. Jim and heath are not normal. I encourage them to continue the survey without me and I exit the cave. Later, they tell of a room with the date 1936 inscribed on the wall. The passage continues to what Jim calls the Mud Mines area and eventually exits near the Epiglottis. Over 1,148 feet of passages are surveyed, making Farmer's Cave the largest and longest in Lee Creek Valley.

August 5, 1991

Continuing with the park resource inventory, I schedule a fish survey with the US Fish and Wildlife Service Co-op unit at the University of Arkansas. The coop leader and several graduate students arrive around 9 a.m. I lead them to a pre-selected hole in Ellis Creek. Team members assemble the gear then wade in to shock the hole. The level of electricity is designed to kill all the fish which is the most accurate way to sample the population. It is only one pool out of many and will be repopulated with the next heavy rain.

As fish float to the surface, they are scooped into buckets. Later the fish will be taken to the university to be sorted by species then counted. The survey helps resource managers determine stream health and how best to manage rare or threatened species. Eight species are collected from Ellis Creek of which Big-eye Shiner,

Central Stone Roller, Green Sunfish and Long-eared Sunfish are the most numerous. Only one Striped Garter and four Redfin Darters are collected from this pool. Bluntnose Minnow and Creek Chub Sucker conclude the list. Oddly no Small-mouth Bass or Log Perch are collected, though I have seen both on previous visits.

The team locates to a predetermined spot in Upper Lee Creek. Here the count is higher. Eleven species are collected including one Green-sided Darter and one Brook Silverside. It is exciting to see these species which until now have remained hidden in the dark quiet pools. The survey reinforces the fact that this valley is biologically diverse. There are many creatures here I may never come to know; Yet every action taken, be it development or habitat management affects so many lives. These streams must be protected for future generations of Green-sided darters if only for the joy they bring when discovered.

August 10, 1991

After a week of temperature in the upper 90s and even 100° the heat wave breaks with a high of only 87. It could not happen at a better time. Ten of us set out on Butterfield Trail for the second annual summer backpack trip. Weather aside, the trip is otherwise routine. We catch a few fish, swim at every convenient hole, and visit the usual sites. We erect tents around 4:30 p.m. at Junction Camp. In my rush to get the group going, I failed to pack parts to one of the rental tents. Due to this error, I relinquish my own as a replacement. Just as well. There is little chance of rain, and I would rather sleep out under the stars. I spread my ground cloth and sleeping bag near the fire and prepare supper. As the night wears on, hikers retire one by one to their shelters with little fanfare. Three of us remain, deep in discussion, until the firewood is exhausted.

August 20, 1991

Because of the park's remoteness, it takes a minimum of twenty minutes for emergency services to arrive. If a visitor receives life threatening injuries, there may not be time for EMS to make the round-trip drive. For this reason, a practice run with Springdale-based Medi-flight is conducted. The flight is costly, but when minutes count it may be worth the price. The helicopter lands in the lower picnic area. We discuss routine procedures and examine the craft. If the helicopter returns here on a busy Saturday it will cause quite a spectacle.

September 8, 1991

The inventory of park flora continues into the end of summer and even early autumn to document species that bloom late. I walk the dry bed of Lee Creek. A large pink blossom captures my attention. I examine the plant thoroughly, including the test for fragrance, but quickly find it repulsive. It is identified as (*Pluchea camphorata*) commonly and appropriately named Stinkweed.

Near Cold springs a visitor approaches apprehensively. She hands me a plastic bag containing marijuana which she reports finding near the cave. I radio the incident to Tim and Brent who respond immediately to that location. Suspicious characters are seen entering Devil's Den. The cave reeks of marijuana. Two boys are questioned, but there is no physical proof to connect them to the illegal substance.

September 12, 1991

Much work is still needed to document late summer and fall plants. One thing I did not learn from my college botany class is that more plants reproduce in summer and early fall than those that bloom in spring and early summer. To get a complete inventory of the park's flora, not only do I need to apply field botany to three seasons, but also spatially – to every conceivable habitat. With this in mind, I set out to hike the Yellow Rock Trail and discover a dainty purple flower on the dry sandstone ledge opposite Devil's Teapot it is (*Agalinus skinneriana*), a somewhat rare Gerardia and member of the figwort family. Several deer are seen along the walk, as well as fourteen species of birds. I continue my search in the evening around the lake finding Arrowhead (*Sagittaria montevidensis*) and Climbing Buckwheat (*Polygonum convolvulus*) in bloom. The evening concludes as it should, in the Mayfield area with the sounds of Whip-poor-will and Great Horned Owl.

September 14, 1991

Frequent campers Dennis and Kathy Shelton are here again for a visit. They invite Susan and I to Fayetteville for pizza. On the long drive home, Dennis and I catch a glimpse of an animal crossing the road that looks so much like a Mountain Lion that it leaves us momentarily speechless. For many years I have believed a breeding population of Mountain Lions no longer existed in Arkansas. In fact, this is the conclusion of the Arkansas Game and Fish Commission. What we have just seen suggests otherwise, but neither of us is bold enough to admit it. I can't report it because we have no evidence whatsoever. My credibility would decrease, and at dusk is the worst time to argue my case – poor lighting and all.

September 15, 1991

Off duty and out of uniform, Jessee encounters a belligerent man walking through his yard with a butcher knife. Since we are in uniform Jessee calls Tim and me to investigate. We approach the man and question him. He says he is digging mushrooms. We inform him of regulations which prohibit collecting or disturbing natural features of the park and trespassing in restricted park areas. He continues his resistance. Insisting that he has every right to collect mushrooms on public lands, including at a park residence. Finally, we convince him to leave. He is last seen heading for the Ozark National Forest where few are merely held accountable for their actions.

September 17, 1991

In preparation for the construction of a gate, I measure the opening of Farmer's Cave. Now that the cave is surveyed and owned by the park, we believe it is important to regulate its visitation. In recent years, the cave was left open to vandalism, beer parties, and injuries. Graffiti mars the walls, and beer cans and candy wrappers breed in the darkest recesses. Gating the cave and regulating entry would benefit everyone. Spelunkers would be better prepared for entry and would be less likely to vandalize and litter the cave. Other benefits to spelunkers include the comfort of having rescue personnel know their itinerary, and the enjoyment of having the cave reserved for their exclusive use.

September 19, 1991

While I continue to pursue the Farmer's Cave gate proposal, Harry manages to acquire funds to install an alarm inside Big-eared Bat Cave. It was determined that a gate would negatively affect the movements of the endangered Ozark Big-eared Bat in this cave, therefore an alarm system would be the next best thing. The US Fish and Wildlife Service appropriated $10,000 for its construction and installation. It will be the first alarm system of its kind. Now if someone wanders beyond this "Do Not Enter" sign their light will trip the alarm. The signal is carried by cable to an antenna above the cave which is sent to another outside the visitor center. This second antenna is connected to the alarm inside. When the alarm sounds, we immediately proceed to the cave to catch the perpetrators. Since Big-eared Bat Cave is one of only three known hibernacula, it must be protected against intrusion. A substantial population of Ozark Big-eared Bats could be destroyed with one careless entry.

September 21, 1991

The Arkansas Mountain Bike Championships begin this morning with a grueling cross-country race. Incidents requiring first aid increase throughout the event, and the trail claims many bikes.

September 23, 1991

This evening, I walk the field north of Washington County Road 61 (upper Mayfield) to look for birds. Brown thrashers are normally uncommon, but I observe a dozen. Perhaps they are a transient group looking for new territory. Three deer wander off as I approach the pond in the north corner of the field. I sit at pond's edge to watch bats drink water on the wing. Barred Owl and Eastern Screech-owl converse. I howl just to hear the echo. The Mayfield area brings out the wildness within.

October 12, 1991

Harry and I arrive early to the visitor center this morning to organize the annual fall backpack trip. Fourteen hikers assemble in his group, and I take 17. After a shuttle to Sandy Gap, we hike to Moonshine Cave. From here we descend the road to Blackburn Creek. The road continues downstream to the Arnold homesite where we stop to rest. A two-story chimney is all that remains of the John and Ellen Arnold homesite circa 1910 to 1929. Ellen was one of Francis Marion Mannon's many grandchildren, and daughter of John Hezekiah Johnston who owned the bluff shelter now called Moonshine Cave. The Arnolds were not the first to live here. Ellen's uncle Ulysees Grant Johnston built the home in 1892 for his wife Minerva Jane Mannon. To understand how intertwined families became in these hills it should be noted that John's wife Martha Emmaline (Mannon) was Ulysses' wife's sister; and furthermore, John Arnold's brother, Will, married Nancy (Mannon), Martha and Minerva's youngest sister.

It is especially busy in the Ozark National Forest today. We meet other hikers, mountain bikers, equestrian and ATV riders. Camp is established at Rock Hole. Afterwards, we take a short excursion up Mill Creek hollow. I am told a substantial waterfall can be found here. After pursuing the hollow for a mile, we give up the search. The lack of rain is blamed for the waterfall's disappearance. We do manage to see a Black Rat Snake, Winter Wren, Yellow-bellied Sapsucker, a small flock of Dark-eyed Juncos and a couple of Northern Flickers.

October 13, 1991

Upon returning from the hike, I learned that Tim responded to a fatal accident yesterday. An elderly lady was walking along the dam with her grandchildren, then suddenly lost balance and fell fifteen feet to her death. Tim, along with two off duty nurses, tried unsuccessfully to revive the woman. It is the second death to occur at Devil's Den during my tenure. Death – accidental or self-inflicted – is a part of the job for which no one prepares. My heart is soft to the untimely death of a snake ran over on the road, or the rabbit that becomes food for the vulture, how much more so for a fellow human being abruptly departed.

October 14, 1991

Tim, Jessee, and I return to the scene of Saturday's accident to make a full report. I photograph the ledge from where the woman fell to illustrate its height. Below, blood-stained rocks mark the point of impact. As Tim recounts the incident, I am still deeply disheartened to think something so tragic could happen at this tranquil place.

George and I guide David Herman, Arkansas Game and Fish officer, to Big-eared Bat Cave. If a trespasser is caught, it is David who will be called to issue the citation. He will need to know the location of the cave and how the alarm works. Once in the crevice and well hidden from the trail above, we hear voices. Three teenagers approach, and we hide to observe their reaction to the closure. Upon reaching the entrance, one of the boys reads the warning sign. The three discuss whether to enter anyway. One suggests the sign is a bluff and that the alarm does not really exist. For five minutes they debate, then decide not to enter. One of the boys cannot resist throwing a rock into the cave to see if the alarm will sound. David appears and catches him with a rock in hand. "You're not really going to throw that rock, are you?", he asks. "Oh, no sir!" the startled boy answers.

George and I step out from hiding and the boys are completely surprised and apologetic. I congratulate them on making the wise decision, entering would result in a fine of up to $50,000. I take the opportunity to educate them on why this cave is closed.

October 20, 1991

A horse died in the campground last night. Apparently, it was not properly tethered and became tangled. The rope strangled the horse and cut its jugular which caused it to bleed to death.

October 21, 1991

With a donation from CCC Company 3795 Reunion Association and a grant from the Arkansas Historic Preservation Program, we have embarked on an interesting project. The park staff agrees to erect six wayside exhibits and build a self-guided trail complete with brochure, through the CCC camp ruins. Each of us has been assigned the text for one exhibit, and together we will work on the largest exhibit to be placed at the trailhead. I volunteer to write text for an exhibit at the overlook. For inspiration, I sit at the viewpoint and ponder the appropriate interpretive message for this, the first structure built by the CCC at Devil's Den. The rockwork is designed to blend with the bluff so that the pavilion looks like an extension of it. It is a simple but massive structure.

October 23, 1991

Jay Soule is back for a visit, and we waste no time heading to the Mayfield area for a little birding. A recent mowing of the field has made it more attractive to the birds. Jay and I watch a sharp-shinned hawk hover and soar.

October 25, 1991

For many years, interpreters here have been telling stories about a man named Logger John. I am told such a man once lived in Lee Creek Valley, but over time, history has obscured the facts and left room for embellishment. Every valley needs a legend, every campfire needs a story, and I am determined to uphold this one. This evening the program is one of storytelling for a group of girl scouts. Such an audience assures any ghost tale a successful presentation. The Legend of Logger John (Keck version) is as follows:

Back in 1873 there was a man folks around here called Logger John. He was larger than average. Some say he was over seven feet tall without boots. No one knew where he was from. He just kind of showed up one day looking for work. Because of his size and apparent strength, Logger John was hired by the local mill hence the nickname. Logger John was a quiet fellow, and most were afraid of him because of his size, strength, and mysterious origin. A photograph was never taken of him, but he was described as having long hair and an unkept beard. Some have said he only had nine toes, but this fact was never substantiated. He had big hands and ears and a scar on his upper lip, barely noticeable through his greasy mustache. Other than these imperfections, he was not considered an unsightly man.

Logger John had a cabin not far upstream from here. It was a small one room structure with a fireplace in the wall opposite the door. Those who occasionally passed by his cabin would recall frequently report seeing a deer gutted and hanging from the porch roof. Logger John primarily made his living off the land. There were rumors he could paralyze a deer with fear just by looking into its eyes. He had the same effect on most people. He wasn't a mean spirited fellow, but this reputation developed.

One evening the local drunk stumbled by Logger John's cabin and made off with a piece of venison. Later the old boy bragged about it in town. The next morning, he was found dead on the Blackburn Road. Folks began to accuse Logger John of the drunkard's untimely death. The next day a cousin of the deceased confronted Logger John about the incident, and even went so far as to call him a bloody murderer. Logger John turned and looked his accuser straight in the eye. Bystanders swore that the accuser fainted dead away, yet Logger John never laid a hand on him, but word spread that he was somehow to blame.

From that day forward a dozen different stories were told about Logger John, and there wasn't a soul in all of Lee Creek Valley that didn't fear him, or fear for their life should ever they be in the vicinity of his cabin. Logger John didn't show up at the mill after that incident, and he pretty much kept to himself. Folks didn't see him for days and weeks, but some said they heard him chopping wood up on Yellow Rock Ridge.

When a young girl disappeared one October evening, the community immediately assumed Logger John had captured her. A posse of mostly vigilantes organized. With torches, shotguns, and courage from which only moonshine can give, several of the men marched up to the ridge to Logger John's cabin. As the men neared the cabin, they could see smoke coming from the chimney. A flicker of light from the fire could be seen through the cabin's only window. Dusk had come and gone. A full moon was rising over Mount Olive. Logger John's axe was leaning against the cabin near the door. A raccoon and two possums were hanging on the outside wall. The blood dripping from the carcasses suggested a recent kill.

The men stopped at the edge of the clearing, concealing themselves behind a thicket of buckthorn and briar. Not seeing Logger John, they called out to him, *"Logger John, if you're in there get out here now. We want to have a talk with you!"* I seriously doubt that talk was what they had in mind. No answer came from the cabin, but a shadow passed in front of the window. Several seconds passed, yet each seemed like an hour. The men shouted again. Still there was no answer, but this time the light from the fire was gone. All was dark except for occasional moonlight breaking through the charcoal-like clouds.

The men decided one of them would have to go in and make Logger John come out. Zeb, the bravest of the mob, was persuaded.

He stood up, took a swig of moonshine, and hollered to the cabin, *"I'm coming in!"* Zeb walked cautiously across the open ground to the front of the porch. Not a sound could be heard coming from the cabin. Only a nearby screech-owl made any sound at all. As Zeb climbed the first stair, it creaked under foot. Slowly he took the next, which brought him squarely on the porch. He can hear the blood dripping from the carcasses to his right. On his left was Logger John's axe. With one hand he reached for the axe. With the other he carefully opened the door. Like the step, the door gave way with an eerie sound. Zeb pulled the door wide but couldn't see a thing inside. From the faint moonlight through the single window Zeb saw a shadow move across the back wall. Without thinking he rushed the shadow with the axe raised.

Outside, the men could hear a dull thump ...and then another! Suddenly a loud crash was heard and then nothing more. Seconds passed, minutes passed, and then one of the men hollered to the cabin, *"Zeb are you OK?"* The men knew something was wrong but were too afraid to approach the cabin. Each turned and ran back down the valley into the darkness. Early the next morning, the men returned with the sheriff. Daylight brings courage, and the men approached the cabin directly. The door was open, and the raccoon and possum were gone. Inside lay Zeb with an axe embedded in his chest. Rivulets of blood ran across the crooked floor. In the corner of the cabin near Logger John's bed, lay a large human ear. Zeb had both of his. Little speculation was needed to determine whose ear it was. Logger John was nowhere in sight. The sheriff placed the ear in a small canvas bag and took it for evidence. A warrant for the arrest of Logger John was made, and all of south Washington county was on the lookout.

The upper Lee Creek Valley was in a state of hysteria. Logger John's cabin was burned by a mob later that week, and men from surrounding communities accompanied by bloodhounds combed the woods for days, but Logger John was never found. Several months later strange occurrences began. Occasionally, locals would hear the thump of an axe, but when they approached the area from whence it came, only silence was found. Once a deer was discovered gutted and hanging from a tree near Sawmill Hollow. For many years on the anniversary of the murder, dogs would suddenly howl and then just as quickly run whimpering under their master's porches. The strangest thing of all occurs on cool October nights when fog begins to roll up Lee Creek Valley. Campers have reported hearing a whisper outside their tents. *"Who's got my ear?"* the voice would seem to say. Not a few sleeping campers would awake to this and the tugging sensation on their ear.

October 26, 1991

Nearly 5.5 inches of rain have fallen the past couple of days. Another camper reports hearing strange whispers outside her tent late last night. The Sheriff's Office called this afternoon to inform me of an armed robbery which took place at the scenic overlook a few hours ago. An Asian man was approached at the Arkansas Highway 170 overlook by two men on motorcycles. They demanded his wallet and watch at gunpoint. Instead of reporting the incident to us right away, the man drove all the way to the authorities in town. We comb the park for suspects, but the trail is at least two hours cold.

November 3, 1991

Peggy Rennie, facility manager, reports waterfowl on the lake. I rush down to confirm the sightings and find a Wood Duck and a Lesser Scaup, the latter of which is the first sighting on park record.

November 9, 1991

Harry and I along with a few friends leave Devil's Den for a week of backpacking in Utah. Now a tradition, the trip has become the best way to rejuvenate our minds and put a long season behind us.

November 19, 1991

After 2.5 inches of rain this past week, the huge stonewall across from the old bridge abutments begins to collapse. What has remained unmovable for nearly 57 years seems to be crumbling before our eyes. Fortunately, the boulder with the cross commemorating the death of Eddie Cornelius still stands.

November 24, 1991

For the second time in as many weeks, the bat alarm sounds. We race to the cave but find no trespassers. Harry suspects a weak battery or lightning as the cause.

December 5, 1991

Jessee informs me that the department is close to deciding on my proposal to gate Farmer's Cave. Two and a half months have passed since the proposal was submitted.

December 15, 1991

All year, I have been focused on completing a comprehensive park resource inventory. I am working on the geological section of the report, which requires frequent trips to remote park areas. My task today is to find the contact zone between Pitkin Limestone and the Cane Hill Member, which consists of shale, siltstone, and fine-grained sandstone. I deduced from earlier geologic maps that the best chance to find an exposed contact is in the Ellis Creek drainage. After stumbling around for nearly an hour, I find tan-colored beds of shale resting unconformably on Pitkin Limestone near Ellis Creek fault. Its specific location is on the east bank in the southwest 1/4 of the northeast 1/4 of section 27, north of the park boundary about 150 yards.

December 16, 1991

Continuing the geological inventory, I locate and excavate a six-inch inch vein of Baldwin Coal on the fifteen-mph curve of Arkansas Highway 170. Given the rate of erosion, soil should cover my excavation in a few months, but for now those passing will see this rare outcrop.

December 18, 1991

This morning, I load the Trooper with the usual tools of exploration and set out to locate a way into upper Lee Creek Valley from near Blackburn Cemetery. My maps are a bit sketchy on roads descending from Blackburn to the east Bank of upper Lee Creek. I stop at a farmhouse for directions, but no one answers, although music is heard coming from the upstairs window. Through trial and error, I find a road deeper into the valley. I stop at another house. A woman answers the door cautiously. I ask if the road in front of her house leads to the valley and if so, may I have permission to pass. She confirms the road descends to the creek, and even though it crosses her land the road she says is considered public. I thank her and return to the Trooper.

The road descends gradually at first, then becomes narrow and steep. The grade cuts into a shelf of the bluff which slants toward the valley. It feels as if the Trooper might roll at any second. After several hairpin turns and hair-raising maneuvers the road levels out to an unusual site. Smack in the middle of the woods I find an old junk bus, van, sheds, and piles of debris. I have reached Ruth's place. I have heard of it, but no description compares to being on site. While she no longer resides here, one cannot pass without the feeling of being watched.

The road forks, and I head south. I proceed as far as possible, but fallen trees blocked the way. With pack, I continue on foot. My destination is the sawmill site at the park's north end. My map will be complete once this road is surveyed.

I reached the site and continue south across the bluffs to Bridger Falls. I ascend this hollow to the park's east boundary then north. Bluffs hem in the hollow. Here the highest fall in upper Lee Creek is found. I estimate the two-ledge fall to be 60 feet. The fall and bluffs are unnamed, but my map requires some designation. Since the old mill is just down this intermittent stream, it should be named

Sawmill Hollow and Sawmill Falls. Following the bluff around to the west, I can climb to the top. From this the largest sandstone glade in the valley I can see two miles south to Imp's Leap Ravine. I returned to the vehicle by sheer guesswork, descending the hill to within thirty yards of the Trooper. Satisfied that my map is now complete, I return by way of the treacherous hill to Blackburn.

December 20, 1991

At 6:30 p.m., park employees and their families gather at the visitor Center for the annual Christmas party and feast. Keith, who recently moved to Idaho and the same who accompanied me to Tulsa in a snowstorm (March 1989) is staying at the park and also attends.

Chapter 6: An Expert

January 1, 1992

The phone rings (12:05 a.m.). The new year is only five minutes old. It is someone hoping to make cabin reservations. The book opens this morning for reservations through December, and these 13 cabins are in high demand. Unfortunately for this caller, reservations are not accepted until 8 a.m.

Now it's 7:30 a.m., and in addition to taking reservations by phone, the park office is open to take them in person. Visitors form a line outside the office, at 8 a.m. the rush is on. Like piranhas in a feeding frenzy, visitors struggle to secure their cabin reservation. For hours, people around the region will be hitting the redial button on their phone, hoping to get through. When they do, it's like winning the lottery.

January 2, 1992

The big day is here; Susan and I move into cabin six. As soon as the previous guests check out, I begin the laborious process of moving out park furniture and giving the cabin a thorough cleaning. Cabin six is located on a hairpin curve of the upper loop, a fact with which I am not thrilled. Despite its proximity to the road, it is much nicer than cabin four. A bedroom on the east side faces the curve. We choose the other with sunset views. Although sunsets are hard to come by in Lee Creek Valley, Susan and I can claim the vantage. The east bedroom will come in handy for guests, but for now it will serve as a library. In the middle of the cabin is a living room with a native stone fireplace over 7 feet wide. Like all the cabins at Devils Den, the walls are knotty pine with oak beans. A stone patio, grill, and picnic table also face west and overlook the valley. We are moving because time and prosperity have filled our closet to the rim. Cabin four has become cramped and has always lacked room for company.

January 4, 1992

Moving and cleaning completed, we spend our first night in cabin six.

January 5, 1992

We wake early to the sound of little feet running above the rafters. At first the sound is a little spooky. Bridger picks up on the scent and becomes alarmed. I calm him down, while at the same time try to convince Susan our home is not infested with Norway Rats, but the harmless and native Southern Flying Squirrel. These nocturnal rodents become just another reminder that we are, after all, living in their forest.

January 11, 1992

Unlike last year, the annual winter backpack trip promises to be well attended as the weather is excellent. The temperature reaches 54°. Brent and George lead one group on the usual route of the Butterfield Trail. My group, forever off the beaten path, shuttles to the first county road leading east from Highway 170. It consists of backpacking veterans Rick and Alan Hembree, Ed Hall, Chris Morgan, Bob Willett, Chris Venema, Carl Matthews, David Wimberley, Perry Thomas, Chuck White, Jeff Yoder, and two females (Tracy and Angie) from Missouri. Usually, gender of the group is even, but no one seems to mind the obvious imbalance.

The first highlight of the hike is the old Wright homesite. It is one of the few log homes partially standing. Half dovetail notching places its age around 1880. Just beyond, a jeep road descends five hundred feet to the valley floor. We follow this to the junction of the road north of camp area "A". I have maneuvered the Trooper on this descent a couple of times but swear never to do it again. On the previous trip, I nearly rolled it. Great erosional ditches make the road extremely hazardous. On foot it seems less critical.

Reaching the valley, we rest and continue our discussion of the pioneer history. There are a half dozen homesites in the vicinity, a half-mile north of the park. After conversation and a handful of

M&M's, we strap on our thirty-pound packs and continue north on Lee Creek Road. At the Creek crossing, we pose for a group photo. I suppose it is incorrect to call it a creek crossing as it is dry now. We stash our packs on the opposite side, and hike to U.S. bluff.

We pass Jim's cabin and proceed to the Bubble Hole. On this visit I find the water more turbulent than last. The group is impressed and for good reason. Few places on Lee Creek are as unusual. We ford the creek a third time to reach old Bethlehem church site. Lunch is eaten beside the graves. It may seem inappropriate to dine in a cemetery, but I think that cemeteries are a great place for spiritual reflection and introspection. Beyond the old baptism hole, we march. Another mile or so and we find ourselves at the confluence of Lee and the intermittent stream of U.S. Hollow. We scale the Bluffs that Jessee, George and I visited over two years ago. The group appreciates the climb as I lead them to one bluff shelter after another. The afternoon sun illuminates south-facing alcoves, providing a welcomed sanctuary.

I lead the group to the sawmill site by way of Ruth's place. I swear someone is watching. The others can sense it too. It is only the wind and the thousand images that come to my mind when passing this post-apocalyptic of broken vehicles, appliances, dilapidated sheds, and jars. There must be a thousand glass jars!

Camp is established and fuel gathering delegated. The night is cool and promises to bring precipitation. Once again, I have left my tent at home. How could I have failed to heed the weather forecast? We each take our place around the ceremonial fire to discuss the usual topics. until a light rain disrupts the ritual. Bob takes pity on me and offers the north half of his tent. I accept gracefully. The group harasses me for not bringing shelter, but I can take comfort in the fact that my pack is six pounds lighter than theirs.

January 12, 1992

Morning reveals continued drizzle. Last night's low reached 34°. I slept warm and dry. All the men are up and fixing breakfast, while giggling is heard from Angie and Tracy's tent. They are struggling to apply the morning cosmetics before making an appearance. Are you having trouble finding an outlet for the curling iron? I ask. Of course the girls can give a ribbing as well as they can take. Not only are they good-natured, but proficient backpackers as well.

Breakfast consists of oatmeal and coffee. Chuck prepares pancakes, which to our amazement, are delicious. There is no escaping the drizzle. We pack and head for camparea. area "A" via Bridger Falls, Fossil Flats, and Lee Creek Trail.

January 13, 1992

Four inches of snow has accumulated today.

January 23, 1992

Few corners of the park are left unexplored, but there is one I have failed to see. In the southwest 1/4 of the southeast 1/4 in section 27, there is an intriguing drainage. I hiked to where the intermittent stream forks, and then take the north. Upon reaching the park's western boundary, I follow it south to the next fork. Steep banks rise from the stream making it difficult to go up or down. Hidden deep in the back of this south fork is a huge sandstone outcrop. At the base, a small shelter and crevice are found. A spring with good consistency flows from the shelter and is the predominant source of water for the drainage. Downstream, water cuts deep into layers of shale and flushes like a water slide. Despite the quick descent, a few pools exist prior to Ellis Creek. Downstream of the confluence with Ellis, Pitkin Limestone outcrops. I examined them meticulously for fossils or anything else of interest.

Few Archimedes screws are found, but I discover two small limestone caves. One appears to have been walled-in with stacked boulders, which now lie in a crumbled pile. The other, just a few yards upstream, shows potential but requires a belly-crawl. My intention this afternoon is to explore the drainage in this 50° weather, not spelunk. I'll leave the cave for another day.

January 29, 1992

Returning from a photography shoot at Dotson homesite, I stumble upon a rock foundation between Lee Creek and the Fire Road. The chimney is crumbled but still evident. This site has remained hidden for two reasons. For one, it is off the beaten path and camouflaged by a thick stand of cedar. Secondly, it does not appear on turn of the century maps. It must be very old. It is directly across from the Mannon and Taylor homesites of 1839. John Eaton was also among these families and his homesite has never been located. Could this be it? More research is needed.

January 30, 1992

Evenings are best spent walking in the Mayfield area. Yellow Rocket (*Barbarea vulgaris*) foliage is already sprouting, and wood frogs are chirping from the north pond. I must go and investigate. Sneaking through the underbrush, I advance within view of the water. The frogs do not see me, thus continue their chorus. I count over 100 soaking and singing as if March had come.

February 1, 1992

The bat alarm sounds, and we hurry to the cave to catch the culprits. If the colony of Ozark Big-eared Bats are disturbed now, it could be disastrous. We reach the cave exhausted, breathing air so cold and quickly that our lungs fail to make proper use of it. We catch five spelunkers but decide to let them go. It seems there is another passage into the cave not posted. Harry knew of the passage but did not think a sign was warranted because the passage is so obscure. In fact, it is so narrow it has earned the name "Harry's Squeeze." We explain to them why the cave is closed. Harry will place a sign here first thing tomorrow.

February 3, 1992

The temperature reaches an unbelievable 70 degrees!

February 9, 1992

The nearly uneventful winter is ending. Visitors fighting off
cabin fever arrive in great numbers. Last night, vandals struck. A
coke machine was knocked over.

February 12, 1992

Sandi calls at 5:30 a.m. at Jessee's request and asks me to provide
backup for him. While getting ready for work, Pat notices an odd
flickering of light across the street inside cabin eleven. She wakes up
Harry and tells him that someone is breaking into a cabin. Harry
calls Jessee and then he walks over to investigate. Harry observes a
man exiting and questions him. By the time Jessee calls me to the
scene for additional backup, the intruders have made their escape.
Jessee gives pursuit, but unfortunately the chase ends when we reach
maximum range of the radio. Returning to the cabin we discover
that the bathroom window is broken where the two suspects entered.
Nothing is missing but we find a coke bottle and an unflushed toilet.
Jessee returns 20 minutes later having given up the chase in Winslow.

This evening, I walk the lawn of camp area "A" to see if anything
is blooming. Bluets (*Houstonia caerulea*), and Hairy Bittercress
(*Cardamine hirsuta*) make an appearance. Bluets are among my
favorite early blooms. These four-petaled, baby-blues are fun to find
growing in the shadow of taller plants like dandelion, deadnettle and
henbit.

February 13, 1992

While patrolling the south end of the park, I stop to talk with a
survey crew from the highway department. Their plan is to upgrade
Washington County Road 61. A local politician has promised to
extend Arkansas State Highway 220 to the park. I have no idea why
this is suddenly important. No one lives along the road and the
construction would be expensive and environmentally destructive.
If paved, another major park entrance would result. What purpose
would this serve? Residents of Van Buren and Fort Smith will most

likely access the park via the new Interstate already under construction. Devil's Den State Park is off the beaten path, but if it is to remain one of Arkansas' wildest and most natural parks, getting here should require some effort.

February 14, 1992

A Northwest Arkansas publication names Devil's Den as the best place to take a family, hike a trail, and camp. It will remain so if we guard against excessive development.

February 16, 1992

With radio and field guide, I patrol the Devil's Den Trail. Several visitors are here to enjoy a warm Sunday stroll. I walk the loop trail in the opposite direction (clockwise) to encounter visitors face to face. It gives them an opportunity to ask questions and to report incidents. When not involved in conversation, my nose is to the ground in search of flowers. My list grows longer as Harbinger-of-spring (*Erigenia bulbosa*), Common Chickweed (*Stellaria media*), Pale Corydalis (*Pseudofumaria alba*), Harvey's Buttercup (*Ranunculus harveyi*) are added.

Over the radio I listen to traffic between Brent and the visitor center receptionist. It appears that a hit-and-run accident has occurred on the 15-mph curve of Arkansas Highway170. Brent calls ahead to warn West Fork and Greenland law enforcement units of the suspect. Fortunately, no one is injured, and the suspect is pulled over in Greenland.

February 21, 1992

Weather continues to improve, spoiling us on a spring which does not officially begin for another month. Sunny and 71°. Susan and I take the mountain bikes along Woody Plant Trail. White Trout Lilies break through decomposing leaves, and Harvey's Buttercup sprouts on rocky ledges.

February 22, 1992

Another weekend finds me patrolling Devil's Den Trail. Near the crevice area I hear the first Eastern Phoebe of the season. How can it not be official? Spring is definitely here.

February 23, 1992

Projects today include reorganizing the herbarium in preparation for a busy season of collecting and rewriting the Farmer's Cave gate proposal. The first one did not seem to get a response.

Bill Peck dropped by the cabin for conversation. I met him for the first time while living at cabin four. Actually, it was Bridger who got us acquainted. Bridger ran to the cabin to investigate the arriving guests. I was worried he would jump all over them, but there was Bill scratching Bridger's ears. Bill and his wife are from Louisiana and visit the park once or twice a year. Today he presents me with a Louisiana lottery ticket, knowing that such luxuries are not to be had in the *Land of the Opportunity*. I scratch the card and win a dollar, not quite enough money to cover the cost for the drive to Louisiana to claim it. At closing time, I make a round through the park. A Boy Scout troop is rappelling off Devil's Teapot, the site of our proposed and disapproved mountaineering permit area. I can barely bring myself to tell them they are in violation of park regulations.

February 25, 1992

Poker night. Harry, Jessee, and I gather at Tim's for a few hours of five-draw, Low Chicago, Mexican Sweat, and Jacks-or-better/trips-to-win. The pot rises and falls and comes and goes. To keep the game friendly and to prevent losing a bundle we keep the limit to a three-quarter bump. Dealer antes for everyone, and pennies are not permitted. After a bag of pretzels, and a dollar to my favor, I mosey on home. That's about the extent of a ranger's social life since half of us will be reporting to work first thing in the morning.

February 28, 1992

Susan and I continue our evening walks. She is beginning to remember flower names from last year. Toothwort (*Cardamine concatenata*), Spice Bush and Annual Bluegrass (*Poa anna*) are blooming on the Devil's Den Trail. Yesterday, False Garlic, (*Nothoscordum bivalve*), American Elm (*Ulmus americana*), Winged Elm (*Ulmus alata*), and Red Maple (*Acer rubra*), were in bloom in the Mayfield area.

From the picnic table near the suspension bridge, we watch vultures arrive one by one at the huge Sycamore (*Platanus occidentalis*) below the maintenance building. On late night rounds, I observe a Nine-banded Armadillo and a rare Gray Fox in the headlights of the park truck.

February 29, 1992

Weekday is recorded as a typical, sunny Saturday. I unlock vehicles for visitors, patrol Devils Den Trail, and respond to the alarm at Big-ear Bat Cave. Once again I find no intruders, but the trip is not wasted. Golden crown kinglets are observed near the crevice. Overhead, I count at least a hundred Snow Geese making their way up the valley.

March 1, 1992

77°. Visitors come in countless mobs. Every parking lot is packed, and people are shoulder to shoulder on the trails. Even July 4th is not so busy as today. I spend the day unlocking car doors for visitors, and I'm getting pretty good at it.

March 6, 1992

This evening, I leave for Mountain View and the Ozark Folk Center. For the past year and a half, I have been organizing a National Association for Interpretation (NAI) Region VI Workshop along with good friends in nearly every outdoor education and conservation agency. Over the next few days, interpreters from six states will meet to share innovative ideas and advances in the profession, problems, and common solutions. It is time to see old friends, make new contacts, and get recharged for the upcoming season.

March 14, 1992

A pair of Common Goldeneyes are enjoying a peaceful morning on the lake. They will be gone within the hour as campers awake and walk the trail.

As I sit down to lunch, the phone rings. A truck has just overturned on one of the Arkansas State Highway 74 switchbacks. I rush to the scene expecting the worst. The truck has completely flipped and camping gear lies scattered. Miraculously, no one is hurt.

On evening rounds, Tim and I run campers out of the Mayfield area. A young couple from New Jersey begs us to let them stay, but to do so would only open the door to more problems. Every time an exception is made it backfires. They are upset because the tent and campfire are already built. Although tempted to give in we stick with policy. They express frustration with us yet refused to understand the issue. For instance, if visitors were allowed to camp anywhere, there would have been a dozen or so already camping here, and the area would no doubt be trashed and eroded. This area is special precisely because camping is not permitted wildlife are abundant, the scene is grand, and the park retains some charm. We advise them to go down the road to the Ozark National Forest if a remote free campsite is what they seek.

March 15, 1992

Crime is on the rise. Thieves hit camp area "A" early this morning. Several ice chests are missing.

March 20, 1992

Floyd Gabbard, a regular visitor to the horse camp stops by. He is one of the few who having grown up in Lee Creek Valley still lives in Northwest Arkansas. He shares stories and photos of Wain Dotson family of whom he is related. The most interesting photos and stories concern Otis and Otto the Dotson Twins. Frequently, Wain would send the boys out to work, and off they would go for a swim instead. Stories of the boys moonshining, fighting, farming, and galivanting are the stuff from which popular novels are written.

March 21, 1992

Black-and-white Warblers, Northern Rough-winged Swallows and Louisiana Waterthrushes have returned to celebrate the first full day of spring. Yellow Rocket is just now in bloom despite the appearance of foliage in January.

March 22, 1992

The weather plays a dirty trick. Snow falls and sticks to the grass. In January, we basked in 60° weather; In February, many days were in the 70s; and just two weeks ago the temperature reached 83°! ...and now snow?

The sudden cold weather catches a young man off guard. Apparently, his ride left him yesterday, so he spent last night and this morning in the park. The cold temperatures prompted him to break into Harry's cabin. Harry was out of town at the time. A note promising to pay for damages is found inside the cabin this afternoon.

March 24, 1992

This morning Harry and I dismantle a relic of the Devils Den Trail. For nearly 15 years, a deck overlooking a deep hole in Lee Creek has been a major attraction. The hillside has been collapsing for years and recently has deteriorated beyond the point of safety. Fish Overlook is unbolted board by board and carried across the Creek.

March 26, 1992

A trace of rain is recorded this morning, but the local meteorologist promises 69° or better. Jessee shuttles me to Blackburn where I plan to spend the day exploring Drip-off Hollow. Much of the land is private, yet virtual wilderness. Armed with pen, paper, sandwich, and water, I make my descent and leave the side of the road almost immediately. One of my goals is to document the many species in bloom. Except for flowers the first leg of the journey is uneventful. Twenty-five species are found along with four neotropical migrants (birds).

On first encounter, the intermittent stream is just a trickle, but quickly grows as other tributaries converge. The hollow's first interesting feature is a shale slide where water shoots the curves and falls from a four-foot ledge. From here, Drip-off Hollow earns its name. For the lack of better, I call this first geologic feature Shale Canyon; although I suppose it is more of a shut-in.

About one quarter mile downstream another feature, perhaps the most fantastic, is encountered. The stream, now running like a small river, leaps from a ten-foot ledge. Guarding each side of the waterfall are bluffs some twenty feet in height. Palmer's Saxifrage grows thick on the moist lip of the bluff. To fully appreciate the grandeur, I must go below. To do so requires walking along the bluff downstream for several hundred yards. Finally, it gives way to a slope suitable for descending.

I hike upstream to the base of the falls, jumping from one rock to the next. From close range, I see it is possible to go completely behind. I am tempted to do so, but it will require wading into a pool of unknown depth. A large, pointed rock leans against the east side of the fall. I experiment with names for the waterfall: Pointed Rock Tilted Rock or Arrowhead (Falls). I settle on the latter, not convinced of its justice.

Further downstream the bluffs give way to steep banks of moss and fern. To the east another stream joins. A short distance up this hollow reveals yet another waterfall greater than the previous. Yellow Trout Lilies bloom by the dozens within the splash zone. obviously, this will be named Trout Lily Falls.

Continuing, the next feature of interest is in a drainage from the west. A waterfall of 10-12 feet is found 25-30 thirty yards off the main creek. I call it Quick Creek Falls.

Curiosity and rain persuade me to climb the west bank to a bluff shelter. From the creek, the shelter appears small, but surprisingly I find it 25 feet deep, 40 feet high and nearly forty yards long. I find a dry comfortable rock, eat a sandwich, and admire the size of this hidden retreat. It would have made a good home for prehistoric people; therefore, I label this feature "Good Home Bluff."

My suspicions are confirmed. Lithic flakes and Wild Turkey bones split lengthwise to access the tasty marrow are found around my feet. I have discovered an archaeological site and must tread carefully. I gather a few pieces of evidence, place them in an empty sandwich bag, and mark the location on a topo map. The first opportunity I get, I will present them to the Arkansas Archaeological Survey.

The rain ceases and the sun appears briefly. The next feature in Drip-off Hollow is a sharp "S" curve in the creek. The first curve is bordered by a 35-foot bluff. The second holds a pool of considerable depth. An unusual Hawthorn (*Crataegus* sp.) colony grows along the bank, and the location is noted as "Hawthorn Corner."

The final dramatic feature along Drip-off Hollow is immediately off the creek to the west. Here a waterfall is so close to the main channel that its splash nearly reaches the main creek. I call it Creekside Falls. Not since I first visited Quail Valley have I found an area so impressive and packed with hydrological and geographic wonders. In the years to come, this valley will be posted, clear-cut, or even resettled by the dozen landowners now holding title to some portion of it. I am satisfied to have seen its pristine condition. If I were politically omnipotent, I would draw park boundaries to include Drip-off Hollow. Of course, if I were omnipotent, I would also include the entire watersheds of Blackburn Creek and Lee Creek.

Departing Drip-Off Hollow, the hike continues down Blackburn Creek. A huge bluff borders the south side not far from the confluence of Drip-Off. Shelves of shaly-sandstone stair-step to remnants of the original Blackburn Road. The width of the road has decreased over the past 60 years due to encroaching cedars, but horseback and ATV riders have inadvertently kept it open.

I searched the west bank for evidence of a supposed cemetery. I cannot find it. I do find what appears to be the remains of a still. Bricks around it have various names imprinted:

EVANS &HOWARD/ST LOUIS

MITCHELL/ST LOUIS NO.1

A.P. GREEN/OZARK D.P.

And ST. LOUIS/V&FROO/STANDARD

Someday I will research the meaning of these.

The only other purpose of this exploration not yet accomplished is to find a location to camp during the spring backpack trip. I reconnoiter the west bank for over a mile but find no perfect spot, although a few will suffice. I pass a long alluvial flat overgrown with Ohio Buckeye (*Aesculus glabra*). Dutchman's breeches are uncommon in the park but growing here in abundance.

I climb the ridge separating Blackburn and Lee then descend into the park, following the drainage of Twin Falls. A triumphant day of discovery concludes just prior to sunset.

April 2, 1992

Susan and I make a trip to town for supplies. I take the opportunity to visit the Arkansas Archaeological Survey off Dixon St. I present the sandwich bag of flakes and bones from Good Home Bluff. We compare records and legal descriptions. Consequently, a survey was conducted there by famed archaeologist Samuel Claudius Dellinger back in the 1930's. Records show many artifacts such as mine were found. Not everything was taken, and many insignificant items were left scattered on the surface. I'm excited that the site has remained so undisturbed for the past half century, yet disappointed that I am not the first to discover it. Dellinger recorded the bluff as "Klondike."

April 12, 1992

Wildflower Weekend is a success. Wagon rides yesterday were well attended, thanks to Lindel who provided the means to conduct them. This morning, twenty-five wildflower enthusiasts have gathered with field guides and lunches to hike to Fossil Flats and Puccoon Bluff. Orange Puccoon was in bloom last Saturday and should still be. We leave at 10 a.m. for a three-hour tour. Around the walk-in camp I hear the familiar *beee-bzzz* of the Blue-winged Warbler. Red-eyed vireos have arrived, and I think I hear the shrill cry of a Broad-winged Hawk, which if true, will be the earliest park record. Lunch is eaten by the blue-green waters of Lee below Puccoon Bluff. Dwarf Dandelion (*Krigia virginica*), the smallest of the dwarf dandelions, blooms on rocky outcrops. On the return trip, we have the fortune of spotting a Blue-Gray Gnatcatcher's nest high in a Sweet Gum (*Liquidambar styraciflua*). The nest is built with lichen and cemented with spider webs. Both the bird and nest are small but a joy to see.

April 13, 1992

Living at the corner of the cabin loop enables me to walk Bridger without disturbing visitors. Bridger and I walk the ravine below our cabin which Susan has given the name Cabin Creek. I listen to birds while Bridger smells each leaf and rock. I love my dog but sometimes he can be pretty dense. Fortunately, today is one of those times. While exploring, I spot a raccoon not more than twenty feet away. If Bridger sees him there will be hell to pay. He is not too experienced with wildlife, having spent most of his life indoors. The raccoon clearly sees us but remains perfectly motionless. I try to distract Bridger from the tree, but he continues in that direction. He smells something interesting but cannot locate the source. He walks right past the tree without so much as a glance at the paralyzed raccoon. On other occasions I have walked Bridger within 15 yards of a deer without him even knowing. The deer of course are terrified and frozen. Occasionally, Bridger will spot a deer, squirrel or passing vulture, and will explode with pseudo terror, tugging at the leash, slobbering and barking. Bridger has never caught a wild animal, and while this might be good for the park, it can't be good for his self-esteem.

April 14, 1992

Work continues on the new CCC Interpretive Trail. The trail begins at the chimney beside the pavilion. The chimney is all that remains of the Recreation Hall. In this building CCC enrollees played checkers, cards, and ping pong, as well as read and listen to music. Outside recreation included boxing, horseshoes, and baseball.

From here the trail crosses the road and passes through what used to be the Infirmary. According to camp records, 80% of the enrollees spent at least one day in the Infirmary during July 1935 through September 1936. Four enrollees spent over 70 days here. most were proud, hard workers. The cabins, dam, and community building are evidence of that; But there were some who shirked a task by faking an illness. Those who did were called Goldbrickers, which was early twentieth century slang used by the military. Since CCC camps were run by the military, the term was frequently used often humorously. For example, Thanksgiving Day menu included roast turkey a la goldbrick.

Stairs to the Infirmary can be found, but nothing else. Adjacent to this, the ruins of the kitchen, mess hall, and root cellar are found. The grease trap is a monument to the mess hall. Here, enrollees scraped their plates before departing. After a hard day of sculpting and transporting thousand-pound boulders, I doubt much food was left to scrape. Nearby, a concrete floor serves as a reminder of the kitchen. Eastern Redbuds grow between the cracks.

The cellar is nearly intact. Vegetables and other dry goods were stored here. To the right is a concrete platform where garbage cans were kept. Trucks could easily back up to this miniature loading dock. Much of the waste was transported to remote parts of the valley one such dump is located on the Dotson home site. The dump was likely created after 1938 when Lucinda Dotson sold their land to the government. Another dump can be found north of the amphitheater. By virtue of their age these two are now considered historical thus future sites for archaeological surveys.

The next feature on the trail is the shower/latrine facility. For some reason, this structure was built in the same permanent style as the cabins and community building. All other camp buildings were temporary, wooden frames. In the 1950s or 1960s this building was dismantled. The current theory suggests that it outlived any proposed use and fell into disrepair.

The trail continues to cabin 14, which was originally used as CCC Company 3795 headquarters. When the cabins were remodeled in the late 1970s, cabin 14 was completely rebuilt from its stone foundation.

Around the corner, three concrete generator pads are present. The three gasoline generators (LeRoi, Continental, and Westinghouse) operated on eight-hour shifts to supply electricity to the entire camp. The area immediately north was the location of the barracks. There were eight in total, two 20-man and two 30-man barracks here and the same north of the Infirmary. Two-hundred enrollees were sheltered during each six-month term. Local Experienced Men (LEM) also served here but lived elsewhere. Other personnel included army officers, and national and state park officials.

When completed, the trail will be a quarter mile in length. Construction and renovation will require a considerable amount of work, but plans are to dedicate the entire project during the CCC Company 3795 reunion.

April 18, 1992

The past couple of days have brought periodic showers. It appears it will continue during the spring backpack trip currently underway. No one seems to mind, and everyone is geared for the hike. We had planned to organize two groups, but since several have cancelled their registration, Tim and I lead the same group. Many regulars return, but a few beginners are in attendance including a local journalist.

The reconnaissance of Drip-off Hollow a few weeks ago has proven helpful in planning the weekend's route. We shuttle to Sandy Gap and hike downhill to the John Hiram Johnson homesite and Moonshine Cave. At the cave, we meet three teenagers who camped last night inside the shelter. A fire built against the structure has stained the stone and mortar. The teens have neither interest in preservation, nor any inkling of its historic value.

We take the road to Blackburn Creek, dropping packs at its edge. A side trip to the Bluffs and homesite discovered March 26, is next on the agenda. We then follow the Creek downstream to the John Arnold homesite. The chimney has collapsed considerably since my last visit. Lunch is eaten on the bank where the Creek turns drastically east. Ed Hall and I tally a list of wildflowers encountered. The number reaches forty-five with the promise of another half dozen species expected.

We ford the creek twice within a few hundred yards and proceed to the Francis Marion Mannon homesite. We establish camp east of hidden valley in the basin below Flat Rock Hollow. Bluffs on the north create a small shelter. I did not pack a tent, and rain is still a possibility tonight. Fortunately, a bluff shelter with sandy floor is found, and I take full advantage.

After supper I lead a night hike to a vista west of Quail Valley. The moon periodically peeks through clouds and illuminates Blackburn Creek, 350 feet below our perch.

April 19, 1992

We break camp around 9:30 a.m. and hike to Vista Point for a tour of Phoebe's Cave.

Beyond Falls Hollow and the graves, rain intensifies. On the way to Arkansas Highway 74, we meet others recreating in the foul weather. A mountain bike race sponsored by a local group is in progress. Every 15 yards, we yield the road to passing racers. A solid sheet of rain greets us at the highway. Everyone is soaked but the visitor center is just a mile away.

April 25, 1992

Once again, I am called away from lunch to respond to an emergency. A girl has fallen into Devil's Icebox. I'm sure the fall was painful, but there are no apparent injuries. After receiving special attention, she pretends the pain is critical. It is not my job to guess, and the situation is treated seriously. We extricate her to a waiting ambulance.

April 26, 1992

Morning rounds often present interesting challenges. Nearing the group camp facility, I hear music being played too loud. All visitors must be treated without bias, yet everyone in this group drives a Harley, wears black leather, and exhibits subversive tattoos. As I approach, I imagine the possibilities. Either they will comply or have me for breakfast. The only thing they are likely to respect is courage. Today is a good day to die.

I directly confront the leader." *I share your taste in music"*, I say, *"but unfortunately many of our guests do not. If you would, please turn down the volume."*

"No problem", says the big guy *"We didn't realize it was so loud."*

I thank him, turn, and walk away.

"Say, have you had breakfast yet? We're just about to have some ...one." he says.

The group erupts in laughter. It is the first time I have ever turned down a free meal.

May 1, 1992

The CCC Interpretive Trail is complete. Wayside exhibits are in place, and brush is removed from the ruins, increasing visibility. Today, I have the privilege of guiding the first interpretive tour. A high school class from Pea Ridge has come to learn about the Great Depression and CCC era.

Don Simmons, interpreter from Lake Chicot State Park, has arrived to assist with the annual birders weekend event. He is one of the leading birders in the state, and on many occasions has steered me to a lifer. The first program takes place at Mayfield glade. Participants are instructed to bring lawn chairs and binoculars. I lead them to my sacred bluff, overlooking Lee Creek. The purpose of this evening's activity, entitled <u>Bird Performances</u> is simply to be attentive to the sights and sounds. It is an hour of silence broken occasionally to interpret a bird or song.

May 2, 1992

The early bird walk begins at 7 a.m. Among the die-hard birders are Karen Garrett, Paula from Fayetteville, and Jay and Carol Soule. At least 35 species are counted, but the best sighting is a Gray-cheeked Thrush (life bird 255). Separating this species from the more common Swainson's Thrush can be difficult.

Programs continue back at Mayfield. Several species, rare elsewhere in the park, are common here, including Northern Shrike Eastern Meadowlark, Prairie Warbler, LeConte's Sparrow, Vesper Sparrow, and today's unusual sighting of a Scissor-tailed Flycatcher. This flycatcher is the state bird of the adjacent Oklahoma and a bird of the Great Plains. The Lee Creek Valley is considered the eastern edge of its range.

May 3, 1992

Birding continues around the lake. At 10 a.m., we organize at Yellow Rock Trail Head with binoculars and lunch. Only five birders attend, but small groups are often more successful. In addition to Scarlet Tanagers and Tennessee Warblers, we find other treasures along the way. Prairie Parsley, a species more common to the Great Plains, is found on the trail's south-facing bluff. Lunch is eaten in the shade of a cedar high atop Yellow Rock. With binoculars, I watch helplessly as a black Chevy truck drives across Lee Creek to the walk-in camp. Not only is this vehicle illegally off road but is driving over a hiking trail. If I had a radio I would alert Tim or Brent. By the time I could get down there the truck would be gone.

After lunch, the group climbs down a crevice below Yellow Rock and down a ravine to the fire road. Immediately below Yellow Rock, I add another species to the bloom list.

Yellow Monkey Flower is particular about its habitat. It requires a protective bluff overhang and a moist shale base. This small member of the Schrophulariaceae or Figwort Family is found in only five Arkansas counties. The next nearest colony is in the Rocky Mountains.

May 9, 1992

Most birders left earlier this week. Another group arrives today. On morning rounds, I encounter a half dozen people near Yellow Rock Trail with heads turned skyward and binoculars permanently fixed. They are the Dogwood Trails Audubon Society from Fort Smith. I exchange greetings and ask the standard question, "What are you looking at?" "In the top of that Sycamore, there is a Cape May Warbler" answers Sandy Berger, president of the group. I jump out of the truck and look. There it is! Life Bird 256. Cape May Warblers are rarely seen this far west. It is a park record for sure.

May 22, 1992

Memorial Day weekend and another season in the trenches begins. Reports of vandalism and theft are coming in already.

May 23, 1992

It could not have happened at a worse time. The department has seen fit to decommission our law enforcement ranger. Jessee, Tim, Harry and I will begin late night patrols. More reports of theft are filed this morning. After the evening program, I put away my interpretive hat and slip into my enforcement facade. For the most part they are the same; However, congeniality is ineffective when confronting most delinquents. I patrol the park until 1 a.m. then trade with Jessee. Traffic continues through the park at all hours. Some are campers looking for a site, but at 3-4 a.m. most are juveniles looking for the cave, a party, or something to steal. As my shift ends, I pass a speeding car, daring me to follow. What would be the point?

May 24, 1992

Ballgames on holiday weekends are always interesting. Over 100 people attend; over half come to play. The field is so crowded there is nowhere to hit the ball. I bat four times. Incredibly, the first two result in doubles. The third time I am out at first base, and the last is a pop fly to center field.

May 31, 1992

I barely complete the evening program before the entire audience gets caught in the rain. One quarter inch falls overnight.

June 1, 1992

Before my shift begins, I walk Yellow Rock Trail to collect Sampson's Snakeroot (*Orbexilum pedunculatum*) for the herbarium. For some cruel reason, it only grows at the farthest point from the trailhead. Dotted St. John's Wort (*Hypericum punctatum*) and Pale Purple Coneflower (*Echinacea pallida*) are also blooming.

June 6, 1992

Two new plants were added to the park list this week. I find Bluntleaf (*Galium obtusum*) while leading an interpretive walk on Yellow Rock Trail. Last Thursday, I found (*Scuttellia elliptica*) one of the skullcaps in the mint family.

June 7, 1992

Jessee is off today, but always ready for duty. Just before the daily softball game he hears banging at the amphitheater, 40 yards from his residence. He observes three boys breaking locks off the speaker cases. One speaker has already been removed the other is disconnected. Just before he approaches, the boys attempt to flee but Jessee catches them, grabs their car keys, and makes them wait while he calls for backup. We questioned them but they refused to confess where the speaker is hidden. They are taken into custody, and later, the speaker is recovered from the woods nearby.

This evening, an 18-month-old girl fell palms first into a campfire in area "A".

June 9, 1992

The crowd gathers for the interpretive hike to Yellow Rock shortly into the hike, I realize the group is inordinately quiet, almost uninterested. Naturally, I assume it is me who is failing to interest them. I pull out all the stops and give my best effort. The group follows, listens, but is slow to interact. There is no feedback, positive or negative – which now that I think about it – is a form of feedback. I set out to interest myself and hope they will follow my example.

Wild Bergamot (*Monarda fistulosa*) is in bloom. It is somewhat of a rarity here and the flowers are fragrant and showy. Growing beside this mint is a new species for the park list, (*Dacus pusilla*) or Rattlesnake Weed. "*Why do you suppose it is called this?*" I asked the group. No one seems to know or care. It's time to shut up and head for home.

After work, there is no better method to relieve stress than wading rapids with a rod and trusty lure. I work my way upstream east of the highway bridge. This evening's catch and release includes seven Green Sunfish, one Largemouth Bass, and one Longear Sunfish. I have almost forgotten this morning's dreadful hike.

June 13, 1992

Late night patrol continues. A car with steamy windows is parked at the CCC Overlook. I pull in beside and ask the driver to lower his window. Somewhat surprised, he fumbles for clothes and composure. "*Good evening. Are you folks planning to spend the night?*" I ask. "*No sir. We are just enjoying the view*", he says. "The park closes at 10 p.m. to non-registered guests", I state as if quoting from policy.

What harm is there in being in the park after 10 p.m.? Whenever I'm placed in a situation to enforce a park regulation, I ask myself why does the regulation exists? Most policies are easy to justify, for instance those related to resource protection. Other policies such as the requirement to register to hike the Butterfield Trail or being in the park after 10 p.m. to listen to owls or to star gaze requires scrutiny.

The park is a facility. Like all facilities there are hours of operation. Businesses which operate 24 hours a day have employees working those shifts to keep the operation going. Devil's Den State Park does not (although it seems we are trying to do so just that). If someone becomes injured on the trail at midnight, they will expect park personnel to come to their assistance. Never mind that rangers will give assistance whenever possible. The larger question becomes, is this reasonable? Staff size is barely sufficient to handle the business of the day let alone a night shift.

I ask myself, what harm is there in coming to the park to "park", or in hiking to Yellow Rock to enjoy a full moon at 2 a.m. On the other hand, there are the times when local kids come to drink, explore caves, steal a sign, or sneak into the pool. The 10 a.m. rule gives rangers some means of restricting and preventing these activities. Honest visitors surrender some of their rights in an effort to control those who would abuse the public resource. It is the age-old dilemma of balancing personal and societal freedoms.

I could ignore the couple at the overlook, and go about my business, but as sure as I do I will meet with others who should be ejected. Then I must wrestle with the double standard. It is difficult to create a rule and submit everyone to it without looking petty, hard-nosed, or mean. Am I now to become the judge of who can stay and who must go based on appearance, best guess, or excuse.

The only justice in having park interpreters patrol until 1 a.m. is the opportunity it provides to view wildlife. Most mammals in the park are nocturnal. As I make the rounds from one side of the valley to the other, I keep a list of what is seen, when, and where. Eight White-tail Deer, two Raccoons, two Whip-poor-will and one Chuck-wills-widow are recorded. It is a slow night.

June 14, 1992

Once again I am successful in unlocking a visitor's vehicle. It is scary to think how easy the job is with the right tool. Is anyone really safe? My Trooper is incredibly easy to break into, second only to the 1973 Ford pick-up that I owned previous to that.

The sign at the suspension bridge clearly states, "NO JUMPING." Two young boys learned the hard way why this rule exists. After repeated jumps both lose their balance and fall into the Creek their injuries are not severe, but I advise the parents to have a physician examine them.

June 15, 1992

The first official tour of Farmers Cave commences. It is a momentous occasion. The tour is limited to 10 spelunkers, and quickly reservations are booked. One by one, both young and old enter the dark humid underworld. Within the first leg of the tour, all known wildlife species are encountered. We find Eastern Pipistrelles, crickets, and both cave salamander and Dark-sided Salamander. Mud cakes our shoes, knees, hands, and belly. We bathe continuously in this underground stream, but still, it finds its way into our hair fingernails and mouth. I lead the group as far as the Pentagon, the last of the big passages.

June 19, 1992

Nearly an inch of rain falls this afternoon, cancelling the softball game. The rain ends just in time for the evening program. After an hour of persuading an audience of 68 to take up birding, I begin night patrol. It is a slow night for traffic, but not for wildlife. Thirteen deer, 6 raccoons and 1 armadillo are counted along the roadsides.

Around 12:30 a.m., Jessee calls on the radio to report an accident near Hogeye involving Heath and Jay. I drive over and pick them up. Recent rains have made the roads slick and caused Heath to lose control on a sharp curve of State Highway 265. No one is hurt but the car will need some work.

June 20, 1992

On late patrol again. At 1:30 a.m. (June 21), just before heading home, I swing into the lower picnic area. An old truck is parked near the maintenance gate. As I take down the license I hear a loud metal crash from the direction of the old shed. A man walks toward me silhouetted by the headlights. Quickly, I called Jessee for backup, not knowing what foul play may be in store at this hour. The man approaches and I greet him with caution. Suddenly, two other persons appear. Just before Jessee arrives I resolve the situation. The man had worked at the park years before and remembered that the garbage bins were a good place to see raccoons. This former employee, his girlfriend, and another man decided to come see them. I ask what the metal crash was, and he confesses to banging on the bins to scare the raccoons. It is 2 a.m., dark, and lonely. I'm exhausted and I cannot recall ever feeling so ill-prepared for a situation. I have no weapon, no partner, and no real experience facing an armed thief should this have been the case. I am a park interpreter, teacher, artist, and evangelist, not an armed law enforcement ranger. I'm in this profession to *open the eyes of the blind*, and to help park visitors commune with the natural environment, and to share the treasures of the Lee Creek Valley.

June 23, 1992

it is better to be creative and informative than just informative, or so I thought. On the program schedule, I announced today's hike with the title that is sure to catch attention: "Death March to Holt Ridge Vista." "Not for the faint of heart," I add. The Vista is truly spectacular but gained at a price. From trailhead to ridge lay 450 vertical feet. Should I be surprised when only four show up for the hike? Jay and Carol Soule and Doug Brown and son from Parsons accept the challenge. Oddly all four are from Kansas, a state not known for steep elevations. After a grueling march, we rest at the vista. No one dies despite the program title. Instead of returning via Hell's Half Mile we descend a wooded ravine. "We should not waste this opportunity to see something different," I tell them. To my good fortune, the route harbors Pinesap (*Montropa hypopithys*), Lopseed (*Phryma leptostachya*), and Arkansas Bedstraw (*Gallium arkansana*), three plants needed for the herbarium.

June 26, 1992

Evening programs grow in attendance. Over 100 visitors have come to hear the interpreter speak. Is this large attendance due to the title which I have selected? Do most find interpretive programs entertaining and rewarding? Have they come to alleviate campsite boredom? I would like to believe they have come to hear me, but we are strangers. The evening program is much like a church social, friendly, and relaxed. I am the park's pastor.

To break the monotony and loneliness of late-night patrol, Dan Sharon volunteers to ride along. I assigned him the task of recording tonight's wildlife sightings: 10 deer, 4 raccoons, and 2 armadillos.

June 28, 1992

A man and woman went horseback riding yesterday, and as of this morning, have not returned. A search is organized with the Strickler Volunteer Fire Department and the Washington County Sheriff's Department. As we begin, Channel 40 news arrives.

We divide into teams. Strickler volunteers and I search Holt Ridge, but within the hour the riders are found near Fall Creek. Everyone is anxious to hear their story, especially the media.

It seems they were riding Holt Ridge horse trail when they stopped to talk with ATV riders. These riders directed them to a shortcut. After wandering for hours, they dismounted and began on foot. Shortly after, they lost their way back to the horses, but eventually found campers near Fall Creek. Here they spent the night on cold hard ground.

To divert attention from their own poor judgment, they blame the park for inadequately marking the trails. It is this spin that the TV crew presents. Never mind that several cardinal rules of backcountry travel were broken: They acted upon the advice of others; They left a marked trail for an unmarked Trail; They were improperly equipped or prepared to spend the night in the elements; each wrong decision cascaded into a more serious situation. Most of the equestrian trails lead away from the park jurisdiction and into the Ozark National Forest.

July 1, 1992

As the years pass, I realize the value of leaving the park and remaining out of touch on days off. Living here eventually takes its toll, especially during the busy season. I spend the day in town, catch a movie, and tour the mall. On the way home, I stop for mail at the visitor center. Harry tells me that a horse is stuck in the crevice area. Tim, Jessee, Ted, and two horsemen are at the scene trying to remove it.

Upon arrival, I find everyone drenched in sweat, trying desperately to extract the horse, sunk deep between the sandstone walls. I arrived just in time to see the horse lift her head, roll back her eyes, and take one last breath. All at once there is a silence. "We've lost her" Ted says.

Ginger was her name. She is the third horse to die during my tenure. The riders were attempting a shortcut from Vista Point to camp by way of the crevice area which is designated "Foot Traffic Only. The horse misjudged the crevice and fell. For a while she was not injured, just stuck. but the panic set in and she scrambled deeper into the crevice.

July 2, 1992

The equestrians return to remove the dead horse, but now the task has become impossible. The carcass is stiff and bloated, and the area is too remote to utilize heavy equipment. Short of cutting the horse into manageable pieces, there is only one thing to do, cover it with lime, and bury it with boulders and leaves. It is not the solution we want, but all others seem impractical.

July 3, 1992

In an effort to make peace with the regular July 4th crowd – the very ones who toilet-paper the park every year – Susan and I accept their invitation to this evening's potluck dinner. It is traditional for the rangers to attend. While we are giving our best effort to patch the rift that has come between us, several of them sneak off to TP our cabin. Since they know where we are, they can execute their prank in confidence. Susan and I return home an hour later to realize we have been duped.

July 4, 1992

The annual Devil's Den games begin at 8:30 a.m., but I can barely find the enthusiasm. Steve Short, one of the more respected visitors and July 4th regular, rides with me during the late-night patrol. We encounter several members of the TP gang attempting to add to yesterday's work.

July 10, 1992

The final touches are added to the CCC interpretive Trail. Tom Jopling and his son Josh volunteer to place numbered posts at the various interpretive stops. Thanks to their hard work, the trail is officially complete.

Dan and I continue routine night patrol. Wildlife sightings this evening include Eastern Screech-Owl, two Barred Owls, six White-tailed Deer, one Raccoon, two Nine-banded Armadillos, one Red Fox, and two Eastern Cotton, all are seen within four hours.

July 13, 1992

Monday, 91° with clear sky. I try to put the long summer behind me, but realize it is only half over. Instead of the student who frets over a short summer vacation, I grow more restless as the season drags on. To escape the crowds and responsibilities, I schedule a four-hour hike to Quail Valley. Only one visitor shows.

The woman is from Fayetteville and has made a special trip to attend. It seems awkward to lead an interpretive hike for one, but clearly it will do us both good. We strap on daypacks and catch a shuttle to Holt Road.

As we walk, the barriers which often exist between strangers disappear. We discuss wildflowers and Ozark history, but eventually turn to philosophy and personal dreams. She reveals that she is recently divorced from an abusive alcoholic, and what it has taken to build a new life. I share with her my dissatisfaction with work of late and my desire to travel West.

We reach Quail Valley and rest at the edge of the falls. The conversation continues through lunch and over the next two miles. Hours later, having said all there is to say, we go our separate ways. It is ironic that two people having shared such personal pain, hopes, and dreams, are not likely to ever cross paths again. Park life can be that way, yet the advantages could not be greater. Each of us in our limited encounters primarily sees only the good in one another.

July 17,1992

More regulars arrive for an annual family reunion. Reunions have their advantages and disadvantages. The best part is, Harry and I have little trouble finding softball players. The downside is trying to enforce regulations when outnumbered fifteen to one.

I have watched one member of the reunion mature over the past four summers. This year, the boy experiments with alcohol. On evening patrol, I notice a light down by the amphitheater. I pull over, park, and walk down the trail. I see three boys near the stage and inquire as to their activity. They make a dash for the woods and attempt to hide in a ditch. I round them up finding one too inebriated to stand. Another is drunk, but the third is trying to make the others sober. They beg me not to tell their parents. In trade, I make them clean up their vomit, promise not to drink in the park, and head straight for camp.

July 18, 1992

Day two of Bat-O-Rama III. The highlight of the weekend comes this evening when a presentation on Lechuguilla Cave. Emily Davis-Mobley is the speaker. Over 275 people attend her presentation on the cave and her successful rescue a year ago last April. It is the largest attendance ever assembled at the amphitheater. The night becomes even more memorable when state parks director Greg Butts awards Harry a commendation for his work on bad education and protection.

July 19, 1992

After lunch, Greg makes time for me to show him a few of our projects. I give him the grand tour of the Mayfield area, stopping to view special sites. I show him the Farmer/Pool homesite, Mayfield glade, and Farmer's Cave. I discuss with him our desire to gate the cave and regulate its entry. We enter the cave as far as the Epiglottis. There are pips and crickets on the walls. Voices are heard deep within the cave, so we wait and watch. Two young men are on their return from the Garage. One of them smacks his head on the ceiling. The other slips down a muddy bank into the creek, each swearing as they fall.

After witnessing this scene, Greg does not hesitate to approve the gate proposal. It is obvious to him and has been to me for nearly a year, cave entry must be regulated for the safety of the visitor and for the protection of the cave. I cannot speak for Greg, but I am far more interested in saving the cave. I believe in the freedom to take personal risks, no matter how ill-equipped or skilled some visitors may be. A cave permit system does provide an opportunity for the park to inform the spelunker of what to expect and how to safely enjoy the cave while protecting the natural resources within.

July 20, 1992

Construction begins immediately on Farmer's Cave gate. While Keith Wells goes to town for portable welder and supplies, I begin clearing debris from the opening. Half of all cave gates are compromised, rendering them ineffective. It is up to Keith and his welding skills to build a vandal-proof gate. He returns around noon and begins. By evening, the frame is complete.

July 21, 1992

Keith and I continue welding and painting the gate.

July 22, 1992

By noon the project is complete. I add the final touches, a lock and chain. Keith poses in front of the gate for a photograph. A new routed sign reading: FARMERS CAVE | CLOSED FOR STUDY is placed behind the gate. Until a permit system can be approved, the cave will remain closed except during interpretive tours.

July 25, 1992

A local Boy Scout troop has adopted part of Devil's Den Trail under the leadership of an eagle scout candidate. Several weeks ago, he and I discussed the need to rebuild the badly eroded switchbacks at Twin Falls. It seems nothing short of barbed wire will prevent hikers from cutting them (the switchbacks). The CCC constructed switchbacks to make the walk easier and to prevent erosion; but modern visitors are in too much of a hurry to be concerned with erosion. Every year the switchbacks need repair. I ask the scouts to make repairs that might last several years.

More than a dozen boys along with a few fathers, put in over sixteen man/hours on the project. Large boulders are moved in and strategically placed. Obsolete trails are brushed with briars and Bois d' arc branches. At day's end, we step back and admire the effort. For how long will this project channel the onslaught of ascending, descending, and hurried hikers? Few will appreciate this unique area, or the bloodroot, wild ginger, trillium, and yellow trout lily that grow here. We could erect a sign to read PLEASE STAY ON TRAIL, but signs are destroyed or stolen faster than trails are eroded. I know today's work will not last, but I get some satisfaction in knowing that we have temporarily thwarted the process of deconstruction and won back some of the battlefield. It is a fight no ranger can surrender.

July 26, 1992

Farmer's Cave gate lacks one essential feature to make it resistant. Ted and I discussed construction of a concrete base. This should prevent entry by tunneling. Already someone has busted off the lock and entered the cave. It appears a heavy rock was used to simply smash it open. I place a new lock on the gate, this time attaching it to the chain on the inside. Vandals may be able to reach the lock, but will not be able to crush it. The battle continues.

July 31, 1992

Don Crank contacted me several days ago about surveying the park for ferns. He and his friend Dolores arrive, and I lead them to the upper crevice area. Ferns have always been a fascination to me, and I want to learn the names of the less common. Don is a self-taught expert which gives me hope. Ferns are difficult to identify. They reproduce by spores and have no flowers. From a distance, one fern might look like another, unlike most flowers whose corolla color, number of petals and leaf morphology often give it away.

As we walk, Don recites their scientific name. I recognize the common ferns: Maidenhair, Ebony Spleenwort, Maidenhair Spleenwort, Christmas, Resurrection, Walking, and Hairy Lip Fern. Don locates the more difficult to identify narrow-leaved glade, silver glade, marginal shield, and bladder.

It is entertaining to discuss botany at this level. He teaches me the terms, and I help him identify flowering plants. Three-bird orchid is discovered, along with two other species. Dolores observes and muses at our childlike pleasure.

August 3, 1992

Around 5 p.m. a visitor reports smoke coming from the laundry building. Tim rushes over and opens the door to be greeted by a face full of toxic smoke. I follow with an extinguisher. The room is so smokey that we cannot find the source. Flames are not apparent. While Jessee prepares the hoses, Tim and I take shifts returning to survey the situation. It appears that rags in one of the dryers have ignited. Jessee connects the hose and enters full blast. Another ten minutes and the park could have lost the building for a second time. The first was in the spring of 1988 about eight months before I started working here.

August 8, 1992

Since the first of the week, two inches of rain have fallen.

Water crested the second level of the CCC dam on August fourth. The past couple of days, temperatures have been fairly reasonable, and the weather sunny. All these conditions set the stage for a perfect hike. The third annual summer backpack trip is upon us. The group consists of my older brother Doug and his son Christopher, as well as many regulars: Paul, Dan, Ed, Chris, Rick, Perry, and a few newcomers.

We arrange for a shuttle to Mill Creek high in the Fall Creek watershed. This is Clyde and Phyllis Ulm's land. Clyde personally guides us to the falls for which the hollow is famous. The first waterfall is interesting enough. A thick sandstone ledge supports a fall of 20 feet. It is possible to walk under the fall without so much as catching a splash. We pose for pictures and rest on a fallen log at the pool's edge.

There is much more to see, and time is slipping. As Clyde departs for home, we strap on packs and continue downhill. Once Locust Creek is reached it is clear we have missed the trail to Curiosity Bluff. Paul, Dan, and I separate from the group and scout upstream. The bluff is not found, yet something better is. We return with word of a perfect swimming hole, guarded on three sides by a five-foot ledge. Locust Creek slips over the ledge, creating a pool exceeding seven feet in depth. Upstream, the creek runs over 50 feet of flat sandstone bedrock. The whole scene, deep in wilderness is one of paradise. Recent rains both fill the creek and awaken the foliage.

Paul is the first in the pool, then Doug and I. Eventually everyone joins. We take turns jumping from the highest ledge then simultaneously for the camera. Waves rock the pool and continue long after our departure.

Rick returns from scouting to report the location of Curiosity Bluff. Apparently we walked right past the trail. Curiosity Bluff is a 40-foot sandstone bluff with a crevice, iron concretions, and sculptured alcoves. On close examination one can imagine faces and objects on the tortured rock. Underneath, the sand is dry and powdery. It would have been and probably was a great resting place of many early travelers. We return to our packs. It is nearly 1 p.m., and we have seven miles yet to hike.

Locust Creek joins Fall Creek – a raging torrent. We follow it to the confluence, then Lee Creek to Junction Camp. A hot day wears on. The trail, muddied from the rain and horses, and interrupted by many crossings, grows longer. At each crossing I remove my socks and boots and slip on sandals. At first it is a novelty, but after a while becomes a hassle. The others abandon the quick-change routine in favor of the direct approach. The advantage of crossing frequently is the opportunity to cool off and wash the mud from boots and ankles.

After several miles, everyone tires. A long break is required. Along a gravel bank beside Fall Creek and in the shade of a Sycamore, we collapse. A few replenish their water bottles; some recline for a nap and the rest soak in the creek. One of the newcomers is showing signs of fatigue. Without a word he drops his pack, and saunters into the creek, jeans, boots, and all. In the cool rapids, he floats with eyes closed.

The jeep trail seems endless. Around each corner I expect to see the county road and low water bridge. "It's just around the corner", I say so many times that even I lose faith. Finally, we reach it, but the accomplishment is anticlimactic. Over two miles still separate us from Junction Camp. The hike continues through a maze of ATV trails and mud holes crusted with algae. The mercury rises to ninety degrees, but humidity is the greater enemy. The hike becomes like a trail of tears without the sobbing. The line of hikers stretches for half a mile. We are a flashback of the Donner Party; oxen being driven into endless salt flats. But once Blackburn Creek is spotted a stampede commences.

At Junction Camp, we unburden our baggage. Half the group retires while the other rushes for the waterhole. I am leading the charge. Rick and Perry are missing. After fifteen minutes I leave the cool turquoise pool to search for them. One-quarter mile back I meet them. Perry's knee and the heat have taken a toll. Rick in the sweep position remained with Perry to assist as needed.

Supper consists of bacon and biscuits fried in grease. I had planned to eat these tomorrow, but the heat has completely thawed the bacon. After supper, we celebrate Christopher's tenth birthday with a cupcake and candle. He is quite a backpacker, never once complaining of the long hike. Moments later he is fast asleep.

Doug, Dan, Paul, and I play cards. The others have given out. Snoring can be heard in the distance, but no one will admit to it come morning. Eventually the four of us retire. I spread my tarp between two cedars, roll out the Therm-A-Rest, and lay my aching bones. An hour later, I wake to the rustle of leaves near my head. Aiming my flashlight towards the sound I catch an Opossum frozen in its tracks just three feet away. We stare each other down for about 20 seconds, then I shoo him away.

August 9, 1992

At 6:45 a.m., I heat a breakfast burrito on my butane stove. Most are ready to leave by 9 a.m., but two hikers keep us waiting until 10:20 a.m. I lead the group across Lee Creek and uphill to Camp Meeting Cemetery. As we wander through the area I relate the story of the great flood of Anna.

The hike continues north along Lee Creek, including five crossings, and stops to swim and fish. From here the route follows horse trails now virtual quagmires. The death march continues. There can be little positive comment about the last leg of the journey. At times we are forced to walk knee deep in mud or wade through briars around the edges. Once beyond the floodplain, we discover the Highlands offered little relief. The hills are mud slides, made treacherous by foot-deep hoof prints. A couple of hikers nearly twist their ankles, and one falls headlong into the muck. By 2 p.m. the ordeal is over.

August 11, 1992

As an interpreter and public servant, I have taken the words of Matthew 5:44 to heart. (*Love your enemies and pray for those who persecute you*). Keeping this command can be very challenging. This afternoon, I learn that two of the families involved with the annual Fourth of July toilet paper raids have written letters aimed at destroying my career. Public employees are easy targets, primarily because government agencies go a long way to please their constituents. In many cases, the word of the visitor outweighs the word of the employee. Fortunately, this is not the case today. Apparently the two letters (practically xerox copies of each other) were so filled with outlandish charges the department dismissed them forthright.

August 21,1992

Several friends have visited this week which helps to overlook last week's persecution. On Monday, James and Lydia visited. Bob and Sherry are camping, and we had them up to the cabin for steaks and conversation yesterday. Tonight, Dennis and Kathy arrive.

August 22, 1992

Two new plants are found in bloom on the upper cabin loop: Nuttall's Tick Trefoil (*Desmodium nuttallii*) and Cuspidate-leaved Tick Trefoil (*Desmodium cuspidatum*) are added to the checklist, bringing the total number in this general up to 10.

August 27, 1992

Susan and I eat a leisurely breakfast in the park café. It is a real treat to have such a romantic place so near to home. The cafe is quaint, only a dozen tables. Four provide a view of the lake, another four face the sunrise and huge rose bushes along a split rail fence. The others are situated in the center of the room beneath huge beams. A native stone fireplace dominates the north wall while a 1930s gas pump attracts attention in the corner. The original glass has been replaced with a plexiglass aquarium filled with goldfish. The tables, chairs, and building are other products of the CCC.

Each year we are fortunate to employ the best cook in the area. The food is made from scratch and served straight from the kitchen. Many years ago, the cafe served evening meals, including steak, shrimp, and Italian dishes. Today, its hours of operation include breakfast and lunch only. After a hearty breakfast, we walk beside the lake lamenting the end of the restaurant season. Sandpipers glide along the shore. Soon, even birds will leave. Many have already.

August 28, 1992

Dan and I try a new approach to late night patrol. Enforcing the 10 p.m. quiet hours rule from the vehicle can be difficult. Most campers lower their voices and radios on our approach, then simply return the volume after we pass. Tonight, we go undercover. With lawn chairs, Mountain Dew, and a bundle of wood, we sit around the fire in a vacant site. Oddly no noise is heard the entire evening. Perhaps our cover has been blown. No matter, we accomplished our goal, and enjoy an evening filled with conversation and stars.

August 29, 1992

Tonight, I concentrate on quieting camp area "A" by walking the loop several times. The first round is to remind everyone to turn down their radios. The second is to check for compliance, and the third is to create the impression that the ranger is omnipresent. Rounds continue in camp area "B". Another radio is blaring from site 25. I approach, flashlight in hand, and announce my presence the woman raises her head and returns a hello. I explain to her that the radio can be heard throughout the campground and ask her to lower the volume. "I will as soon as you leave", she says. At first I find it a strange request, but then she confesses to being naked under the blanket.

August 30, 1992

The program this evening is an owl prowl held at the Mayfield area. I am the first to arrive. I walk the fields collecting thoughts, yet confuse them with dreams of Canyonlands, the San Juans and Sawtooths. I need a break from the long hot crowded summer. Contrary to popular belief, most interpreters do not enter the profession to hear themselves talk. It is because above all we love the land, every inch and aspect. The profession is a way to remain in touch with it. Lee Creek Valley is a wonderful refuge; However, at times it is claustrophobic. I need open spaces. Until I stand on some unnamed mountain peak or canyon rim, the Mayfield area must suffice. Here I can see the hills instead of being swallowed by them. Nighthawks and bats maneuver between beige colored grass and a purple sky.

Only four attend the prowl. The campgrounds are nearly empty as schools reopen and visitors conclude vacations. A young father and his two children have come to hear the owls. I must not fail them. I place the recording of an Eastern Screech-Owl ten yards away. The tape plays for a minute, and then we listen for responses. The first one calls and then another. several are heard far away, but these first two interest us. They seem to be calling each other. Suddenly one flies in and then the other. One is in the gray phase, the other in red (or more accurately rust). both are so intent on each other and neither appears to see us. I shine the light on each for comparison. There is no need for further interpretation, often it is best to let nature speak on its own behalf. Barred Owls add to the chorus.

The children and father are excited, having seen something truly wonderful. They thank me for the program and head back to camp. I remain until the last owl is silent. Few evenings have been better spent.

September 4, 1992

One more weekend and the summer will be behind us. Dan and I patrol together one last time. Wildlife sightings are slim, but we observe a striped skunk near the park entrance sign on Arkansas Highway 74. The traffic slows early for a Friday night.

September 7, 1992

The last program of the season, the traditional softball game, begins at 10 a.m. far less attended than the games played Saturday and Sunday. Most visitors departed early this morning. After two hours of battle Harry's team captures the season's final victory. I must wait over eight months to exact my revenge. By 5 p.m. the park is silent. Employees gather one by one at the pool for a farewell to summer party. Although this season is over, everyone knows October is just a cooler version of July. There's no point thinking about that now; Harry and I leave tomorrow for the annual trip West. Soon we will follow a setting sun to Colorado's Snowmass wilderness.

September 19, 1992

The Arkansas mountain bike championships are in full swing. The races are directed by Tim and officiated by Steve Shepherd. Normally, my job is to handle routine business, and when time permits, document the activities on film. This year Tim has scheduled me to lead an interpretive bike ride.

I organized the group in camp area "A". Single file, we ride the fire road, make frequent stops to discuss the historic sites and catch our breath. The route provides them with a sneak preview of tomorrow's criterion race.

September 20, 1992

Before the race, Jessee and I station ourselves at Fossil Flats. It is here that most bikers will find trouble. The Creek is nearly dry, but drizzle dampens the smooth bedrock. We are here to photograph the best spills and to provide first aid to the worst. The first group of racers reach the crossing, and nearly everyone wrecks. A few overconfident bikers attempt to stay in the saddle but are unsuccessful. Even knobby tires are no match for the algae-covered limestone. After all bikers have passed, Jessee and I throw gravel on the bedrock to increase traction. We line the route with flagging.

On the second lap, more bikers cross safely, but others still look for shortcuts. One decides to leave the marked route. Slipping on the unaltered bedrock he falls, bruising hip and ego.

By the third round everyone takes the crossing seriously. Only two bikers wreck. One pins his right arm beneath as both he and the bike slam to the ground. The wreck appears brutal, so Jessee and I rush toward him. I take three steps, slip, and slam to the ground, breaking the fall with my arm. Instinctively, I yell and grab my elbow in pain. Referring to my injury, a spectator turns to Jessee and says *"You've got an elbow here!"*

Am I broke? I ask, thinking he has seen the bone protruding through the skin. I am in so much pain that I don't even think to look for myself. By the time I recover, the wrecked biker has regained his feet and limps away to complete the race, issuing obscenities as he goes. My elbow hurts like hell, and my clothes are soaking wet, but I'm OK. After the awards ceremony, the park is once again silent. Susan and I have supper at Jay and Carol's campsite where they have hidden during the weekend to avoid the hundreds of bikers.

September 25, 1992

The annual Arkansas State Parks superintendents banquet begins tomorrow at DeGray Lake Resort State Park. This year, interpreters and their spouses are invited. Susan and I travel by way of Arkansas Tech University my alma mater, and down scenic Arkansas Highway 7 at Russellville. Across Lake Dardanelle I can see the state park where my interpretive career began on April 27, 1985. Two hours later, we reach the entrance to DeGray, where I served from October 1, 1986, through December 16, 1988. Six years ago, I called this home. I climbed every hill, examined every flower, and searched for its fascinating history.

But now I feel like a stranger. I can still remember what it was like to work here, but this place no longer remembers me. I have been replaced by other stewards. I cannot help but regret the day Lee Creek covers my footsteps. Interpreters, rangers, and superintendents take possession of their assigned park. When we speak of that place, we say "my park." I have seen too many park professionals fall into the trap of thinking it will always be their park. It won't. It never was. My calling is not to build a fort around the treasure chest and repel the tourist; my purpose is to help them reach deep into the chest and touch every nugget and coin.

September 26, 1992

After breakfast and speeches, employees posed for pictures on the lodge deck. A moment in history is captured. Later in the afternoon, a few of us tour the lake. Here among the islands and coves, I spent many evenings adrift, interpreting for visitors. As we pass Blackbird and Armadillo Island, Turkey Roost and the Cove of No Return, I recall the good times. I remember watching a deer swim 300 yards from shore to an island. I experienced one of the top three sunsets of a lifetime, now plastered on a postcard in the gift shop. Park Interpreter Duane Moren steers the boat west, bringing us within view of two Bald Eagles and an osprey. Duane also remembers that sunset. He was in the front of the boat providing interpretation, while I was steering the boat and taking the sunset photo.

September 29,1992

Now that the off season has arrived, Tim, Kim (seasonal employee), Jessee, and I find time to reinstate the weekly poker game. Card games give us a chance to unwind, discuss park issues in a comfortable atmosphere, and listen to some old records. Tim's collection is sufficient to satisfy any taste. As the refreshment goes so does the money. One moment, I am up a few bucks then down a few. I come home two dimes ahead.

October 2, 1992

Civilian Conservation Corps Company 3795 alumni usually meet every odd year in late June. This weekend several have gathered. We are invited to their fish fry this evening, and Harry, Brent, and I attend. I am drawn from one conversation to the next, collecting tidbits of history. The men share dozens of stories from their days as enrollees. They recall pranks, dances, and social events that highlighted the times. A decade from now, few of these men will be with us, and I will remember then, I have been a part of something rare this day.

October 4, 1992

A couple of squirrel hunters report a fire on Holt Ridge. With a radio and backpack pump, I follow them into the scene. The fire is contained within a hollow tree but it's difficult to extinguish. I returned for Jessee and additional tools. 20 minutes later we are back with more water, a ladder, and chainsaw. After watering without success, we pack the holes with mud to deprive the fire of oxygen. This too fails. The only solution is to fell the tree, break it open, and put the fire out directly. A cigarette stuck inside the tree initially caused the blaze.

October 10, 1992

Doug, Christopher, and Jennifer my niece, arrive early for the fall backpack trip. Jennifer, not yet six years old has never been backpacking. The group consists of varied ages mainly children and parents. We shuttle to Mount Olive at 9 a.m. and the hike begins.

The route includes Mount Olive school site, Bridges gravesite, Vista Point, and Quail Valley. There are new features on the agenda which include a fracture west of Phoebe's Cave. We probe various holes looking for the one reported to be as long as Devil's Den. In a small hole beneath a sandstone shelf, we find it. The fracture is similar to the last half of Devil's Den, with many ups and downs. Cave Orb Weavers are present and too numerous to count. Rick and I alternate the lead. At one point the floor drops twelve feet. Rick scrambles down to give an assessment. The cave continues, but measures one third the length of Devil's Den.

Around noon, the group gathers at Quail Valley for lunch and rappelling lessons. Paul and I packed the gear for just such an occasion. We begin by demonstrating knots tying and the proper use of equipment. Before allowing the children to rappel, I require them to pass an oral test. I fire a battery of questions and scenarios at them, and until they answer all correctly, none will step into a harness.

We start the rappel on a small block with little incline. Everyone goes afterwards, we move the ropes to a forty-footer, but only half the group musters the courage. I stress the importance of recognizing one's limitations, and to quit when it is reached. Rappelling is, after all, supposed to be fun. There is no room for peer pressure.

We play around the bluffs all afternoon. As the sun sets we head to the upper quarry. Beneath a grove of Loblolly Pines, we camp and build a fire. Supper is eaten in the dark followed by a night hike to Holt Ridge Vista. The moon lights our way. We reach the vista and find the fires of camp area "E" dancing in the valley. Voices below are carried up the ridge. Between the moon and the moment, I can't help but howl. Everyone joins. The echo carries for several seconds and bounces off Hurricane Ridge. Campers in area "E" howl back. Minutes later, coyotes are heard barking to the south.

Back at camp I engaged in a game of spades. The fire flickers as a cool breeze sets in. The cards are nearly impossible to read but the game continues. In the dark, my opponents, as well as my own teammate, fail to realize we have lost the hand. I'll let them know in the morning.

October 11, 1992

After breakfast, we police the area for trash. Earlier this week, I collected litter around the campsites. Now we extend the radius to the entire quarry. For many years hunters and locals have dumped trash here. We collect every can, bottle, and wrapper we can find. After the hike, Ed and I will return with the truck to haul the bags away.

October 18, 1992

With Ozark Heritage Weekend fast approaching, it is good to receive visits from many Lee Creek Valley descendants. Glenn and Irene stopped by yesterday with additional Mannon family history.

Today I talk with folks who lived on the John Zinnamon place and others who've descended from Charlie Redfern. Myrtle and Desmond share with me their experiences growing up in Lee Creek valley during the 1920s and 1930s. Both attended Mount Olive school. Desmond recalls the first one, a log structure, and Myrtle talks about the framed building she attended. I drive them to the site and take notes of their memories.

October 19, 1992

Channel Five will be broadcasting from Artist Point this evening and has asked Tim and me to discuss fall foliage on camera. It is cold and windy on the back deck of the little gift shop. As the cameras are being set, we discuss the show's angle. After a short interview the TV audience will be invited to phone in with questions.

All goes smoothly until the caller asks, "If you could be any tree in the forest, which would it be?" After a long pause I answer Sassafras. Tim votes for Sweet Gum after some awkward discussion on the subject, the interview ends just in time to salvage a little dignity.

October 24, 1992

Ozark heritage weekend begins with a guided hike to home sites north of camp area "A." In attendance is a great great granddaughter of Moses Mannon. The programs continue with an auto tour to historic sites throughout the valley.

October 30, 1992

Today, Phyllis retires from her receptionist position at Devil's Den State Park. During lunch break we give her a proper sendoff. Over the years Phyllis has been a mainstay. Visitors know her well and counted on her humor. To the staff, she was known as "Sarge" – Always quick to keep us in line. As a test of her good humor, Phyllis was fired (Jokingly) over thirty times, and yet every day she returned for work. Certainly, a chapter in the park's history is closing.

November 7, 1992

The Arkansas Native Plant Society pays the park a visit. I lead them to the crevice area, hoping to identify some wildflowers of interest. This late in the year almost nothing is in bloom. We manage to find Elm-leaf Goldenrod (*Solidago ulmifolia*), a few asters, and ferns; however, even for this group, plants take a back seat to the fascinating geology of the crevice area.

November 13, 1992

Friday the 13th does not go uncelebrated as Jessee and Sandy host the bonfire and chili supper. As the evening wears on children gather around to hear the Legend of Logger John. Just telling the story on such a night gives me a chill.

November 14, 1992

One never knows when the next piece of park history will surface. Buck Ham, the son of early Superintendent Keith Ham, stops in to show me several family photos taken here in the late 1950s and early 1960s. The family lived in what is now the visitor center. Several of the photos contain scenes of recreation, one showing a concrete diving platform and the swimming beach. Of greatest interest to me is the picture of the temporary low water bridge used during construction of the present-day bridge. All the photos are priceless, revealing aspects of the park few of us knew. Buck donates them, requesting that they be used in future interpretive exhibits.

As a child, Buck probably gave little thought to what role the family photos would play in protecting park history nor that thirty years later the photos would be so valuable to park historians. Photos taken today or tomorrow may have little meaning or value; but if I place them in archives for 30 years, suddenly they become the key that unlocks a thousand questions: How have we treated our rare and special places? Is overcrowding still a management challenge? Have visitors given new names to new or popular places? Do we recreate the same?

November 16, 1992

During lunch I am called to respond to a wildfire on Holt Ridge. With radio, pump, and rakes I head to the location accompanied by two young men who inadvertently caused the fire. Unlike the stump that caught fire six weeks ago. This one is serious.

According to the men they were four-wheeling along Butterfield Trail when they noticed a line of fire behind the Jeep. Realizing the jeep was burning they bailed. A punctured gas tank and spark from a rock started the fire. Seconds later the jeep and woods were ablaze.

Once on site, I radio the office as to its location and extent of the fire. We attack the fire at its flanks, working persistently toward the head. By the time reinforcements arrived the fire is 50% contained but constant winds keep it well fanned. Within 30 minutes, Forest Service personnel with chainsaws, leaf blowers, and pumper truck arrive to finish the job.

A Forest Service official prepares to write the hunters a citation, but I convince him that they have suffered enough. Both men have lost all their gear, and the jeep is a total loss. I advised the hunters to find a way to remove the charred vehicle or they may yet receive that citation.

November 25, 1992

Around 7:45 p.m. a vehicle towing a pop-up trailer from Louisiana runs off a switchback along Arkansas Highway 74. At 8 p.m. the phone rings. As is often the case, there is only one Ranger to respond to a crisis. Tonight, I draw a short straw. Considering that the car slid several feet over the embankment and is resting almost vertically, I am amazed to find everyone uninjured. Our first priority is to remove the trailer. Once this is accomplished I attempt to pull the vehicle up the embankment with the Isuzu Trooper. Having done so before, I feel sure I can do it again. For 15 minutes I struggle with the gears, but the car will not budge on the last attempt, the rope slips off the tow hook, cutting through my bumper. With the bumper ruined and clutch nearly in flames we leave the project to the professionals. Within the hour, a wrecker arrives and concludes the matter. Once it is sitting back on the road the vehicle is examined. Amazingly only a piece of plastic molding is damaged. In fact, the Trooper fares far worse.

December 16, 1992

Cherry Knob is the second highest hill within view of the park. Hurricane Mountain is two feet higher. Four-wheel drive roads crisscross Cherry Knob, but I have never explored them. Tim, Jessee, and the others are familiar with the area from past mountain bike events. The knob is a favorite among hardcore bikers. On a whim, I decide to take the Trooper on an outing and end up here. The best access is off Washington County Road 217 at the top of the hill. On the right lie several piles of glass. Ten years ago, this glass along with other debris was illegally dumped. On the left, two 4x4 roads diverge. I take the right. It is well traveled and a safe bet for starters. The road gradually descends the ridge in and out of clearcuts. Occasionally, a stone wall or homesite is encountered but little else. Near the end I come across two small eerie dwellings. A cardboard bear plastered in the window startles me and was probably put there for that purpose. I returned to the second fork and continue. From the appearance of this one the road has not been traveled in years. Cedars choke the edges and briars inhabit the roadbed. Through the trees, I can just barely view Lee Creek Valley. Holt Ridge is far more interesting, but at least I have satisfied my curiosity.

December 20, 1992

Barbara Hale and her husband Tom pay me a visit today. She is a genealogist and historian at the Fayetteville Public Library. Quite some time ago I put my query in the paper asking for information about the Hale family and the homesite north of camp area "A." In her possession is the entire Hale family genealogy, or so we thought. In all our searching, we cannot find a link between her family and

Greenfield M. Hale who lived here in the early 1900s. Barbara suspects Greenfield is somehow related to a branch of the family killed in the great flood of Anna.

· December 22, 1992

In preparation for the winter hike next month, I scout Ellis Valley for a campsite. Very few options are available so I will probably leave it to a vote. At Farmer's Cave, I discover that the sign is missing. Somehow, someone was able to reach through the bars and take it. Later, Brent and I take the park 4X4 to Sawmill Hollow near Zinnamon church (not to be confused with Sawmill Hollow in the northeast corner of the park). I am looking for a place to start the winter hike. It is hoped that we can hike the entire Ellis Creek drainage, but the north end is privately owned. Brent shows me where to begin our descent and remain on his father-in-law's land.

This afternoon a domestic disturbance is reported. At 2:30 p.m. the young woman in Cabin four tells Harry she was assaulted during the night by her live-in boyfriend. He had been drinking all night and struck her two-year-old daughter. During the fight that ensued he took her $1800 diamond ring and threw it down the hill. Later, a Washington County deputy arrests the man, but the ring is not recovered.

Chapter 7: Restless

January 2, 1993

The Farmer's Cave permit system gets its first official test today. A party of six complete the form as I issue hard hats and gate key.

January 12, 1993

Harry and I, along with Rex Roberg from the Arkansas Game and Fish Commission, get organized at the Visitor Center for the annual bat survey. There are more caves to check this year and less help than last. Traditionally, the count begins in Big-ear Cave. Harry and Rex take the lead, and I follow with the recount. Here we find 59 Big-ear Bats – one shy of the highest count taken in 1975 and 1988.

The survey continues in "J" Cave, named for Jessee and for the shape of the passage. No Big-ear Bats are found, but the cave proves worthy of the effort. We count four northern Long-ear Bats – a new one for my list. The cave also harbors one Indiana Bat, another endangered species. Next is Puckett's Cave, named in honor of Bill Puckett, whose research has contributed to the management of Big-ear Bats, primarily in Oklahoma and Arkansas. Since this cave regularly harbors endangered species, Harry has decided to close it to the public as well. I have not previously explored Puckett's Cave. Then again, I never knew where to look. Sightings continue as we add four Big-ear Bats, and 38 Indiana Bats to the list. Harry is excited to find such a large colony, and his voice quivers while explaining how to identify the species. Look for the pink nose he says.

At the end of the day, we tally 63 Ozark Big-ear Bats, 40 Indiana Bats, four Northern Long-ear Bats and, and 529 Eastern Pipistrelle Bats. Best of all, I add 3 new caves to my list.

January 13, 1993

Jessee receives a call from the department this morning to inform us that we are under investigation. It seems there was a hit and run in Fayetteville, December 22, and a witness identified our 4x4 plate number. Shocked at the accusation, we each strain to remember where, when, and what we were doing over three weeks ago.

Keeping a personal journal has its advantages. I examine last year's volume and reconstruct the day. Between my journal entry, gas log sheets, and the incident report concerning the domestic disturbance everyone is able to reconstruct their day. We are of course innocent. The vehicle was never more than five miles from the park. Clearly it is a case of mistaken identity.

January 16, 1993

The regulars assemble at the visitor center for the fourth annual winter backpack trip. Most have attended at least eight of our seasonal hikes. It appears the backpacking program at Devil's Den has become a club, but it is good to see old friends.

There are two groups this year. Brent and George lead the first along Butterfield Trail while I take the second down Sawmill Hollow and into Ellis Valley. Out of the 15 hikers only one is female.

The Creek is up, or at the very least, normal for winter. We descend the hollow by way of an old logging road. until it becomes overgrown and unrecognizable. Our first break is taken at the confluence of Ellis east and west forks. I revisit the homesite, stonewalls, and picturesque falls of each fork where I fell in love with this valley in March of 1991.

A few miles and several crossings later, we established camp on the creek's west side near large bluffs. The site is soft and grassy, nearly dry, and strategically located to water and abundant firewood. We set up tents, then prepare for further exploration.

First, I lead the group to the homesite I discovered on October 10, 1990. I have yet to determine who lived here. Research is endless and each day adds another list of projects. The hike continues to all my secret places. I cannot help but share with these longtime friends the truly special haunts and hideaways of the park. I'm confident they will come to treasure them as well.

We return at sunset, build a campfire, and huddle around it to cook the evening meal. We have been fortunate today. The weather has been perfect; however, night will bring a certain chill. I prepare a package of dehydrated beef stew and recline in the Therma-lounge chair. We stay with the fire, trading political and religious views until the sleeping bags can no longer be resisted.

January 29, 1993

A fire is reported this afternoon just beyond the Overlook on Arkansas Highway 170. The grass is extremely dry, but we respond and control it within a few minutes. A tossed cigarette is most likely the cause.

January 30, 1993

Another fire is set, this time intentionally. Fire is a great management tool if used properly. In an effort to restore the appearance of Farmer/Pool homesite, I burn the brush between the site and the county road. After the area is cleared, the jonquils planted here over fifty years ago will thrive.

January 31, 1993

The warm weather has caused several wildflowers to appear. Dandelion (*Taraxicum officinale*) bloomed on January 17, Hairy Bitter Cress (*Cardamine Hirsuta*) on January 27, and today I find bluets (*Houstonia ceaerulea*) and Pale Corydalis (*Corydalis sempervirens*) setting new records.

February 9, 1993

In an attempt to finish the second edition of the natural resource inventory before weeks end, I work late in the visitor center. Around 10 p.m., I locked the door and head for home. Driving away, my headlights catch the shadow of a human crumpled against the wall below the payphone. My first reaction is one of startled fear. "Is everything alright?" I ask. She nods affirmatively. The dark shadow reveals a young lady of approximately 17 years old. She speaks with little more than a gesture. *"I'm waiting on a ride"*, she says. I offer to wait with her until they arrive, but she declines.

February 10, 1993

On the way to town, I learned that Jessee, Tim, and Harry are responding to a crisis in camp area "A" related to last night's encounter with the teen. At the scene, Jessee explains that the girl to whom I spoke came to camp with her recently paroled boyfriend. Over the course of the evening both got high on spray paint inside the tent. After the boyfriend became violent, she ran to the visitor center and called for a ride. The boyfriend took her car, but later returned to continue sniffing paint.

Jessee approaches the site and asks the man to exit the tent. He appears at the door twice but refuses to comply. He is still under the influence. Considering this, the fact that he is a kickboxer, and recent criminal offender, Jessee treats the situation with extreme caution. The man is delirious, belligerent, and paranoid. At one point he grabs a sack from the car and runs into the woods. I follow from a safe distance to determine what and where he is hiding. Jessee takes this opportunity to search the car. He finds a homemade knife, spray paint cans, and several plastic bags used to cover the head when breathing paint fumes. Everything, including the car, is covered in gold paint a sad and permanent reminder of a camping trip gone awry. The man returns as a Washington County deputy arrives. Outnumbered five to one he allows us to take him into custody without further incident.

February 13, 1993

The idea that parks are possessions of the people is one which I strongly promote. Everyone must feel a sense of ownership in order for parks to survive. It is when the public loses this bond that the responsibility falls heaviest on bureaucracy. When agencies take a stronger interest in the parks than the public a fortress mentality develops. Each visitor must believe it is his or her duty to remove litter when they find it, to move a fallen limb in the trail, or to report observed violations.

This afternoon I am pleased to meet a visitor who agrees with this philosophy. She encounters bikers on Devil's Den Trail, clearly posted for foot traffic only. She confronts the young boys and explains why bikes are not permitted. They ignore her because she has no enforcement authority.

The woman reports the incident to me, and I investigate. I find the bikes parked at the entrance to Devil's Den Cave. Since the boys are nowhere in sight (probably in the cave), I push the bikes back to the office. Another visitor, also upset at the bikers, offers to assist. Later, the boys arrived at the visitor center to report their bikes stolen, but instead of filing a report they are subject to a lecture on proper park ethics The entire incident restores my faith in visitors that understand their role as steward and partner with park rangers.

February 15, 1993

The annual Arkansas State Parks interpreters meeting begins tomorrow at Village Creek State Park, followed by the National Association for Interpretation region workshop in San Antonio, Texas. It is a good time to be leaving. Devil's Den is hit by unexpected snow and ice, reminiscent of the events of March 5, 1989. The power flickers all day. Before leaving, I store up an abundance of wood for Susan in case the electricity fails for several hours. Without electricity she would have to heat the cabin with the fireplace, cook with the camp stove, and light the house with kerosene. I would relish the opportunity if not for one night, to live a more primitive life. Susan, on the other hand, does not share that sentiment – no judgment implied. I feel a little guilty leaving her for almost 3 weeks under these conditions.

March 5, 1993

It is good to be back in the valley after several weeks on the road. I have missed much. White Trout Lilies have already bloomed. How many other natural events have occurred during my absence? I take pride in announcing the first flower of spring, and first arrival of neo-tropical bird species. This morning, two hundred snow geese fly over. Of course geese are not migrating in from South America, but it is a spring event that is rarely seen, given the forest canopy.

March 7, 1983

After nine months of planning, the first RV Elderhostel held in Arkansas begins at Devil's Den. Elderhostel is an international program offering educational opportunities to older students, mainly for students 50 years old and older. We will conduct three courses for 18 students during the week. Our program is unique because it is the first to offer classes strictly to RV campers. Traditionally, Elderhostel programs are held in universities or private lodges. At 3 p.m., students arrive for registration, supper, and social event.

March 8,1993

Classes begin at 8:30 a m. Harry conducts the first class on *Bats, Caves, and Crevices*. Later in the week he will lead the group into a cave to see bats firsthand. I instruct the second course entitled *Plantasia*. Several guest speakers will address the group this week, including Don Crank, Carl Hunter, and Bob and Julie Holland.

After lunch, we begin the third course *Basic Backpacking*. The subject is introduced while hiking to Yellow Rock. Later in the week, Brent and I will lead them on an overnight hike. The evening concludes with a campfire presentation on the wonders of Arkansas. most of these hostelers are first time visitors and a proper introduction is in order. Among the group are couples from Oregon, South Carolina, South Dakota, Pennsylvania, New Jersey, New Mexico, Montana, Texas, and Oklahoma.

March 11, 1993

The Elderhostel is going well, and the weather has cooperated until today. Of course it turns bad during the backpack trip. At 2 p.m., with gear organized and group assembled, we shuttle to Holt Road and begin. I lead them along Butterfield Trail and interpret Ozark history. After a small detour to Vista Point, we arrive at Quail Valley and camp beneath the shelter bluff.

Our group consists of seven, excluding Brent and me. The other hostelers either have a better sense or less adventure in their blood. Faye Kelly is the youngest at age 62. She chooses to make the hike without her husband. The oldest is 70. There are two couples and three individuals; Women outnumber men. The winter weather creates a social atmosphere as we gather around the campfire "Montana Bob" shares his jokes and each reveals personal experiences and political views. Differences in age and social background are completely forgotten. We are family now, if only for the trip. As sleet turns to snow I cannot remember a more magical winter night.

March 22, 1993

Jessee catches three boys killing bats with firecrackers in Devil's Den Cave. Instead of leveling a fine we require them to watch two hours of programs on the importance of bats. I am pleased to see their reaction following the programs. Not only do I detect some sense of guilt but more importantly, an attitude of appreciation for bats.

March 24, 1993

The spring hike is not for another three weeks, but I must soon determine a route. Since I have the day off, and both Bridger and I feel the urge to explore, we scout a route to Blackburn's Bluff. I would like to find a place to camp somewhere in this vicinity, but after walking the ledges and benches for an hour, we find nothing suitable and abandon the goal. Besides Bridger is too dry to make scent.

After lunch I strike out alone. Bridger is as they say, dog tired. Whenever I need space, I find myself walking in the Mayfield area. I am nearly always rewarded with a good sighting of a bird or flower. This time the rewards are abundant: Fish Crow, Cedar Waxwing, Great Blue Heron, Red-tailed Hawk, Eastern Meadowlark, and Loggerhead Shrike.

The Loggerhead Shrike is a park record. I watch him catch a small snake and impale it on a honey locust. I have heard of this hunting method but have never witnessed it until now. Two other rewards are offered for my efforts. I hear the first Louisiana Waterthrush of spring, and find an antler, shed but not eaten. Only a few rodent teeth marks are evident.

March 28, 1993

Mike Mlodinow arrives for a little birding. I join him after work in camp area "A" and find him chasing a Bewick's Wren. I have seen one in Oklahoma, but I would like to confirm it here. It will be another park record this week. Up and down, then up again, the wren keeps us busy. Finally perching and singing, the bird provides Mike and me a satisfying look. Later Mike locates a Vesper Sparrow. While not a park record, it is definitely a life bird for me (#363).

March 29, 1993

Red-headed Woodpeckers are back after an absence of two years. Bridger and I see one on our morning walk. Somewhere downhill a Black-and-white Warbler is calling.

April 2, 1993

A search of the park reveals a total of 40 species of wildflowers currently in bloom.

April 11, 1993

To the untrained eye, it would appear spring is just arriving. The oaks are flowering, and most understory trees are fully leafed, attempting to catch sunlight before the canopy develops. I find it hard to categorize a season. To some, one season ends when another begins, but there is overlap. According to the calendar, spring began March 20. Appearances would suggest that now is the first obvious day, but I prefer a more liberal interpretation. Spring begins when dormancy ends. For witch hazel, it begins roughly January 11. For most of the oaks (blackjack, post, white, red, black, and chinkapin oak) spring is today. For these oaks, summer starts when flowers no longer give pollen to the wind. In late September, the leaves ceased to be of service to the trees, and autumn begins. Dormancy is the figurative "Seventh Day." The elements of creation patiently wait in the stillness, until celestial powers summon them once again to burst forth and reproduce (spring).

April 12, 1993

I find it best to tackle the morning memos and endless paperwork with coffee and birds. I sit outside the office on the old CCC bench and listen to the constant chatter of Carolina Chickadees, Tufted Titmice, and Red-bellied Woodpeckers.

Each spring day requires more time in the field. So much is happening, I can scarcely record it all. Near the "Bowls" I see a Broad-winged Hawk, my earliest sighting. On the footpath to the old CCC well, a Woodland Vole pays a visit from the underworld. I observe it for nearly ten minutes before it returns to a fresh tunnel.

April 16, 1993

For the past five years I have studied the flora of the park. I have amassed dozens of field guides for reference, collected nearly 100 new plants, documented the blooming of some 400 species, and compiled a checklist of over 600. After a while one begins to believe he is an expert, even taking a subject for granted. Tomorrow the Arkansas Native Plant Society will attend a field trip here, but this evening two members arrive early to examine plants along Devil's Den Trail. It is a rare opportunity to discuss park flora and present my work for peer review. I am embarrassed to have mistakenly called wood rush a sedge for the last few years. *"Sedges have edges and rushes are round"*, according to my botany professor. I am pleased to learn of a new species of bittercress. Walking with the experts gives my study a renewed purpose. I have not yet mastered this subject.

April 17, 1993

Over a year has passed since I last wandered the woods of Drip-off Hollow. I return today with a group of backpackers on the annual spring trip. It may well be my last secret. We begin the hike in a light drizzle at Blackburn cemetery. I show them the gravesite of Francis Marion Mannon. Many of the backpackers have previously visited his homesite. One of the hikers noticed an unusual headstone which reads Bill Tanner 1772-1894. We speculate as to the authenticity of the dates, which would make old Bill 122 years old.

We descend the hill east of the cemetery to an old homesite. Once the creek is reached we search for the clearest route. There is no path, and bushwacking is the order of the day. Since the route is downhill, no one complains. The Creek is up, and every ledge produces a spectacular waterfall, the first of which is Shale Canyon. We break for snacks and pictures. From their expressions and comments, I am content that we have chosen this route.

By the time we reach Arrowhead Falls, the group is somewhat separated. Bushwacking takes its toll. I find a suitable place to descend the bluff. Rick lowers a rope to provide greater security while climbing down the muddy ledges. After everyone has made it safely we head for shelter beneath the bluff. The drizzle turns to rain. Younger hikers wade the creek and soon I join them. I cannot pass up the opportunity to revisit Trout Lily Falls. The rain lets up a little and we continue.

The creek gains strength as smaller intermittent streams join. After crossing numerous times to avoid thick underbrush, I realize my intended destination will not be reached. The children are showing early signs of hypothermia. I decide to shorten the route and reclaim the steep and slippery ridge. Our party becomes disjunct, and several are one hundred yards behind. In the drizzle, half the group remains while I return to check the progress of the others. Once I rejoin all hikers, I inform them (to their delight) that we will camp at the first suitable site. Tired, wet, and chilled, the group continues to a level bench two-thirds of the way to the ridge. We come to a cedar glade with adequate space and natural shelter. Immediately we turn to the task of erecting tents. Within five minutes, I am inside changing into dry clothes.

The next three hours are spent in relative solitude, napping, reading, or otherwise passing the time – except for Rick who has managed to get a fire going. Around 5 p.m. I wake up to find the drizzle unyielding. Preferring not to cook in the rain, I drag my stove inside ignoring the safety warning label on the tent flap. The rain ends around 8:45 p.m., and we gather for the traditional fireside chat. Barred Owls and Whip-poor-wills serenade our retreat to sleeping bags.

April 18, 1993

I wake to find the sky completely transformed. Temperatures rise with the sun to celebrate a blue canopy. Everyone takes the opportunity to dry their gear. Not a tree in sight is left undecorated. Wet bags, tents, and clothes give the appearance of a tornado through a laundromat. After coffee, oatmeal, and musical performance by Rufus-sided Towhees, we break camp. The final chore is disguising the fire ring so as not to leave a trace. I am sure we have spent the night on private property.

Since the intended route was abandoned yesterday, I have no real agenda for today. Bushwacking continues. Despite my best efforts I cannot avoid leading the group into larger colonies of BlackBerry, greenbrier, and cedar. The serendipitous route is not without its highlights. We find another home site and split rail fence at least 60 years old.

We emerge from the wilderness to a familiar logging road, leading to Moonshine Cave. A group of equestrians from the park are assembled on the bluff above the cave. I recognize frequent visitor Mike Nees from Bolivar, Missouri among the riders. We discuss each other's route and itinerary. They have just visited the cave and are leaving.

Most of the riders are in the saddle, but as one woman begins to mount, the horse rears up, loses its balance, and falls. The woman becomes pinned between the horse and a tree. We turn toward the screams and watch horrified as the horse kicks and compresses the woman before regaining its feet. Several rush to her aid. In obvious pain, she attempts to stand, but cannot. Bob Horn and another member of our backpacking party are trained in emergency care, and they attend to the woman, while Dan and I summon a backboard and EMS. Harry and Ted arrive with the needed equipment. We return to the scene and prepare the woman for transport. The hike up the mountain is only a quarter mile but extremely steep. It takes ten of us alternating positions, to carry her to a waiting ambulance.

I return to Moonshine Cave for my backpack and the group. For the third time in less than an hour, I retrace the trail up the mountain. We cross the highway at Sandy Gap, descend into Lee Creek Valley, and join Butterfield Trail around mile 1.5. Near complete exhaustion, we cross Lee Creek at the trailhead. The water is knee deep and swift, but by forming a human chain all cross safely.

April 25, 1993

During routine patrol, I stopped to visit Mike at the horse camp and get an update on the injury that occurred last weekend. The word is that when the horse fell it crushed the woman's pelvis and hip. She is expected to make a full recovery.

This afternoon while hiking a bluff above the highway bridge, I find a colony of Shooting Star, (*Dodecatheon media*). Until now, this uncommon flower was found only at Moonshine Cave and Holt Ridge Vista.

April 30, 1993

Susan and I attempt to improve the habitat around our cabin. Yesterday, we enlarged the patio and added a small bird bath. Today we hang a hummingbird feeder, suet, and orange slices. Within seconds a Red-eyed Vireo approaches the fruit, and a Ruby-throated hummingbird drinks from the feeder. It's as if they were sitting on a branch at the edge of the woods, waiting.

May 2, 1993

Day two of the 12th Annual Birders Weekend begins in the Mayfield area. Quickly the group adds Blue Grosbeak, Loggerhead Shrike, and Yellow-breasted Chat to their list. Oddly, we can find no Prairie Warblers, which were common in years past.

After a quick break, I lead a second hike to the upper crevice area. Seven birders ignore the threat of rain. Already a drizzle previews the coming attraction, but serious birders are not dissuaded, especially when a life bird is near.

Off trail above Devil's Den and near Big-ear Crevice, I hear a faint "*zeee zeee zoe zee*." Off-hand I cannot recall to whom this song belongs, but I'm quite sure it is one of the rarer warblers. All eyes scan the direction of the sound. From our vantage point, we can look directly down at a large oak canopy. Suddenly, I detect movement and focus on that location. Black-throated Green Warbler! Besides a glimpse of one in Minnesota this is my second sighting ever and the first for my park list. Nearly everyone in the group adds it to theirs as well. We watch the bird for as long as it can be seen.

At the top of the crevice area, we continue to ignore the numerous Tennessee Warblers, Red-eyed Vireos, and Parula Warblers for the faint sound of something different. Moments later *towit towit towit Teo* is heard. Once again I'm puzzled but we are determined to learn the origin of this song. We entered the ravine at the south end of the upper crevice area. Fallen trees and jumbled boulders hinder easy access; However, every step brings us closer to the music. The bird is singing overhead. We stop and scan the canopy from the forest floor. Minutes later a beautiful black and yellow headed bird pops into view. Hooded Warbler! Although rare, Hooded Warblers were almost always seen during birders weekend; however, this is our first for the past few years.

With two exceptional sightings to our credit the trip is already declared a success. To Imp's Leap we climb. Fantastic views of the Upper Lee Creek Valley can be had from here. Scarlet Tanagers perch below, and we marvel at their brilliant red and black plumage. A squeaky high pitched *eek* is heard. It can only be the call of a Rose-breasted Grosbeak. Two are spotted near the Tanagers. We are in birder's heaven.

May 16, 1993

On Devil's Den Trail, I continue my weekend routine to look for new blooms, to answer questions, and to control the crowds. Near Right Angle Crevice, I pass two married couples in their late teens. One of the girls seems to be in pain so I inquire. "It's just a cramp", the other girl answers. I continue on. Five minutes later, one of the boys catches up to me on the trail and requests assistance. The girl's condition has worsened and requires medical attention. Once again, I inquire as to her trouble. She complains of severe abdominal pain. There is little I can do to diagnose the problem. The only solution is to extricate her to the trailhead where EMS can treat and/or transport her to Washington Regional. After questioning the husband privately, I determined that the girl may be having a miscarriage. She can neither move nor remain but refuses to accept an ambulance, fearing the financial cost. A nosey crowd forms. Before the whole incident becomes a media spectacle, I make the decision for her. We carry her to the trail head as the ambulance arrives. The husband accepts the EMT's assistance and the two are whisked away. The other couple shows open concern for the husband's ability to cover expenses, fearing the loss of his new Chevy truck.

May 21, 1993

A local school group has come to hike, picnic, and play – an innocent outing. Washington County Sheriff's Department calls to inform us that a woman may appear at the park to take her child away. We are not to give her any information. It seems the child is legally in the father's custody. A county deputy and I patrol the park to warn teachers and to look for a suspicious vehicle. None appear.

May 27, 1993

Back in March a pair of Eastern Phoebes chose the shelter of our cabin eaves to nest. We watched them daily and were careful not to disturb them beyond necessity. The eggs hatched in April, and we continued to monitor the progress of our chicks fighting for food, screaming for attention, and growing fatter. Today, most of the young have left the nest to perch on the telephone line. I regret their leaving. Evenings on the patio will be silent without them.

May 28, 1993

The park mailing list continues to grow to over three hundred names. It is good to see so many visitors take a long-term interest in the park. For the past three years, we have struggled to create a volunteer program. The mailing list has helped, but something more inventive is needed to retain and make use of this interest. Several weeks ago, I proposed the idea of developing a nonprofit support group. Pinnacle Mountain and Prairie Grove state parks have already done so, but their support is strong locally; ours is widespread. Still the idea is worth trying. Today I send letters to our park friends, asking them to meet with us on July 10. If there is enough interest, we hope to form the Friends of Devils Den State Park, Inc.

May 30, 1993

The crowd swells as a new season begins. The visitor center is so populated, I find it easier to answer questions outside the building. While engaged in conversation by the flagpole I notice a woman exiting the building. Strangely, she is hugging the wall with her eyes closed. She reaches to the flagpole and faints at my feet. "What's wrong?", I asked her husband. "She's afraid of snakes." He answers. A mere look at them on display has thrown the woman into hysteria. As the family carries her away, I am chastised for not posting warning signs. I imagine what the text of warning sign would be.

WARNING! COMPLETELY STRESSED, TERRIFIED, AND EMACIATED SNAKES INSIDE A LOCKED DISPLAY CASE. ENTER AT YOUR OWN RISK

June 4, 1993

The summer missionaries arrive. Blake and Scott will take their place alongside the others who have served a long, hot season for God in Devil's Den.

I received word that Ross Stinchcomb has died. Ross joined the maintenance crew ten days before I came to Devil's Den in 1988, and just recently retired. A tall quiet man, Ross was one of the finest carpenters the park had ever employed.

June 5, 1993

Today is National Trails Day. To celebrate the event, I have scheduled a work project on Yellow Rock Trail, and I have invited Pepsi Cola of Springdale to provide refreshments for volunteers. At 8:30 AM I gather tools and meet the group at the lower trailhead. Pat Huff, Jean Long, Dennis and Michael Shelton, among others, have come to work. The CCC built switchbacks are badly eroded, and over the years, hikers have destroyed the supporting walls. One by one we carry boulders uphill and rebuild. By afternoon, we put the finishing touches on the project by placing cedar limbs on the edges to discourage off-trail traffic.

June 11, 1993

The Northwest Arkansas Cavalcade arrives for its annual Dogwood ride. I meet with Floyd and continue our discussions about the Dotsons and early valley history. He introduces me to John Pool who also grew up in the valley, but now resides in Missouri.

John is the second son of Charles Parker Pool. It was Charles who purchased the old William James Farmer property, and the same which is now called the Mayfield area. We drive to the homesite and talk. Now only the cellar and a patch of jonquils mark the area where John worked and played as a youth.

I asked John to tell me his story. His father was born in March 1844, in Harrison County, West Virginia. During the Civil War, Charles served in Company D West Virginia Infantry, which was a Union outfit. After the war it is not clear what Charles did, but he eventually landed in Fayetteville in 1915, where he married Clara Bell Straw. John and his brother Charles Thomas were born there. Before John was two, the family moved to Upper Lee Creek Valley near old Bethlehem church. At age seven (1925) they moved here.

John describes his childhood home. There was a two-story white framed house with four-inch weatherboard siding. The front door and living room faced Washington County Road 61, which John says was rarely traveled. A large bedroom and kitchen downstairs faced Lee Creek. Upstairs consisted of two bedrooms. On the south side of the house was a peach orchard, and on the north was a garden and long barn. Downhill on the east side were individual sheds for chickens, smoked meat, hogs, and a spring. The spring and chicken houses are still evident. Further to the north stood a tenant house and a couple other log structures of which no evidence remains.

Across the road from the house was another log building, a blacksmith shop, an apple orchard, and hand dug well. The pecan tree which towers above the road today was a prominent feature then. The road in front of the house has not changed, but sections uphill and downhill are different. In John's day, the road turned at Ellis Creek and followed it downstream before crossing. Uphill from the house, across from the horse camp, the original road is still obvious. The current road is a product of the CCC.

In all, the property consisted of one hundred acres. The family raised chickens, hogs, 30 head of cattle, and 25 sheep. He recalls there being seven or eight horses and mules. In the garden they planted tomatoes and potatoes. The fields consisted of hay, corn, and beans.

I asked John about the wildlife he encountered as a child. He says deer were not seen until after WWII. He never saw a Black Bear or a Wild Turkey in these parts. Common wildlife includes Fox Squirrel, Raccoon, Woodchuck, and Opossum. On one occasion, he stepped on a 13-button rattlesnake in the field across from the house. He recalls kids taking bats from Farmers Cave, stuffing them in their hats, taking them down to the bluff, and fighting them like roosters. Catching fish was a similar matter of waiting until the water was low then throwing crushed green walnuts in the pools to deprive the water of oxygen, and then the fish floated to the surface. The practice was (and is) illegal, but the game warden rarely came around.

At age 89, Charles Parker Pool died in January 1933, a few months before the CCC program was established. His grave can be found at the Friendship cemetery along Arkansas Highway 170. That same year, John remembers how moonshine could be bought for two dollars a gallon and then resold for fifty cents a pint.

When the CCC enrollees came, life changed for the Pools. Relations soured when the government tried to buy their land for $1,300 knowing Charles had paid $2,500. CCC enrollees would hide their automobiles on Pool land, since they were not permitted in camp. John recalls another incident when several enrollees were talking dirty to the Sawyer girls. John was walking down the road with the girls when several CCC boys appeared. One of them pinched a girl's rear. When she turned, the boys blamed John who was promptly yet unjustly slapped. John says he nearly killed the enrollee.

John left the Lee Creek valley during WWII. In 1944, his mother sold the farm. Carthal Edwards lived in the house afterwards. Clara passed away just three years ago at the age of 101. After thirty minutes of conversation, my notebook is full. As the sun sets, John and I head for camp. There are so many questions remaining but must be asked another day.

June 12, 1993

Mike Mlodinow reports seeing a Blue-winged Warbler on the nest. It is our first breeding record, and the latest sighting of the year. Not to be outdone, I observe a Gray Fox, White-tail Deer, Nine-banded Armadillo, Opossum, and Raccoon on evening rounds.

June 19, 1993

Work begins abruptly this afternoon when I'm immediately called to respond to a bike injury. I head to Holt Road, as a light rain begins. By the time I reach the ridge, the rain is blinding. I find the woman huddled under a tree avoiding the rain with no success. Her knee is lacerated but the bleeding has nearly stopped. She hobbles into the truck and explains the incident. Without fear, she rode in high gear down Butterfield Trail. Suddenly the front tire halted on a root and over the bike she went.

June 27, 1993

The park is once again filled with old friends, including Bob and Sherry Horn, and Dennis and Kathy Shelton. I take the opportunity to get their input on forming the Friends of Devils Den.

June 28, 1993

Today's softball injury: sprained ankle. One man shows up in army boots, black jeans, and no shirt. Nearby, his woman watches with a passel of screaming kids. On his way to first base, he attempts to slide, but the boots stop him cold. He limps to the sideline in pain, trying best not to show it. As I help him to the car, two of the children come running with bleeding toes both having cut their feet on the jagged asphalt. Performing a sort of triage, I decided to treat the children first. A nurse camping nearby begins to treat the man and eventually transports him to the hospital. Later, I learned that the man was wanted on several outstanding felonies and was apprehended at the hospital.

July 1, 1993

After a few phone calls I find enough people interested in forming an interim board for the proposed friends group. Chuck White, Karen Garrett, Harry Morgan, and Zoe Morgan have agreed to serve.

July 3, 1993

For the third time in as many years, the park is faced with death. At 3 p.m., Campsite 6 is due to vacate. The next visitors to occupy the site wait for the current occupant to leave. To them he appears drunk and incapable of departing safely. They report the potential problem to the office and Jessee investigates.

Jessee arrives at the site and approaches the vehicle. He announces his presence to a man in the back of the camper. The man looks up, sees Jessee, and puts a gun to his own head. At first, the pop sounds like a firecracker from a nearby campsite, but when smoke rolls from the camper Jessee realizes the gun has been discharged. Falling back to safety, he calls for backup. Brent arrives and they assess the situation. Clearly the man has committed suicide.

Minutes later I arrive with a bed sheet to cover the body. Despite a full campground, no one else is aware of the incident. As EMS, County Sheriff, coroner, and wrecker arrive it becomes obvious. I read the three-page suicide note while a dozen men fill out reports. Over an hour later the investigation concludes and removal of the body is permitted. I reach in with rubber gloves and roll the body over. As the head turns the bullet falls to the floor and is collected for evidence. We place the body in a black rubber bag as the wrecker positions itself to remove the vehicle. Within minutes of our departure the site is reopened and quickly reoccupied. The park is back to normal. It will be some time before I'm back to normal.

July 4, 1993

Another traumatic incident occurs this morning when one of our lifeguards accidentally sprays a chemical in her eye. She is sent to the hospital with fear of permanent eye damage. Later we receive assurances that the eye will heal.

From one trauma to the next. A frantic woman approaches me. She does not know what to do. Her baby stumbled into the campfire. I examine the child for life threatening injuries. While finding none, I determined that they should immediately leave for the hospital. Coincidentally, the same woman who helped with the ankle injury on June 28 leads them into town. Devil's Den might well have a guardian Angel.

July 9, 1993

For the Friends group to succeed, there will be a certain amount of legal work to process. Nonprofit and incorporation procedures can be expensive and difficult; Therefore, I must secure the *pro bono* assistance of an interested lawyer. Susan suggests calling Jim and Dianne Boyd since they are attorneys and own property near the park. I call and both agree to help. The interim board is now complete. Tomorrow, we put our plan into action.

Interested visitors begin to arrive as early as noon to attend the organizational meeting of the Friends of Devil's Den State Park, Inc. Channel 29/40 and Channel 5 have responded to my news release and are here to cover the event. I give each a fifteen second soundbite. By 2 p.m., the group has grown to thirty, not counting park staff.

I open the meeting, express my hopes for the group, and explain the park's need for such an organization. Our guest speaker is Linda Westergard from Pinnacle Mountain State Park, who was instrumental in starting Partners for Pinnacle, Inc. After a short break Jessee outlines the park's immediate concerns at precisely 4:40

p.m., a motion is made to proceed with organization and to empower the interim board. The road ahead will be long and hard, but today we celebrate. Devil's Den has an official friends group!

July 11, 1993

The thermometer reads 100°. I sit in the shade of the cedars in front of the visitor center and read newspaper articles concerning yesterday's "Friends" meeting. I reflect on the words of park volunteer Dennis Shelton following the event: "You birthed that baby well. Now it is up to us to make it grow.

July 13, 1993

A cabin guest asks if I might be interested in seeing some old park photos. Always on the prowl for tidbits of history, I meet at his cabin to hear his story. After an absence of some 47 years, he has returned to retrace a boyhood vacation in the Ozarks with his own sons. The boys run in and out while he and I discuss Devil's Den of the 1940s. He exhibits several photos taken on Devils Den Trail during the summer of 1946. I immediately recognize the various locations and many of the geologic features have not changed. Cold Springs and Battleship Rock between Parallel Crevice and Devils Icebox are both similar to their 1940s appearance. He relives the memories, while I study other photos including the Blackburn store and the cottage resorts of Mount Gaylor. After an hour of discussion, I convince him to loan the photos so that I may reproduce them for the park.

July 16, 1993

Today's softball injury: bruise to the left shoulder. While pitching to Tim, I take a direct hit.

July 24, 1993

In the past, Eagle Scout projects have been only temporarily beneficial. One Eagle Scout cleaned the caves and crevices, only to find them trashed the following week. Another rebuilt trail switchbacks at Twin Falls only to see them destroyed a month later.

Today we try again. The CCC overlook pavilion on Arkansas Highway 170 has been damaged by thoughtless adolescents who have carved their would-be-lovers name in the posts. Additionally, trees have grown to obscure much of the original view and the trail is considerably eroded. With a long day's work, we are able to restore the overlook to a respectable appearance. How long it remains is anyone's guess.

August 2, 1993

With the Friends group in its organizational stage, our first task is to draft a constitution. Borrowing from the bylaws and structure of Partners for Pinnacle, I complete the first draft.

August 7, 1993

The interim board meets to discuss and edit the constitution for the Friends of Devil's Den. Halfway into the meeting, Jessee and I are called away to respond to an injury in the Ozark National Forest. We receive a report that a woman and teenage boy were riding somewhere east of Cherry Knob when the boy fell off his horse. The extent of the injuries and the boy's location are unknown.

The afternoon heat is sweltering. Dust swirls along the trail, penetrating the eyes, nose, and throat. Around every corner we catch a spider web in the face. Horseflies add insult to injury. It becomes apparent that the boy is farther down the trail than expected. Jessee takes the medical bag and continues; I head back for the car to rendezvous at the bottom of the mountain. Shortly, EMS and Strickler volunteers arrive and are updated on the plan. We establish a base at Zinnamon homesite. Minutes later, Jessee locates the boy and reports the injury to be minor – a broken wrist at the worst. An off-duty doctor arrives, and I send him up the trail to meet the party. An hour and a half later, we returned to find the board meeting concluded.

August 8, 1993

A family requests permission to release a baby Blue Jay in the park. They have been raising it at home but have grown tired of the responsibility. They want assurances for its safety. I tell them there are no guarantees. Any number of predators might snatch it. To ease their concerns, I suggest releasing the Blue Jay at my cabin where I can monitor it.

At lunch I find the bird sitting over my patio on an oak limb chirping continuously. I tell it to keep quiet or prepare to meet every stray cat in the area.

An hour later a child brings this same baby Blue Jay to the office and reports finding it in the playground. This will not do. I have to relocate the bird to the most remote area of the park; however, having imprinted on humans I fear it will return within a day or two.

August 11, 1993

On the way to town, I round the 15 MPH curve of Arkansas Highway 170 and see Tim on the shoulder. Three others sit on the bank and a fourth lies in the grass. Closer, I see an old pickup overturned deep in the ravine. Tim and one of the lifeguards are performing triage. I immediately pull over and give them a hand. One of the patients has a cut ear and arm; another two individuals have lacerations on their legs. The driver lies at the edge of the woods. He appears to be inebriated, on drugs, or both.

Once the injuries are stabilized, we investigate the crash. It appears three were in the cab of the truck; one was thrown through the windshield; two others were riding in the truck bed and were tossed into the trees as the vehicle flipped. Beer cans litter the area.

As we reach the driver, he stumbles to his feet and runs into the woods. EMS and local law enforcement arrive and control the scene. I lead West Fork and Washington County deputies on a search to find the driver. Walking down the Old Road Horse Trail I find him lying in the leaves. He is exhausted, under the influence, and probably injured. I wait for armed backup. Earlier, one of the officers attempted to place the suspect in handcuffs but he bolts. This time however he is outnumbered and surrounded. An officer grabs his feet, and a struggle begins. Even in his condition, it takes four of us to fasten the cuffs. On the way to the car, he threatens revenge, shouting *"I'll remember you! I never forget a face!"*

August 14, 1993

I could not have picked a hotter or drier weekend for the summer backpack trip. There is little enthusiasm as we begin the march to Fossil Flats and Sawmill campsite. Plans for the day include swimming as much as possible. Only three pools on all of upper Lee Creek contain water (if algae crusted fish pee counts as water). At the first pool, I give a fishing demonstration. Green Sunfish and Long-eared Sunfish cooperate. As soon as the camp is established we return to the swimming hole, nearly a quarter mile downstream. Here, two hundred yards below Fossil Flats, the water is cool and deep. A spring provides a constant supply. We swim for hours, then return to the campsite for an afternoon nap. Two hours later the heat drives us back to the hole. We are all thoroughly roasted. My sunburn is the worst in recent memory. By evening, I am too sick to eat or shuffle cards. Sleeping is out of the question.

August 15, 1993

Having tossed and turned all night in pain, I rise early. By 9:30 a.m. we are back at the visitor center, thus ending the shortest and most miserable backpack trip of my life.

September 17, 1993

Mink is rare around these parts, but I catch a glimpse of my first while on evening patrol.

September 19, 1993

As usual, the Mountain Bike Weekend is a success. During the criterion races, I am stationed at the Gravity Cavity or Whoop-dee-do. It is my job to control the crowds and give emergency medical assistance. Unlike previous years, no injuries are reported. Located north of the Walk-In Camp, bikers race up and down a 15-foot vertical ditch. A crowd gathers, waiting for the first good wreck. All the riders pass superbly.

As the event concludes, Harry and I depart for the San Juan Mountains and its signature peak – Rio Grande Pyramid.

September 29, 1993

Late this evening while stopping at the visitor center to collect my mail, I meet a tourist from California. The conversation continues for an hour and a half. Fern McHenry is a California State Park Ranger taking a cross country sabbatical on motorcycle. Like me, Vern exhibits signs of burnout. We talk about the pleasures of working in an adventurous outdoor environment, and the frustrations of mounting bureaucracy and crime. Crime has always been a part of the park scene, but it seems more so these days. Perhaps it is we, and not the situation, that has changed. Years of trying to fix the park, only to find our work undone by vandals and thieves is demoralizing. It is therapeutic to share these feelings with one who understands.

October 2,1993

Susan hit another deer today while climbing the grade of Arkansas Highway 170. This one damages the left fender and headlight of the Cavalier.

October 3, 1993

Mike and I confirm a Merlin sighted at Mayfield. Since it is the park's first record, we are hesitant to make the declaration. For new records or species sightings, it is critical that there be a 100% level of confidence. That comfort level begins with two or more natural resources specialist agreeing.

October16, 1993

Thunderstorms flare at 5:30 this morning. The fall backpack trip is in jeopardy. Despite the rain, two dozen arrived. We wait out the rain as long as possible. Harry and I torture the group with slides of our recent trip to Colorado. By 10 a.m. I decide we must either cancel the hike or depart. The rain persists. We take the park shuttle to Holt Road and trudge along in full raingear to Mount Olive. We reach Quail Valley around 11:30 a.m. and huddle under a bluff for a snack. After reaching a consensus, we decide to make Quail Valley our camp. There's enough shelter along the bluff to keep us dry should the rain continue. The rain ceases two hours later, and several decide to pitch tents in the open. Under partial sunlight, we hike the bluffs west of Quail Valley and down to Quarry Falls. We spend the evening around the fire. I fix freeze dried Polynesian chicken with rice and beg for chocolate. My food cache consists of supper, coffee and little else. I hope to supplement my diet with leftovers from others. If I am unsuccessful, fasting is an option. The rain returns at dark.

October 23, 1993

Although the park was officially 60 years old last Wednesday, we celebrate today during the Ozark Heritage Weekend. After our hike to homesites, everyone gathers at the visitor Center for birthday cake. Over 75 visitors, friends, and employees attend. Just the mere mention of "free cake" nearly causes a stampede.

The first official Friends of Devil's Den State Park, Inc. meeting begins at 2 p.m. I introduce the interim board and take nominations for officers. Harry Morgan is elected president, Benny Nettles is vice president, Jack Miller is treasurer, and Karen Garrett is secretary. Years from now we will look back on this day as the beginning of a new Devil's Den. For many years national parks have had the support of nonprofit citizen groups such as the Eastern National Parks and Monuments Association. Until recently state parks have not been so fortunate. Visitors must take more than a passive role to ensure their future success. In hard times many state parks across the country have closed or severely cut services. If there is organized support, this may not happen. Following the meeting, 25 individuals and families join.

October 25, 1993

Another routine laundry night ends abruptly. On the way home, I am flagged down by a cabin guest who believes her friend may be having a heart attack. I instruct her to go back inside while I call EMS. At the scene, Tim and I examine the situation. An older lady sits on the bed holding her chest but seems stable for the moment. Strickler Fire Department and EMS arrive. Quickly, the scene becomes crowded as nearly a dozen people respond to the scene. To preserve some dignity for the woman I ask the volunteers to wait outside as I myself leave the scene to the more than competent EMS personnel. Later I am informed the woman was observed and released in good condition.

October 30, 1993

The Friends group holds its first workday. A light snow fell yesterday and remains this morning. Flurries continue as Pat Huff, Keith Wells, Benny and Jonathan Nettles and I begin the Mayfield cleanup project. Our goal is to convert, as much as possible, the old Buddy Mayfield homesite back to the wilderness. There are two barns, a hunter's cabin, and trailer to clean and a mile of barbed wire to remove. We build a bonfire to burn the debris and to warm our hands. By day's end one barn is clean fencing around the trailer is removed and all the junk is hauled away. Considering that Buddy spent most of his retirement developing the site, it will take several days to complete this ambitious project.

December 11, 1993

After a year and a half without a park ranger, the department finally fills the vacant position. During the interim, all of us shared the enforcement duties. Jerry Smith joins the Devil's Den family, but he will be living outside the park. He represents the first new addition to the park management team since my arrival nearly five years ago.

Chapter 7: Restless

January 3, 1994

The temperature is too low to walk the dog this morning. Instead, I risked letting him relieve himself unattended. Bridger is not bothered by the chill and quickly wanders off to explore, ever attentive to the movements of deer. None are spotted. Minutes later I call for him, but he fails to report. It seems I must experience the cold after all. Walking the upper cabin loop, I observe Bridger on the lower loop visiting Rosie, Harry's adopted mutt. Rosie was one of the strays saved after thoughtless locals dumped her in the park. Her siblings were not so fortunate.

January 15, 1994

After spending a week bedridden with flu, I regained some strength. That strength will be tested today and tomorrow as I can find no volunteers to lead the 5th annual winter backpack trip. I begin the day by oversleeping, and as usual have procrastinated the packing of gear. Most hikers have already arrived, albeit fewer than expected. Many registrants are no doubt discouraged by a forecast predicting snow and ice.

There are no virgin backpackers in attendance. The eight veterans include Bob and Donna, Ed, Rick, Perry, Kevin, Doug, and Christopher. Our route – by now a familiar one – begins at the fire road in camp area "A"; However, few have explored the falls, crevices, and faulted sandstone blocks below Yellow Rock. Packs are left by the road while we visit this area.

We establish basecamp at the sawmill site – a second home to these hikers. Tents are erected, wood gathered, and lunch consumed. In my haste to pack, only Hershey kisses are available for lunch. As usual mercy is taken upon me and some cheese and crackers are offered.

The objective of this hike is to explore the bluffs of Sawmill Hollow, which I briefly visited in December of 1991. A small logging road leads east, uphill. At the end of the road, we veer to the left on the bench, working slowly toward the main bluff. I had forgotten how massive the outcrop is. Even the camera's wide-angle lens fails to capture it. I photograph the group walking under the icicles. The bluff overhangs some 20 feet and cedars dangle from the thin sandstone ledge. Gradually the hollow narrows and joins the opposite bluff. The high fall persists in the axis of the hollow.

Part of the group descends to the base of the falls while the rest maneuver around them. Along the ledges sand lies in thick dusty piles. Neither rain nor splashing from the falls can reach or dampen the ledge. Until now, only deer and beetle tracks have disturbed the sand. Now ours will remain until antlions plow them beyond recognition.

At the first feasible location we ascend the north bluff to its bench. Already views into Lee Creek Valley are afforded, but I am well aware of the vista that awaits. Patiently, the group follows. The large red and white oaks give way to post and blackjack and eventually to farkleberry and grass. I collapse on the clumps of grass and gaze south to Yellow Rock. Within minutes everyone is basking in the silence. Turkey Vultures carried by updrafts cruise overhead. For such a cold morning the glade is quite the bed of warmth. Doug and Perry have fallen asleep. I am not far behind.

I could easily spend the night here. Often I wish there were no agendas. I could remain at vistas such as this until absolute boredom overcame me. I would not depart until the scene could offer no more inspiration, poetry, or solace. It seems I'm always pressured by the need to keep to some schedule or complete a time-sensitive task. In the grand scheme of things, what could possibly be more important?

One by one I sense the group's desire to leave, each having reached their threshold of inspiration. We gather gear and begin the descent. We reach Sawmill Camp and prepare for supper. I rarely skimp on supper. Even in the rush to pack I have not failed to bring a package of dehydrated sweet and sour pork with rice, Folgers coffee singles and Hershey's kisses.

The wind stirs, and as expected, the clouds emerge. We are reminded of the forecast. Perhaps the snow will hold off until tomorrow. Plenty of wood has been collected and the fire is stoked. Small gusts blast the campfire, sending sparks against my tent and clothing. "You're on fire!" Doug yells. "Yikes!" I say slapping myself silly.

We remain at the fire's edge until precisely 10 p.m. as if it were some important goal. Final preparations are made for bed, including one last hand warming over the coals. Inevitably I have forgotten to pee. It will be a long night.

January 16, 1994

Sleet begins at 4 a.m. Each hour passes reluctantly. I have not slept. Despite this fact I managed to remain in the bag another four hours. At 8 a.m., Doug and Rick reignite the fire. It is now convenient to get up. The sleet is unrelenting. All our gear is coated with ice, and I suspect each of us will carry a pound of it out. By 10:40 a.m., we reached the vehicles and head for home. Already the roads are near impassable.

January 18, 1994

The snow and ice continue to disrupt travel in and out of the Upper Lee Creek Valley. Susan attempts Arkansas Highway 170 but stalls out a quarter mile shy of the ridge. By afternoon the postal lady arrives, signaling the road's accessibility. Mail on a snowy day is like Christmas, and it might as well be. Today's mail includes a thousand-dollar donation to the Friends of Devil's Den State Park, Inc. from the Morgan family.

January 25, 1994

Over five years ago, Harry and I measured the length of Devil's Den Cave. In preparation for a publication on the park's geology, we return to develop a more accurate map. The plan is to make a drawing based on compass measurements. To simplify the process, I bring my mini-cassette recorder to make verbal notes and avoid cumbersome notebook and pencil. Within the first three minutes, I drop the recorder rendering it useless. Harry waits while I return to the office for pen and paper. Two hours later we reemerge from the fracture with dim lights and muddy pages filled with numbers. After lunch, I strive to make some sense of it.

February 1, 1994

Clyde Hopkins stops by with his mother to discuss valley history. Clyde was raised south of the park near the community of Lee Creek. His home was the site of a small plantation during the Civil War. Clyde tells of being born in what was once the slave quarters. We sift through page after page of genealogical information photos and clippings, a gold mine of valley history. I am tempted to take on a dozen research projects but restrain myself. Lee Creek community is over eight miles south and is in another county. There is already too much work within the park; However, I do not refuse the invitation to visit the old artesian well.

We take the Trooper south on Washington County Road 61 and turn left into Bryant cemetery, just north of the steel bridge. On the north side of this cemetery, we examine remains of the old homestead. There is little left to compare childhood photos. On site, we reach a gate to private property. Clyde knows the present landowner and permission is assumed. As we approach the house, several barking dogs appear. We knock but no one answers, although a radio blares upstairs. There are still places in rural Arkansas where one may be shot at before reaching the porch.

Trusting Clyde, I follow him downhill to the artesian well. The smell of sulfur guides us through the thick underbrush. Finally, after years of staring at this spot on the map, I stand in front of the spring. The water temperature is perfect for bathing, that is if one can stand the smell. Clyde tells of how the well was developed while drilling for oil. For a time, the area served as a little-known health spa. The current landowner has rigged a pump to carry water to the house. From the well, the putrid water flows into a slough and then Lee Creek. Several minnows have found the warm slough preferrable to the frigid waters of Lee.

February 3, 1994

Few corners of the park have escaped me these past five years. I am left with only the undesirable slopes of Ellis Creek for new adventures. North of Mayfield homesite, there is a small pond which I have visited on occasion. The drainage uphill of the pond is yet unknown to me. With a camera and a few hours of sunlight, I proceed. Shortly an Armadillo greets me. We take size of each other and then go our separate ways.

The drainage becomes insignificant near the 1,180-foot contour line. Veering west, I locate an old logging road and follow it until feeling the urge to descend. Choosing neither path nor reason, I scramble down to Ellis Creek. I am rewarded with a few minor geological oddities. A small balanced rock stands in the middle of the woods with no apparent connection to the hill. I find several sandstone slabs with perfect cross sections of ripple marks – an ancient, petrified delta.

The hill gives way to Ellis Creek. I wander downstream to a set of rapids which require contemplation. I find a comfortable rock from which to properly examine them. I'm not sure how much time passes before thoughts begin to stray. To be conscious of the clock would defeat the purpose of the exercise. Suffice it to say I begin to take greater interest in floating sticks down the rapids than in the rapids themselves. Only after depleting my source of wood for boats, do I abandon the creek. At Farmers Cave, I discover the gate has been compromised. There is no telling how many have toured the cave in the absence of some sort of restraint.

February 5, 1994

Hairy Bitter Cress is blooming at the sewage treatment plant, and henbit is close. I can find no sign of bluets, but it is clear, spring has begun. The temperature pushes 60°.

February 9, 1994

Perhaps spring will have to wait. Last night left us with a half inch of sleet.

February 10, 1994

The sleet and snow refused to melt. From a cozy window, I watch gold and purple finches searching desperately for seed below an empty feeder. The local mob of Gray Squirrels had nearly cleaned me out. A few weeks ago, I noticed one with a mangy tail. Now it appears the entire family is suffering. No doubt they are feeling the chill without the rump hair.

February 18, 1994

Occasionally I am the only one on duty in the park, and during these times there is usually a crisis. Tonight is no exception. Just before dark, I am called to respond to a twenty-two-year-old male trapped in Satan's Maze. I quickly throw on a pair of ragged jeans and grab my hard hat and light. Strickler Fire Department volunteers arrive, and we rush to Right Angle Crevice – the exit of Satan's Maze. Admittedly out of shape, I lead the way. Instantly, the mud and I are one. I have not been in this passage since January 1990, and I had hoped never to return. Upon reaching the maze we discover the victim has already freed himself and left the cave by way of the main entrance to Devil's Den. Sore, cold, and muddy, I exit and find the young man sitting at the entrance.

February 19, 1994

Once again, alone, I respond to park emergencies. Around 9 p.m. the weather turns for the worst. Lightning, heavy winds, and rain attack the valley. By 9:15 p.m. I receive a call from the guests in cabin five that a tree has just fallen through the roof. Cloaked in rain gear, I run uphill to investigate. Sure enough, an 80-year-old oak has found a resting place on the 50-year-old structure. One branch punctured the bedroom window, spreading glass over the bed. Another punctured the bathroom roof. Rain quickly fills the pots and pans positioned to catch the largest leaks. In a stroke of genius, I staple Visqueen to the bathroom ceiling and angle it to the tub this will keep the water from running all over the floor and allows me the leisure of dealing with the problem tomorrow. Unfortunately, the cabin guests will have to spend the night on the living room couch. No other cabins are available tonight. If they had gone to bed earlier, they might have sustained injuries from the shattered glass.

February 28, 1994

Since February 5, not a single new species of plant has bloomed. I find a meager specimen of Whitlow Grass at the sewage treatment plant.

An interesting couple passes through the park this afternoon. They are from San Diego, and like most middle-class Californians, are looking for greener pastures. Hundreds of families have found their way from California to Northwest Arkansas (NWA), completing a cycle which began with the emigration from Arkansas in 1849 and again in the 1930s. This couple, however, is headed further east. and they sold their house and furnishings, invested in camping gear, and left for good. After four months of searching for the perfect small town they have found little to suit them. It seems many of us are looking for the same thing: quaint community, low crime, good economy, cultural diversity, progressive idealism, and friendly neighbors. On those rare occasions when just such a place is discovered, it is quickly ruined like miners rushing to a gold strike. Fayetteville, Springdale, Rogers, Bentonville, and Bella Vista have all seen this transformation. I encourage the couple to look elsewhere, not for fear that they will further contribute to the degradation of NWA, but out of hope that they may yet find utopia. Both have kept a daily journal of their adventures which I hope to someday read.

March 8, 1994

Spring is delayed yet again. On my return from a convention in northwest Missouri, I am greeted at the border by snow in excess of 18 inches!

March 10, 1994

Temperatures take a drastic turn, and the ground responds with the blooming of White Trout Lily, Harvey's Buttercup, Serviceberry, and Eastern Redbud.

March 11, 1994

It seems the flowers are in a rush. Everything is poking through the soil. Today, I find Shepherd's Purse, Spring Beauty, Woodland Bluegrass, Dead Nettle, and Harbinger-of-spring.

March 12, 1994

Several weeks ago, plans were made to demolish the old chicken barn in the Mayfield area. For the past year, minor dismantling has occurred. The remaining structure is a worthless eyesore. My greatest desire is to see the entire area restored to some semblance of a park. Today, volunteers with the Friends of Devils Den complete the task. At first only a few arrive at the appointed time, but as the morning progresses 17 volunteers attend. We begin by building a fire to consume the boards. Metals are separated into a pile for recycling. Like ants we work tirelessly building the fire ever higher until its height threatens the field and the heat becomes unapproachable. We break for a quick lunch at the Mayfield glade, then minutes later resume work at a furious pace. Seven hours later the ground is leveled, and within a year or two, only pictures will prove it once existed. One by one, volunteers depart. Pat and I remain to watch the stars and guard the fire. In the quiet of evening, I hear the familiar peent of an American Woodcock. Wildness has returned.

March 13, 1994

On my way to Mayfield this morning, I noticed a broken car window at Devil's Den trailhead. On the radio, Tim and Jessee are discussing other incidents of vandalism and theft. I meet with them and get the full account. At least three vehicles have been vandalized, and one nearly rolled off the embankment. We begin the investigation by listing the stolen items. There had been a number of suspicious vehicles driving up and down Washington County Road 61 last night and this morning. I decided to search Cedar Grove for clues. Two vehicles are parked in the grove; one has expired California plates. I report back to Jessee who is consulting with the county deputy. The deputy heads to the grove while I resume work in the Mayfield Area. Twenty minutes later, we receive word from the deputy that he has five suspects in custody and could use some backup; but upon arrival, we find the deputy has the situation under control. All five boys are handcuffed to the trees while a young female sits in the front seat sobbing and confessing the entire incident.

March 14, 1994

Aromatic sumac, Johnny-jump-up, and Slippery Elm are in bloom.

March 15, 1994

Devils Den State Park has been selected to be a part of a documentary on Arkansas State Parks. Two graduate students from Mississippi State University have arranged an interview. I lead them into the cave and through the upper crevice area, determined to make a good impression. They ask my views on a number of controversial subjects, but I'm not afraid to speak. The truth is more important than my career.

After lunch, the interview continues in the Mayfield area. As we pass the Farmer/Pool homesite I notice smoke rising from the corner of the field. Fire is consuming a couple acres of grass and continues to burn towards Ellis Creek and Lee Creek. I drive to the horse camp where fellow employees are working. Don Ross, Regional Supervisor, calls for assistance and all converge on the scene. It takes nearly an hour to contain the fire, primarily due to high winds and thick underbrush. Damage is light, however, and might be viewed as beneficial.

It is painfully clear where and how the fire started. Although it has been well over 72 hours since we dismantled the barn, the burn pile is still red hot. Wind stoked the coals, which ignited dry grass, fifteen feet away. Ultimately it is I who must take responsibility for the fire. Thankfully, no one gives me grief. The fire provides a welcome diversion, and the students are thrilled to get such video documentation.

March 16, 1994

Spring continues with the blooming of Pale Corydalis yesterday and False Garlic, today. While searching for new blooms, among the weeds of Lake Trail, I hear a strange call coming from a nearby Boxelder. With the sun's glare, I am unable to make a clear identification. I suspect it is a Brown-headed Cowbird or Common Grackle, but the size, color, and call do not quite match either. As if for my benefit, the bird descends from the branch to the lake's edge. Here I clearly see she is neither cowbird nor grackle. I study her for nearly 5 minutes before declaring the first park record of a Rusty Blackbird.

March 18, 1994

Today's blooms include Wood Rush, Early Buttercup, and Rue Anemone.

March 19, 1994

On busy Saturdays, Harry and I try to walk Devil's Den Trail at least once to meet visitors and count the number of flower species in bloom. I find Bloodroot, Yellow trout Lily, False Rue Anemone, and Palmer's Saxifrage. I also observe a half dozen visitors each clutching handfuls of the showiest of blooms. For some reason, few can resist the urge to pick wildflowers. For many it is treated like an inalienable right.

I once heard a ranger asked a mother to caution her children about collecting the flowers in the park. She in turn wrote to the director to insist that this rule be changed. *"How else might children show love for their mother?"* She asks. My response might be: *"Teach them to understand that all of us share this flower, both now and into the future."* Rangers help visitors find, learn, and enjoy the nature of the park.

Visitors rarely have any idea how significant an impact they make when picking a single Blood Root, Dutchman's Breeches Golden, Seal, or Ginseng. The entire Devil's Den colony of Dutchman's Breeches lies within ten feet of the trail (about six plants). Approximately 30,000 visitors walk within ten feet of these flowers. If only one out of 5,000 visitors pick the rare wildflower, the park (a place set aside specifically to protect the flora and fauna) would have failed in its mission, and visitors would suffer the loss of something very special.

March 20, 1994

Eastern Redbud and American Plum are in bloom. I walk into the middle of the Mayfield area. It is the only place to go when woodland claustrophobia sets in. It is Sunday evening, and a warm March breeze caresses the field. Bats are beginning to wake, and I can hear the last faint call of the phoebe. Once again I am determined to sit until I lose interest in the sights and sounds and fragrances of the open valley or until my butt hurts. My main goal is to hear the first Whip-poor-will. I sit for what seems to be an hour, but the goat sucker is not heard this night.

March 21, 1994

During lunch break, I continue my search for blooms and find Bird's-foot Violet, Wood Violet, and Rock Cress.

March 23, 1994

Each day brings more evidence of spring. Several migratory birds have arrived. I add Louisiana Waterthrush, Black-and-white Warbler, Parula Warbler, and Chipping Sparrow to my annual bird count. I am surprised to find Low-bush Huckleberry (*Vaccinium pallidum*) in bloom. The blooming of Grape Hyacinth (*Muscari racemosum*) in Harry's yard and Hop Hornbeam (*Ostrya virginiana*) on the upper cabin loop are on schedule.

March 25, 1994

If a particular habitat is not visited frequently, early blooms of certain species may be missed. Yellow Rock Trail runs through a few of these unique plant communities. I try to walk it every two days, but the steepness of the trail discourages the set schedule. I go when I find the energy. Halfway up the trail this evening, I hear a strange call from the bluffs nearest the highway. I leave the trail and silently walk to the source. High on the ledge, a pair of Rock Doves roost and coo. It is not the typical sound heard from this species. Perhaps some special courtship is taking place. On the return I add Violet Wood Sorrel (*Oxalis violacea*), Rock Crowfoot (*Ranunculus micranthus*), and Blue Phlox (*Phlox divaricarta*) to the list.

March 29, 1994

While leading a group of 33 Elderhostel students on Devil's Den Trail, we observed the first spring sighting of Blue-gray Gnatcatcher and Northern Rough-winged Swallow. Our goal is to locate and discuss the park's native flora, but I can find no new blooms. Later, I continue my search in camp area "E" and find Pear (*Pyrus communis*) and Ground Ivy (*Glechoma hederacea*).

March 30, 1994

Good weather ignites the blooming of Yellow Star Grass (*Hypoxis hirsuta*) Yellow Rocket (*Barbarea vulgaris*), and Missouri Gooseberry (*Ribes missouriensis*). Red Oak (*Quercus rubra*) and Black Oak (*Quercus velutina*) appear to be producing pollen, but the branches are too high for me to see and verify.

April 1, 1994

At 1 p.m., I receive a call to respond to an injury in Devil's Den Cave. From the initial report, I learned that a young female has fallen ten feet at a place called "The Drop". She was heard screaming prior to unconsciousness. Harry, Tim, and I mobilize. I am the first to enter the cave and reach the girl. She has indeed fallen from "The Drop", injuring her head and knee. The bleeding has stopped. After a quick examination, I determine that she is able to move partially on her own strength. Unfortunately, there is little choice. The cave passages are too narrow and twisted for use of a backboard slowly and methodically the girl is brought to the surface.

We provide additional first aid at the visitor center, and then the girl and her friends depart. I sit outside the visitor center on the old CCC bench. I am exhausted, my uniform is soaked, and my hair is caked with mud. In less than an hour I expect to receive one of the most important telephone calls of my life. I must pull myself together.

I decided to become a park interpreter over ten years ago because the profession seemed to offer the greatest amount of time in natural settings. I have always longed to be near the land, to that which is most primeval, and to share my lust for knowledge and adventure. I became enamored with the land on September 2, 1972. I know this because it was the day my family moved to Bella Vista, Arkansas from the concrete, brick, and asphalt jungle of St. Joseph, Missouri. Never in my life had I seen such vast woodlands with immediate access from the backyard. From that wooded ravine, I was able to imagine the connection to the wildness everywhere. Over the years I honed my skills in fishing, trail building, spelunking, camping, and wild food identification. By age thirteen, I felt the calling to spend my life in the wild. Not until I became a second semester college freshman did I finally understand how to make a living within it.

My first visit to the Rocky Mountains in December 1982 changed my life. I learned three valuable lessons: I'm not a good skier; the sport really doesn't interest me; and three, no longer would the wooded hills of Arkansas pacify my restless spirit. I needed real mountains. I returned to the West in June 1984 to spend the summer in the mountains of southwest Utah as a Baptist missionary. After college, I tried again to move West, this time to Craters of the Moon National Monument in Idaho. For three months I lived in basaltic heaven (although many visitors today still view that place as hell burned over. The season ended and I reluctantly headed back east to find work.

Arkansas State Parks saw fit to hire me, but every day I thought of nothing but Idaho, Utah, Colorado, Wyoming, and Montana. There was no nearby substitute for these places. During my search for work in Idaho, I transferred to Devil's Den.

It would not be an exaggeration to say I have thought of Idaho every single day for the past ten years. I have. It is also accurate to state that Devil's Den is the most interesting place I have lived. I am doubtful such another place as this should ever be found again, but today I expect to resume the search in the wilds of Idaho. At 4 p.m., I interview for a job with Idaho Department of Parks and Recreation.

April 2, 1994

Until I hear from Idaho, everything I do here will seem like it is the last time. The 6th Annual Mountain Bike Festival begins today, but my mind is preoccupied. As usual, I guide mountain bikers on a tour of the Upper Lee Creek Valley. My personal goal for the trip is to confirm the blooming of Orange Puccoon. I find two.

April 5, 1994

As the sun sinks behind Cherry Knob, Harry calls to report that an older gentleman has fallen into Right Angle Crevice. This time Harry arrives first, and Tim and I follow with the backboard. By radio, we learn of the man's injuries. The visitor fell twenty feet while peering over the ledge. He landed on his feet which may well have saved his head, not to mention his life; however, the ankle is not so fortunate. By the time Harry arrives, two hikers have helped the man from the crevice. After a quick assessment, we strap him to the board. We reach the parking lot near dark. Hours later we learn how substantial his injuries are. His right foot is fractured beyond repair. Still, it could have been worse. In years past, Right Angle Crevice has claimed both leg and spine.

April 8, 1994

Hiking around the glades yesterday, only one new bloom was found – Rose Verbena (*Verbena stricta*). Today, several more appear, including Flowering Dogwood (*Cornus florida*), Shooting Star (*Dodecatheon media*), Wood Vetch (*Vicia caroliniana*), Pygmy-flowered Vetch (*Vicia minutiflora*) and Prairie Blue-eyed Grass (*Sisyrinchium campestre*).

At 6:30 p.m., I received THE call I thought would never come. There is a job waiting for me in Idaho.

April 9, 1994

The fifth annual spring backpack trip begins. For the first time since I began this annual event, I am not leading a group. Last Christmas, Harry acquired several new pieces of backpacking equipment and has talked me into trading places. Tim leads the other group. After the morning shuttle, Jessee and I drink coffee outside the office. He suspects that I have been offered a job but waits to hear it officially from me. While he is not surprised, both of us realize the end of an era has come. This evening, Susan and I take the Trooper down Holt Road to meet with Harry's backpack group.

We come bearing gifts of popcorn, chocolate, and firewood. During a game of cards, I break the news to Harry. He does not take it well but understands my need to go. His love for the West runs deep. My obsession with Idaho is matched only by his with Utah.

April 10, 1994

The next two weeks will be a rush. There is so much work to be done. I must update the natural resource inventory, publish the latest edition of the vascular plant checklist, and tie up loose ends with the park's history research. There are letters to write, colleagues to inform, and of course packing. All of that will begin tomorrow. Tonight, Harry and I break out the good wine and make a toast to the last five years, camaraderie, to all the trips out West and to the dream.

April 11, 1994

Several migratory birds are heard this morning. Chimney Swift, Yellow-throated Vireo, Wood Thrush, and Scarlet Tanager all make their presence known as I walk Bridger around the loop. I will miss these birds, but I know the West will offer new sightings.

April 14, 1994

The days pass quickly now. Susan and I conclude several commitments today. Reality is setting in. We are leaving. I find myself staring at the walls of the cabin. What fine construction this cabin has. The fireplace, crafted with large sandstone boulders and oak beams, will be mourned. Everything about this place will be missed – flying squirrels scurrying in the attic, gray squirrels robbing the bird feeder, phoebes nesting on the back door eves, raccoons denning in the old tree down the hill. I step outside. In the moonlight, I see a fox standing not more than fifteen yards away. He looks at me momentarily, then scampers leisurely away. I have never seen one this close to the cabin. I am solaced and amused to remember that it was a fox that first welcomed me to the park. Was it the same one? Is he sending me off?

I imagine there is some message in this chance meeting. Perhaps the fox thinks, "Humans – never content, always rushing off to the next new place or experience." The Woodland Indians have come and gone. European-Americans have come, built small farms – lived small lives – and have gone. The Civil War soldiers have hidden in its bluff shelters for a time then marched on. The CCC came, built a park for the ages, now half hidden by generations of deciduous leaves. The tourists arrive in hordes yet slip out the back road by Sunday evening. Rangers and park interpreters abandon old trails to make new ones more than halfway across the continent. The fox sees all this but gives no opinion, no advice. Change comes and goes, but nature remains and earns the right to have the final say in the Upper Lee Creek Valley.

April 15, 1994

Susan and I are awakened at 4 a.m. to bobcat screams. I have not heard this sound since 1979 in one of my favorite ravines in Bella Vista. Why now do so many valley creatures make their presence known to me? Why do I feel the need to anthropomorphize? We search for meaning when none is intended, and we fail to see it *when it cries aloud in the street.*

April 16, 1994

Wildflower weekend begins. I can think of no other special event more enjoyable to end my Arkansas State Parks career. I conduct a wildflower workshop for eight enthusiasts. Today is also the first spring meeting of the friends of Devil's Den. Our greatest accomplishment at the board meeting is to approve funding to send Harry to a bat conference in Arizona. It marks the organization's first expenditure to directly benefit the park and its programs. It is the last time I meet with the group as the park's liaison. Every day is a "last" something or another. It is also a first as I officially join the group as a dues-paying member. Though I will be a few thousand miles away

I can continue to have a voice in the park's mission. I am assigned membership #66. Superstitious folks might think it a sign.

April 18, 1994

There are few reasons not to hold a poker game; Therefore, my resignation will not go uncelebrated around the card table. One last time, we gather at Tim's for some unlabeled brew and seven-card-stud low-Chicago. My sole purpose tonight is to give back what I have so often taken. My parting gift to Tim, Jessee, and Harry is to bluff my way through the worst of hands and lose the $15 I have. By 1 a.m. it is accomplished. Jessee and I dig through Tim's music collection. I find an old Bob Welch album and pass the next hour reminiscing.

April 22, 1994

Earth Day. Over six months ago, I planned to make a state of the environment address in honor of this event, but like many great ideas, I have procrastinated to the point of assuring mediocrity. My mind has been in a thousand places preparing for the move. Twenty visitors attend, some who have known me over the years, most who I've never met. I began by telling the park's story, one which I know so well. I conclude around the campfire with the Legend of Logger John.

Following the program I stop by Harry's cabin. We speak very little of the future, but reflect on past adventures, accomplishments, and the highs and lows of working as an interpreter in Devil's Den. We speak as if something has died, something that can never be replaced. We watch the television coverage of Nixon's death but reflect on another. Harry and I are kindred spirits, but both of us know distance and time will ultimately change that relationship.

Around 11:30 p.m. I returned home to cabin six. It is the last time I can call it home. With all the furniture loaded, the cabin is sterile and empty. Susan has gone ahead of me to Bella Vista to visit with family before the long-haul west. I have only a blanket to spread across the old CCC bed. Every move I make echoes into the other rooms. I open the window to enjoy the breeze. I lie in bed straining to hear the sounds of night. There are none.

April 23, 1994

8 a.m. I am completely packed and down to work. What can be more exciting than one's last day? I have always been fonder of endings than beginnings, sunsets to sunrises. There is no forgiveness on one's last day. The visitor center is hopping. Hundreds pour into the park to enjoy the summer like weather. Most visitors these days have just moved to the area from California or the upper Midwest. Hopefully, what they find is an inspirational place with a fascinating history, both which are worth treasuring and perpetuating. I have one last opportunity to interpret the park. At 10:30 a.m., a group from the Bentonville Educational Enrichment Program arrives. I have arranged to guide them on a wildfire walk. The group leader is Neil Compton, the well-known conservationist and author. It was one of his books that inspired me to explore the secrets of the high Ozarks. It is fitting that we should meet before I leave these hills behind.

Following the hike, I sit back in the solitude of Jessee's office to recover from the heat, packing, stress, and lack of sleep. I feel ill, and I am encouraged to leave early. *"What are they going to do, fire you?"* Harry jokes. I walk to cabin six shed my uniform like an old cicada and open a sack which Harry has given me. Inside is an official 1994 NCAA Arkansas Razorbacks championship hat. I laugh, remembering what Susan told me: If the Razorbacks win the national championship, you will get the Idaho job. She and I had watched nearly every home game this past season at the new Bud Walton Arena. Harry and I had gone to the Delaware State game together.

I park the U-Haul trailer in front of the visitor center and work the final hour. *"Dedicated to the end!"* Harry says. I believe it has less to do with dedication and more to do with savoring the memories. This is the tenth job I have ended in my life, and by far the most enjoyable. But it has been far more than a job. It has been a way of life, one which has consumed me.

Harry and I close the office and take down the flags. Visitors are still using the restrooms, and we both know it could be a while before they leave. Having turned in my keys already, Harry assumes the task of waiting to lock them up. We shake hands and say nothing...nothing more needed to be said.

The Trooper tugs at the heavy U-Haul, filled to the rim with all our earthly treasures. I used to pride myself on packing everything I owed inside the Trooper. Years of living rent-free and two incomes have created the need for a trailer. It takes nearly fifteen minutes to make the grade of Lee Creek Valley.

For the first time in my life, I do not look back to see what I am leaving; avoiding the "Pillar of Salt" moment (Genesis 19:26). I chuckle internally, silently, privately. It's far deeper than that. My mind wanders. I recognize that it is not the "leaving" so much as the going where spiritually called. When Elisha was called to follow the prophet Elijah (I Kings 19:19-21), he was found plowing in his field. As soon as Elijah cast his cloak upon him, Elisha knew exactly what that meant. He made a burnt sacrifice of the oxen, gave it to those around him to eat, and took off after Elijah without so much as a kiss goodbye to his mother and father.

"No one who puts his hand to the plow and looks back is fit for the kingdom of God."

Jesus

A Word About the Calling

This has been a true story of one man's coming and going in a parks career; however, if this is all I have to offer, then I missed the mark. The person of faith will live an intentional life, listening to the still small voice of God calling "follow me." Where we go or how long we stay is an act of faith in the master planner. The Lord said to the prophet Jeremiah, I know the plans I have for you," declares the Lord, "plans to prosper you and not to harm you, plans to give you hope and a future.

I have moved 32 times in my life, many times not of my choosing, but if we seek his will, come when we are called, and trust him in the journey, we will please God and walk with the divine.

The steps of a man are established by the Lord
David

Coming 2026:
CITY OF ROCKS: JOURNALS OF A PARK SUPERINTENDENT

About the Author

Wallace Keck was born in St. Joseph, Missouri, in the last year of the baby boom and coincidentally, the first year of the Wilderness Act. At age seven, the family of six picked up and moved to the resort/retirement community of Bella Vista, Arkansas. In 1972, the journey from Bella Vista to the nearest town (Bentonville) was still a wild one. The school bus routes were chert-covered hill-climbs and low-water crossings that consumed two to three hours each day. Weekends offered free time and woodland places to explore. Every bluff overhang was a potential cave, and every stream promised a secret waterfall. The wilderness began where the lawnmowing ceased. Such was the environment that fostered the boy in the woods to be a ranger and park manager of Idaho's wilder landscapes.

Keck earned a BS in Fisheries and Wildlife Management with an emphasis in Interpretation from Arkansas Tech University. [Note: interpretation and interpreter are terms relating to a profession that seeks to connect visitors to the significance, inherent meanings, and the stories of a place, whether they are natural, cultural, or other scientific discipline]. Keck's 43-year career spanned employment in five public land management agencies in three states, and at eight state and federal parks. Keck served 23 years as the Superintendent of City of Rocks National Reserve in Almo, Idaho. In Devil's Den: Journals of a Park Interpreter encompasses approximately five and a half years of his career from the end of 1988 to the spring of 1994, while working for the Arkansas Department of Parks and Tourism.